PRAISE FOR THE FIRST EDITION, *THE BOOK OF WI-FI*

"A plain-English guide for consumers, a bridge over troubled waters for those who want to go wireless but don't know where to start, what to buy or how to make it all work."
—SACRAMENTO BEE

"Although there are many good Wi-Fi tutorials available in the market these days . . . *The Book of Wi-Fi* definitely belongs to the top notch. The author's practical and fluff-free style liberates this book from the hype and dogmatic tone that prevail in other books."
—IBM DEVELOPERWORKS

"Highly readable."
—LINUX USER AND DEVELOPER

"An outstanding book which gives you a good working knowledge of every aspect of wireless networking and how to set up a small home network or a larger corporate Wi-Fi network with a firewall and VPN."
—FLASHMX.COM

"Covers the issues without belaboring the details."
—DESKTOPENGINEER.COM

"The author has done an absolutely fabulous job of taking complex information and explaining it in laymen's terms."
—BITYARD.COM

"Shines a big bright spotlight on the murky world of Wi-Fi."
—DINGBAT MAGAZINE

"Provides a useful foundation for anyone wishing to set up, use, and secure an 802.11b network."
—LIBRARY JOURNAL

THE BOOK *of*
WIRELESS
2ND EDITION

A PAINLESS GUIDE TO WI-FI AND BROADBAND WIRELESS

by John Ross

NO STARCH
PRESS

San Francisco

Printed on recycled paper in the United States of America

12 11 10 09 08   1 2 3 4 5 6 7 8 9

ISBN-10: 1-59327-169-7
ISBN-13: 978-1-59327-169-5

Publisher: William Pollock
Production Editor: Megan Dunchak
Cover and Interior Design: Octopod Studios
Developmental Editor: Tyler Ortman
Technical Reviewer: Mike Kershaw
Copyeditor: Jeanne Hansen
Compositor: Riley Hoffman
Proofreader: Michael Shorb
Indexer: Nancy Guenther

For information on book distributors or translations, please contact No Starch Press, Inc. directly:

No Starch Press, Inc.
555 De Haro Street, Suite 250, San Francisco, CA 94107
phone: 415.863.9900; fax: 415.863.9950; info@nostarch.com; www.nostarch.com

Library of Congress Cataloging-in-Publication Data

```
Ross, John, 1947-
   The book of wireless : a painless guide to Wi-Fi and broadband wireless / John Ross. -- 2nd ed.
      p. cm.
   Rev. ed. of: Book of Wi-Fi. c2003.
   Includes index.
   ISBN-13: 978-1-59327-169-5
   ISBN-10: 1-59327-169-7
  1. Wireless LANs--Installation. 2. Wireless LANs--Standards. 3. IEEE 802.11 (Standard) I. Ross,
John, 1947- Book of Wi-Fi.  II. Title.
TK5105.78.R67 2008
004.6'8--dc22
                                             2007048461
```

You see, wire telegraph is a kind of a very, very long cat. You pull his tail in New York and his head is meowing in Los Angeles. Do you understand this? And radio operates exactly the same way: you send signals here, they receive them there. The only difference is there is no cat.

—Albert Einstein

BRIEF CONTENTS

CONTENTS IN DETAIL

4
THE HARDWARE YOU NEED FOR WI-FI   43

5
MANAGING YOUR WI-FI CONNECTIONS   73

6
WI-FI FOR WINDOWS   97

7
WI-FI FOR LINUX AND UNIX   115

11
CONNECTING TO AN EXISTING WI-FI NETWORK   195

12
WIRELESS NETWORK SECURITY   211

13
ALTERNATIVES TO WI-FI:
WIRELESS BROADBAND DATA   239

14
SMARTPHONES AND PDAs   255

15
VIRTUAL PRIVATE NETWORKS   265

16
USING BROADBAND FOR TELEPHONE CALLS   285

17
TIPS AND TROUBLESHOOTING   293

INDEX   307

ACKNOWLEDGMENTS

I'm grateful to everybody at No Starch Press for their help and advice as this book moved from idea to print. In particular, Tyler Ortman, Megan Dunchak, Michael Kershaw, and Riley Hoffman have made this a much better book than it would have been without their attention. Any remaining faults in the book are, of course, my responsibility.

Thanks also to Georgia Taylor at Verizon Wireless and Helen Chung at Clearwire, who allowed me to borrow equipment and use their networks, and to all the manufacturers and software developers who allowed us to use photographs of their hardware and software.

INTRODUCTION

This is a book for people who want to use the Internet everywhere—not just in the office or in the room at home where there's a telephone or cable connection, but in the backyard, at the public library, at a highway rest area, or in a hotel lobby. In this book you will learn how to choose the best wireless data service for your particular needs, how to set up your computer for wireless, and how to design and install your own wireless network. We'll also describe some wireless products and services that you might not have known about, such as the ability to make low-cost, worldwide Voice over Internet (VoIP) telephone calls from your laptop computer.

The combination of wireless Internet services and portable computers can make a huge difference in the way we use the Internet. By eliminating the tether to a wired network, we can gather information, watch and listen to streaming video or audio, and exchange messages wherever we might be, rather than only at specific locations. It's no longer necessary to return home or to the office or search for an Internet café or a public library. Like mobile telephones (which use related technology), go-anywhere, always-accessible

Internet services can change the way we live, work, and entertain ourselves. When wireless broadband Internet services work properly, they're practically invisible; just turn on the computer or a smaller portable device such as a smartphone, and a universe of information is immediately at your fingertips. But we're talking about computers, so complications are always possible. In order to help you identify the causes and solutions for wireless connection problems, the first few chapters of this book offer details about how wireless data communication systems work, including the surprising tale of the avant-garde composer and the glamorous actress whose wartime invention provided the foundation of modern spread-spectrum technology.

As you read this book, I hope you will remember that a wireless network, and for that matter, any kind of communications technology, is a means to an end that you use to achieve some other objective. Remember that your original goal was to find out if your favorite team won, invite your friends to a dinner party, read your class notes, or watch the latest YouTube videos. If you have to concentrate on making your wireless connection, you're doing something wrong.

You're in control. The computer and the network should do things the way you want to do them, rather than forcing you to adjust your life or work to meet the machine's requirements. If you have trouble making your wireless connection (or any other computer activity) work "properly," it's almost always the computer's fault, or the fault of the people who designed the hardware and software. The computer and the network are your servants, and not the other way around.

New wireless network products and services are appearing all the time, so the information in this book represents a snapshot of a moving target. Within another year or two, manufacturers will have replaced some of the products described here with new and better models, and the wireless service providers will offer faster connections over wider areas. The specific makes and models will change, but the general principles ought to remain.

The first edition of this book, *The Book of Wi-Fi*, was limited to 802.11b Wi-Fi networks, which were the only practical choice when that book was published in 2003. When I wrote that book, I expected Wi-Fi networks to replace or supplement wired home and office networks, but I did not anticipate that a huge number of additional Wi-Fi hot spots would also cover public locations. In my Seattle neighborhood, I can connect my laptop computer to the Internet at a branch library, half a dozen coffee shops, three taverns, four pizza joints, and a supermarket. Today, Wi-Fi signals are everywhere, and other broadband services offer wireless signals that cover much wider areas than any Wi-Fi network. A few years from now, more and better wireless services will offer even faster connections. The dream of a high-speed wireless service that works almost everywhere is rapidly coming true.

The first three chapters of this book explain how data networks operate, how wireless technology can extend data networks beyond the reach of wired connections, and how Wi-Fi networks work. Next, Chapter 4 describes the hardware needed for Wi-Fi and how to design and install your own Wi-Fi network. Chapters 5 and 6 provide the information you need to use a Wi-Fi network to connect to the Internet from a computer running Microsoft Windows. Chapter 7 covers Wi-Fi clients for the Linux and Unix operating systems, and Chapter 8 provides similar information for Macintosh OS X. Chapter 9 explains how to install and configure Wi-Fi access points, and Chapter 10 covers long-range, point-to-point Wi-Fi links. Chapters 11 and 12 cover connecting to existing Wi-Fi networks and Wi-Fi security.

In Chapter 13, we'll move away from Wi-Fi and describe some alternative broadband wireless services, including EV-DO, EDGE, and WiMAX. Chapter 14 explains how to use Wi-Fi and broadband services with smartphones and other pocket-size computers, Chapter 15 describes virtual private networks (VPNs), and Chapter 16 explains how to use wireless links to place telephone calls through the Internet. Finally, Chapter 17 offers troubleshooting tips and general advice.

Most readers won't read this book from cover to cover, but you'll probably find something you can use in every chapter. In particular, please don't ignore the chapters on security and VPNs—they contain essential information that can keep your network and your data safe. If all your computers use Windows, you can skip the Linux/Unix and Macintosh chapters.

If I have done my job as author, this book will improve your experience with Wi-Fi and other wireless data services. I hope it will help you understand how data moves through the air between your computer and the Internet and how to set up and use your own system for best performance. After your wireless connection is ready to use, you shouldn't have to think about the network at all. Along the way, I hope you enjoy both the book and your time online.

1

INTRODUCTION TO NETWORKING

 Broadband wireless networks are one more step toward the Internet's ultimate destiny of interconnecting everything in the known universe.

A wireless network combines two kinds of communication technology: data networks that make it possible to share information among two or more computers, and radio (or wireless) communication that uses electromagnetic radiation to move information from one place to another.

The earliest Wi-Fi systems provided a convenient way to connect a laptop computer to an office network and to connect computers to a home network without stringing cables between rooms. Today, Wi-Fi and other broadband services allow millions of users to connect to the Internet when they're away from their homes or offices, as wireless signals cover entire metropolitan areas.

A variety of products and services use different methods to accomplish essentially the same objective: wirelessly exchanging network data using radio signals. Each service has a somewhat different set of features, and each uses a slightly different technology. The three most widely used systems are Wi-Fi, WiMAX, and 3G cellular service.

The next chapter explains how these three broadband wireless networks work. But before we go into detail about specific wireless data network services, it will be helpful to understand networks in more general terms.

Moving Data Around

To begin, let's review the general structure of computer data and the methods that networks use to move data from one place to another. This is very basic stuff that might already be familiar to you, but bear with me for a few pages. This really will help you to understand how a wireless network operates.

Bits and Bytes

As you probably know, the processing unit of a computer can recognize only two information states: either a signal is present or not present at the input to the processor. These two conditions are usually described as 1 and 0, on and off, or mark and space. Each instance of a 1 or a 0 is a *bit*.

The form that each 1 or 0 takes varies in different types of communication channels. It can be a light, a sound, or an electrical charge that is either on or off, a series of long and short sounds or light flashes, two different audio tones, or two different radio frequencies.

Individual bits are not particularly useful, but when you string 8 of them together into a *byte*, you can have 256 different combinations. That's enough to assign different sequences to all the letters in the alphabet (both upper- and lowercase), the 10 digits from 0 to 9, spaces between words, and other symbols such as punctuation marks and letters used in foreign alphabets. A modern computer recognizes and processes several 8-bit bytes at the same time. When processing is complete, the computer transmits the same stream of bits at its output. The output might be connected to a printer, a video display, or a data communication channel. Or it might be something else entirely, such as a series of flashing lights. Figure 1-1 is an example of a sequence of bits.

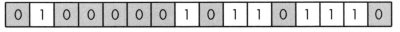

Figure 1-1: These bits form the sequence of A (01000001) and n (01101110).

The inputs and outputs that we're concerned about here are the ones that form a communication circuit. Like the computer processor, a data channel can recognize only one bit at a time. Either there's a signal on the line or there isn't.

However, over short distances, it's possible to send the data through a cable that carries eight (or some multiple of eight) signals in *parallel* through eight separate wires. Obviously, a parallel connection can be eight times faster than sending one bit through a single wire, but those eight wires cost eight times as much as a single wire. That added cost is insignificant when the wires are only a foot or two long, but when you're trying to send the data over a long distance, that additional cost can be prohibitive. And when you're using existing circuits, such as telephone lines, you don't have any choice; you must find a way to send all eight bits through the existing pair of wires (or other media). The solution is to transmit one bit at a time with some additional bits and pauses that identify the beginning of each new byte. This is a *serial* data communication channel, which means that you're sending bits one after another. At this stage, it doesn't matter what medium you use to transmit those bits—it could be electrical impulses on a wire, two different audio tones, a series of flashing lights, or even a lot of notes attached to the legs of carrier pigeons—but you must have a method for converting the output of the computer to the signals used by the transmission medium and converting it back again at the other end.

Error Checking

In a perfect transmission circuit, the signal that goes in at one end will be absolutely identical to the one that comes out at the other end. But in the real world, there's almost always some kind of noise that can interfere with our original pure signal. *Noise* is defined as anything that is added to the original signal; it could be caused by a lightning strike, interference from another communication channel, or dirt on an electrical contact someplace in the circuit (or in the case of those carrier pigeons, an attack by a marauding hawk). Whatever the source, noise in the channel can interrupt the flow of data. In a modern communication system, those bits are pouring through the circuit extremely quickly—millions of them every second—so a noise hit for even a fraction of a second can obliterate enough bits to turn your data into digital gibberish.

Therefore, you must include a process called *error checking* in your data stream. Error checking is accomplished by adding some kind of standard information to each byte. In a simple computer data network, the hand-shaking information (described in the next section) is called the *parity bit*, which tells the device receiving each byte whether the sum of the ones and zeroes inside the byte is odd or even. If the receiving device discovers that the parity bit is not what it expected, it instructs the transmitter to send the same byte again. This value is called a *checksum*. More complex networks, including wireless systems, include additional error checking handshaking data with each string of data.

Handshaking

Of course, the computer that originates a message or a stream of data can't just jump online and start sending bytes. First it has to warn the device at the other end that it is ready to send data and make sure that the intended recipient is ready to accept data. To accomplish this, a series of *handshaking* requests and answers must surround the actual data.

The sequence of requests goes something like this:

> Origin: "Hey destination! I have some data for you."

> Destination: "Okay, origin, go ahead. I'm ready."

Origin: "Here comes the data."

Origin: Data data data data . . . checksum

Origin: "That's the message. Did you get it?"

Destination: "I got something, but it appears to be damaged."

Origin: "Here it is again."

Origin: Data data data data . . . checksum

Origin: "Did you get it that time?"

Destination: "Yup, I got it. I'm ready for more data."

We can leave the specific contents of the handshaking information to the network designers and engineers, but it's important to understand that every bit that moves through a computer data network is not part of the original information that arrived at the input computer. In a complex network, such as a wireless data channel, as much as 40 percent or more of the transmitted data is handshaking and other overhead. It's all essential, but every one of those bits increases the amount of time that the message needs to move through the network.

Finding the Destination

Communication over a direct physical connection (e.g., a wired connection) between the origin and destination doesn't need to include any kind of address or routing information as part of the message. You might have to set up the connection first (by placing a telephone call or plugging cables into a switchboard), but after you're connected, the link remains in place until you instruct the system to disconnect. This kind of connection is great for voice and simple data links, but it's not efficient for digital data on a complex network that serves many origins and destinations because a single connection ties up the circuit all the time, even when no data is moving through the channel.

The alternative is to send your message to a switching center that will hold it until a link to the destination becomes available. This is known as a *store and forward* system. If the network has been properly designed for the type of data and the amount of traffic in the system, the waiting time will be insignificant. If the communication network covers a lot of territory, you can forward the message to one or more intermediate switching centers before it reaches its ultimate destination. The great advantage of this approach is that many messages can share the same circuits on an as-available basis.

To make the network even more efficient, you can divide messages that are longer than some arbitrary limit into separate pieces called *packets*. Packets from more than one message can travel together on the same circuit, reassemble themselves into the original messages at the destination, and combine with packets that contain other messages as they travel between switching centers. Each data packet must also contain another set of information: the address of the packet's destination, the sequence of the packet relative to other packets in the original transmission, and so forth. Some of this information instructs the switching centers where to forward each packet, and other information tells the destination device how to reassemble the data in the packet back into the original message.

That same pattern is repeated every time you add another layer of activity to a communication system. Each layer can attach additional information to the original message and strip off that information after it has done whatever the added information instructed it to do. By the time a message travels from a laptop computer on a wireless network through a local area network (LAN) and an Internet gateway to a distant computer that is connected to another LAN, a dozen or more information attachments might be added and removed before the recipient reads the original text. A package of data that includes address and control information ahead of the bits that contain the content of the message, followed by an error-checking sequence, is called a *frame*. Both wired and wireless networks divide the data stream into frames that contain various forms of handshaking information along with the original data.

It might be helpful to think of these bits, bytes, packets, and frames as the digital version of a letter that you send through a complicated mail delivery system:

1. You write a letter and put it into an envelope. The name and address of the recipient is on the outside of the envelope.

2. You take the letter to the mail room, where a clerk puts your envelope into a bigger Express Mail envelope. The big envelope has the name and address of the office where the recipient works.

3. The mail room clerk takes the big envelope to the post office where another clerk puts it into a mail sack. The post office attaches a tag to the sack, marked with the location of the post office that serves the recipient's office.

4. The mail sack travels on a truck to the airport, where it is loaded into a shipping container along with other sacks going to the same destination city. The shipping container has a label that tells the freight handlers there's mail inside.

5. The freight handlers place the container inside an airplane.

6. At this point, your letter is inside your envelope, which is inside the Express Mail envelope, which is inside a mail sack, inside a container, inside an airplane. The airplane flies to another airport near the destination city.

7. At the destination airport, the ground crew unloads the container from the airplane.

8. The freight handlers remove the sack from the shipping container and put it on another truck.

9. The truck takes the sack to a post office near the recipient's office.

10. At the post office, another mail clerk takes the big envelope out of the sack and gives it to a letter carrier.

11. The letter carrier delivers the big Express Mail envelope to the recipient's office.

12. The receptionist in the office takes your envelope out of the Express Mail envelope and gives it to the recipient.

13. The recipient opens your envelope and reads the letter.

At each step, the information on the outside of the package tells somebody how to handle it, but that person doesn't care what's inside. Neither you nor the person who ultimately reads your letter ever sees the big Express Mail envelope, the mail sack, the truck, the container, or the airplane, but every one of those containers plays an important part in moving your letter from here to there.

Instead of envelopes, sacks, containers, and airplanes, an electronic message uses strings of data at the beginning or end of each packet to tell the system how and where to handle your message, but the end result is just about the same. In the OSI network model (described in the next section), each mode of transportation is a separate layer.

Fortunately, the network software adds and removes all of the preambles, addresses, checksums, and other information automatically so you and the person receiving your message never see them.

However, each item added to the original data increases the size of the packet, frame, or other package, and therefore increases the amount of time necessary to transmit the data through the network. Because the nominal data transfer speed includes all the overhead information along with the data in your original message, the actual data transfer speed through a wireless network is a lot slower than the nominal speed. In other words, even if your network connects at 11Mbps, your actual file transfer speed might only be about 6 or 7Mbps or even less. That sounds like a huge slowdown, but it really doesn't matter in a Wi-Fi network that's connected to the Internet through a 1.5Mbps DSL line or even a 5Mbps cable modem; your wireless link is still able to handle data transfer more quickly than the DSL or cable modem can provide it. On the other hand, if you're using Wi-Fi with an ultra-fast fiber optic connection to the Internet, or if you want to move very large audio, video, or CAD files around your own local network, you will want to use one of the faster Wi-Fi versions, either 802.11g or (when it becomes available) 802.11n.

The ISO OSI Model

As the package delivery example demonstrates, the information itself is only part of the process. When information moves across a network, it's essential that all of the parties involved—the originator, the ultimate recipient, and everything in between—agree that they will use the same formatting, timing, and routing rules and specifications. These rules (also called *protocols*) define the network's internal "plumbing" and the form of the information that moves through it.

As network communication has become more complex, the community of network designers has accepted the International Organization for Standardization's (ISO) Open Systems Interconnection (OSI) model to identify the individual elements of a network link. The OSI model applies to just about any kind of data communication system, including the broadband wireless network that will be described in the rest of this book.

Because everybody in the communication industry uses the OSI model, it encourages hardware and software designers to create systems and services that can exchange information with similar products from other manufacturers. Without the OSI model or something like it, it would not be possible to expect equipment from more than one source to work together.

The OSI model also allows a designer to change just one element of the network without the need to design everything else from scratch. For example, a wireless network uses radio signals instead of cables at the physical layer and adds routing information at the data link layer, but it keeps the existing protocols and specifications for everything else. A complex network (such as the Internet) can use wired connections for one part of the signal path and wireless connections for another.

The OSI model is usually portrayed as a stack of seven layers with each layer acting as a foundation for the layer directly above it as shown in Figure 1-2.

Starting at the bottom, the seven layers of the OSI model are described in the following sections.

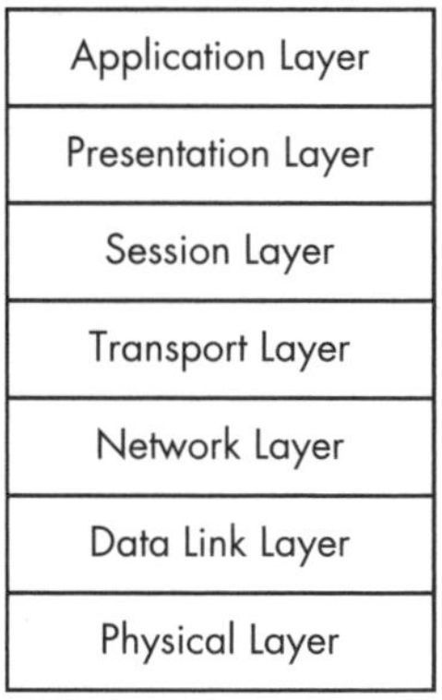

| Application Layer |
| Presentation Layer |
| Session Layer |
| Transport Layer |
| Network Layer |
| Data Link Layer |
| Physical Layer |

Figure 1-2: The OSI network model has seven layers.

The Physical Layer

As the name suggests, the *physical layer* defines the physical media or hardware that carries signals between the end points of a network connection. The physical layer might be a coaxial cable, a pair of telephone wires, flashing lights, or radio waves.

The specifications of a network's physical layer might include the shape of the shell and the pin numbers in a cable connector, the voltages that define the 0 and 1 (on and off) values, the durations of individual data bits, and the radio frequencies and modulation methods used by a radio transmitter and receiver.

The Data Link Layer

The *data link layer* handles transmission of data across the link defined by the physical layer. It specifies the format of each data packet that moves across the network, including the destination of each packet, the physical structure of the network, the sequence of packets (to make sure that the packets arrive in the correct order), and the type of flow control (to make sure that the transmitter doesn't send data faster than the receiver can handle it). Each packet also includes a checksum that the receiver uses to confirm that the data was not corrupted during transmission, as well as the string of bits and bytes that contains the actual data inside the packet. Therefore, it contains the software that creates and interprets the signals that move through the physical layer.

In both wired and wireless Ethernet, every physical device that is connected to the network has a unique 48-bit media access control (MAC) address that identifies it to the network. The header (the first part of the data string inside of a packet) includes the MAC addresses of both the origin and destination of that packet.

The Network Layer

The *network layer* specifies the route that a signal uses to move from the source to the destination independently of the physical media. At the network level, it doesn't matter whether the data moves through a cable, radio waves, or if it uses some combination of both because that's all handled at a lower level.

Within the Internet, the exchange of data between LANs, wide area networks (WANs), and the core Internet trunk circuits occurs at the network layer.

The Transport Layer

Starting at the transport layer, the OSI model is concerned with communication between programs on two different computers rather than the process of moving data from point A to point B. For example, when you view a web page on the Internet, the connection between the browser on your computer (such as Internet Explorer or Firefox) and the webserver that contains that page occurs at the *transport layer* (but the commands you send to the server occur at the application layer).

The Session Layer

The *session layer* defines the format that the programs connected through the transport layer use to exchange data. If the programs use passwords or other authentication to assure that the program at the distant end of the connection is allowed to use a local program, that authentication happens in the session layer.

The Presentation Layer

The *presentation layer* controls the way each computer handles text, audio, video, and other data formats. For example, if a distant computer sends a picture in JPEG format, the software that converts the data string to a picture on a monitor or a printer operates at the presentation layer.

The Application Layer

The *application layer* handles the commands and data that move through the network. For example, when you send an email message, the content of your message (but not the address or the formatting information) is in the application layer. Most of the words, pictures, sounds, and other forms of information that you send through a network enter the system through the application layer.

Summary

In general, data networks have evolved over the last 100 years from very simple (and relatively slow) telegraph services to today's complex high-speed communication systems. One of the most important improvements in networking has been to replace many of the wires and cables that connect individual users to the worldwide network grid (also known as the Internet) with radio signals. Chapter 2 explains how to combine traditional network services with wireless signaling.

2

INTRODUCTION TO WIRELESS NETWORKS

Up to a point, it's quite possible to treat your wireless network as a set of black boxes that you can turn on and use without knowing much about the way they work. That's the way most people relate to the technology that surrounds them. You shouldn't have to worry about the technical specifications just to place a long-distance telephone call or heat your lunch in a microwave oven or connect your laptop computer to a network. In an ideal world (ha!), the wireless link would work as soon as you turn on the power switch.

But wireless networking today is about where broadcast radio was in the late 1920s. The technology was out there for everybody, but the people who understood what was happening behind that Bakelite-Dilecto panel (Figure 2-1) often got better performance than the ones who just expected to turn on the power switch and listen.

In order to make the most effective use of wireless networking technology, it's still important to understand what's going on inside the box (or in this case, inside each of the boxes that make up the network). This chapter describes the standards and specifications that control wireless networks and explains how data moves through the network from one computer to another.

Figure 2-1: Every new technology goes through the tweak-and-fiddle stage.

When the network is working properly, you should be able to use it without thinking about all of that internal plumbing—just click a few icons and you're connected. But when you're designing and building a new network, or when you want to improve the performance of an existing network, it can be essential to understand how all that data is supposed to move from one place to another. And when the network does something you aren't expecting it to do, you will need a basic knowledge of the technology to do any kind of useful troubleshooting.

How Wireless Networks Work

Moving data through a wireless network involves three separate elements: the radio signals, the data format, and the network structure. Each of these elements is independent of the other two, so you must define all three when you invent a new network. In terms of the OSI reference model, the radio signal operates at the physical layer, and the data format controls several of the higher layers. The network structure includes the wireless network interface adapters and base stations that send and receive the radio signals. In a wireless network, the network interface adapters in each computer and base station convert digital data to radio signals, which they transmit to other devices on the same network, and they receive and convert incoming radio signals from other network elements back to digital data.

Each of the broadband wireless data services use a different combination of radio signals, data formats, and network structure. We'll describe each type of wireless data network in more detail later in this chapter, but first, it's valuable to understand some general principles.

Radio

The basic physical laws that make radio possible are known as Maxwell's equations, identified by James Clerk Maxwell in 1864. Without going into the math, Maxwell's equations show that a changing magnetic field will produce an electric field, and a changing electric field will produce a magnetic field. When alternating current (AC) moves through a wire or other physical conductor, some of that energy escapes into the surrounding space as an alternating magnetic field. That magnetic field creates an alternating electric field in space, which in turn creates another magnetic field and so forth until the original current is interrupted.

This form of energy in transition between electricity and magnetic energy is called *electromagnetic radiation,* or *radio waves. Radio* is defined as the radiation of electromagnetic energy through space. A device that produces radio waves is called a *transmitter,* and a complementary device that detects radio waves in the air and converts them to some other form of energy is called a *receiver.* Both transmitters and receivers use specially shaped devices called *antennas* to focus the radio signal in a particular direction, or *pattern,* and to increase the amount of effective radiation (from a transmitter) or sensitivity (in a receiver).

By adjusting the rate at which alternating current flows from each transmitter through the antenna and out into space (the *frequency*), and by adjusting a receiver to operate only at that frequency, it's possible to send and receive many different signals, each at a different frequency, that don't interfere with one another. The overall range of frequencies is known as the *radio spectrum.* A smaller segment of the radio spectrum is often called a *band.*

Radio frequencies and other AC signals are expressed as cycles per second, or *hertz (Hz),* named for Heinrich Hertz, the first experimenter to send and receive radio waves. One cycle is the distance from the peak of an AC signal to the peak of the next signal. Radio signals generally operate at frequencies in thousands, millions, or billions of hertz (kilohertz or KHz, megahertz or MHz, and gigahertz or GHz, respectively).

The simplest type of radio communication uses a continuous signal that the operator of the transmitter interrupts to divide the signal into accepted patterns of long and short signals (dots and dashes) that correspond to individual letters and other characters. The most widely used set of these patterns was Morse code, named for the inventor of the telegraph, Samuel F.B. Morse, where this code was first used.

In order to transmit speech, music, and other sounds via radio, the transmitter alters, or *modulates*, the AC signal (the carrier wave) by either mixing an audio signal with the carrier as shown in Figure 2-2 (this is called *amplitude modulation*, or *AM*) or by modulating the frequency within a narrow range as shown in Figure 2-3 (this is called *frequency modulation*, or *FM*). The AM or FM receiver includes a complementary circuit that separates the carrier from the modulating signal.

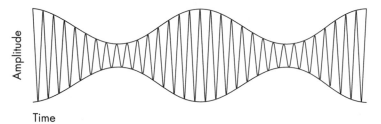

Figure 2-2: In an AM signal, the audio modulates the carrier.

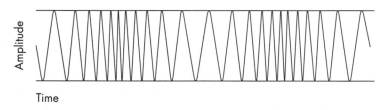

Figure 2-3: In an FM signal, the audio modulates the radio frequency.

Because two or more radio signals using the same frequency can often interfere with one another, government regulators and international agencies, such as the International Telecommunication Union (ITU), have reserved certain frequencies for specific types of modulation, and they issue exclusive licenses to individual users. For example, an FM radio station might be licensed to operate at 92.1 MHz at a certain geographical location. Nobody else is allowed to use that frequency in close enough proximity to interfere with that signal. On the other hand, some radio services don't require a license. Most unlicensed services are either restricted to very short distances, to specific frequency bands, or both.

Both AM and FM are *analog* methods because the signal that comes out of the receiver is a replica of the signal that went into the transmitter. When we send computer data through a radio link, it's *digital* because the content has been converted from text, computer code, sounds, images or other information into ones and zeroes before it is transmitted, and it is converted back to its original form after it is received. Digital radio can use any of several different modulation methods: The ones and zeroes can be two different audio tones, two different radio frequencies, timed interruptions to the carrier, or some combination of those and other techniques.

Wireless Data Networks

Each type of wireless data network operates on a specific set of radio frequencies. For example, most Wi-Fi networks operate in a special band of radio frequencies around 2.4 GHz that have been reserved in most parts of the world for unlicensed point-to-point spread spectrum radio services. Other Wi-Fi systems use a different unlicensed band around 5 GHz.

Unlicensed Radio Services

Unlicensed means that anybody using equipment that complies with the technical requirements can send and receive radio signals on these frequencies without a radio station license. Unlike most radio services (including other broadband wireless services), which require licenses that grant exclusive use of that frequency to a specific type of service and to one or more specific users, an unlicensed service is a free-for-all where everybody has an equal claim to the same airwaves. In theory, the technology of spread spectrum radio makes it possible for many users to co-exist (up to a point) without significant interference.

Point-to-Point

A *point-to-point* radio service operates a communication channel that carries information from a transmitter to a single receiver. The opposite of point-to-point is a *broadcast* service (such as a radio or television station) that sends the same signal to many receivers at the same time.

Spread Spectrum

Spread spectrum is a family of methods for transmitting a single radio signal using a relatively wide segment of the radio spectrum. Wireless Ethernet networks use several different spread spectrum radio transmission systems, which are called frequency-hopping spread spectrum (FHSS), direct-sequence spread spectrum (DSSS), and orthogonal frequency division multiplexing (OFDM). Some older data networks use the slower FHSS system, but the first Wi-Fi networks used DSSS, and more recent systems use OFDM. Table 2-1 lists each of the Wi-Fi standards and the type of spread spectrum modulation they use.

Table 2-1: Wi-Fi Standards and Modulation Type

Wi-Fi Type	Frequency	Modulation
802.11a	5 GHz	OFDM
802.11b	2.4 GHz	DSSS
802.11g	2.4 GHz	OFDM

Spread spectrum radio offers some important advantages over other types of radio signals that use a single narrow channel. Spread spectrum is extremely efficient, so the radio transmitters can operate with very low power. Because the signals operate on a relatively wide band of frequencies, they are less sensitive to interference from other radio signals and electrical noise, which means they can often get through in environments where a conventional narrow-band signal would be impossible to receive and understand. And because a frequency-hopping spread spectrum signal shifts among more than one channel, it can be extremely difficult for an unauthorized listener to intercept and decode the contents of a signal.

Spread spectrum technology has an interesting history. It was invented by the actress Hedy Lamarr and the American avant-garde composer George Antheil as a "Secret Communication System" for directing radio-controlled torpedoes that would not be vulnerable to enemy jamming. Before she came to Hollywood, Lamarr had been married to an arms merchant in Austria, where she learned about the problems of torpedo guidance at dinner parties with her husband's customers. Years later, shortly before the United States entered World War II, she came up with the concept of changing radio frequencies to cut through interference. *The New York Times* reported in 1941 that her "red hot" invention (Figure 2-4) was vital to the national defense, but the government would not reveal any details.

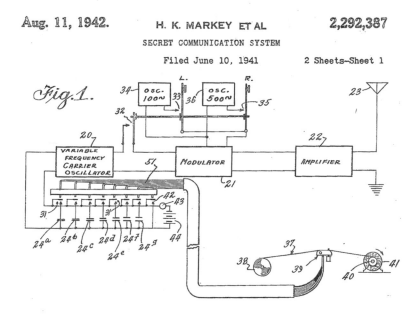

Figure 2-4: Hedy Lamarr and George Antheil received this patent in 1942 for the invention that became the foundation of spread spectrum radio communication. She is credited here under her married name, H.K. Markey. The complete document is accessible at http://uspto.gov.

Antheil turned out to be the ideal person to make this idea work. His most famous composition was an extravaganza called *Ballet Mechanique*, which was scored for sixteen player pianos, two airplane propellers, four xylophones, four bass drums, and a siren. His design used the same kind of mechanism that he had previously used to synchronize the player pianos to change radio frequencies in a spread spectrum transmission. The original slotted paper tape system had 88 different radio channels—one for each of the 88 keys on a piano.

In theory, the same method could be used for voice and data communication as well as guiding torpedoes, but in the days of vacuum tubes, paper tape, and mechanical synchronization, the whole process was too complicated to actually build and use. By 1962, solid-state electronics had replaced the vacuum tubes and piano rolls, and the technology was used aboard US Navy ships for secure communication during the Cuban Missile Crisis. Today, spread spectrum radios are used in the US Air Force Space Command's Milstar Satellite Communications System, in digital cellular telephones, and in wireless data networks.

Frequency-Hopping Spread Spectrum

Lamarr and Antheil's original design for spread spectrum radio used a *frequency-hopping system (FHSS)*. As the name suggests, FHSS technology divides a radio signal into small segments and "hops" from one frequency to another many times per second as it transmits those segments. The transmitter and the receiver establish a synchronized hopping pattern that sets the sequence in which they will use different subchannels.

FHSS systems overcome interference from other users by using a narrow carrier signal that changes frequency many times per second. Additional transmitter and receiver pairs can use different hopping patterns on the same set of subchannels at the same time. At any point in time, each transmission is probably using a different subchannel, so there's no interference between signals. When a conflict does occur, the system resends the same packet until the receiver gets a clean copy and sends a confirmation back to the transmitting station.

For some older 802.11 wireless data services, the unlicensed 2.4 MHz band is split into 75 subchannels, each of them 1 MHz wide. Because each frequency hop adds overhead to the data stream, FHSS transmissions are relatively slow.

Direct-Sequence Spread Spectrum

The *direct-sequence spread spectrum (DSSS)* technology that controls 802.11b networks uses an 11-chip Barker Sequence to spread the radio signal through a single 22 MHz–wide channel without changing frequencies. Each DSSS link uses just one channel without any hopping between frequencies. As Figure 2-5 shows, a DSSS transmission uses more bandwidth, but less power than a conventional signal. The digital signal on the left is a conventional transmission in which the power is concentrated within a tight bandwidth. The DSSS signal on the right uses the same amount of power, but it spreads that power across a wider band of radio frequencies. Obviously, the 22 MHz DSSS channel is a lot wider than the 1 MHz channels used in FHSS systems.

A DSSS transmitter breaks each bit in the original data stream into a series of redundant bit patterns called *chips*, and it transmits them to a receiver that reassembles the chips back into a data stream that is identical to the original. Because most interference is likely to occupy a narrower bandwidth than a DSSS signal, and because each bit is divided into several chips, the receiver can usually identify noise and reject it before it decodes the signal.

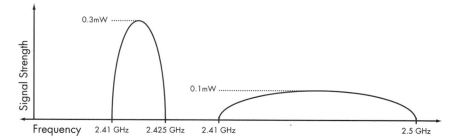

Figure 2-5: A conventional signal (left) uses a narrow radio frequency bandwidth. A DSSS signal (right) uses a wider bandwidth but a less powerful signal.

Like other networking protocols, a DSSS wireless link exchanges handshaking messages within each data packet to confirm that the receiver can understand each packet. For example, the standard data transmission rate in an 802.11b DSSS WI-Fi network is 11Mbps, but when the signal quality won't support that speed, the transmitter and receiver use a process called *dynamic rate shifting* to drop the speed down to 5.5Mbps. The speed might drop because a source of electrical noise near the receiver interferes with the signal or because the transmitter and receiver are too far apart to support full-speed operation. If 5.5Mbps is still too fast for the link to handle, it drops again, down to 2Mbps or even 1Mbps.

Orthogonal Frequency Division Multiplexing

Orthogonal frequency division multiplexing (OFDM) modulation, used in 802.11a Wi-Fi networks, is considerably more complicated than DSSS technology. The physical layer splits the data stream among 52 parallel bit streams that each use a different radio frequency called a *subcarrier.* Four of these subcarriers carry *pilot data* that provides reference information about the remaining 48 subcarriers, in order to reduce signal loss due to radio interference or phase shift. Because the data is divided into 48 separate streams that move through separate subcarriers in parallel, the total transmission speed is much greater than the speed of data through a single channel.

The subcarrier frequencies in an OFDM signal overlap with the peak of each subcarrier's waveform matching the baseline of the overlapping signals as shown in Figure 2-6. This is called *orthogonal frequency division.* The 802.11a standard specifies a total of eight data channels that are 20 MHz wide. Each of these channels is divided into 52 300 kHz subcarriers.

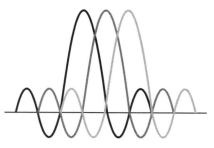

Figure 2-6: In OFDM, the peaks of overlapping frequencies don't interfere with one another.

When a Wi-Fi radio receiver detects an 802.11a signal, it assembles the parallel bit streams back into a single high-speed data stream and uses the pilot data to check its accuracy. Under ideal conditions, an 802.11a network can move data at 54Mbps, but like DSSS modulation, the OFDM transmitter and receiver automatically reduce the data speed when the maximum transmission rate is not possible due to interference, weak signals, or other less-than-perfect atmospheric conditions.

The more recent 802.11g specification was designed to combine the best features of both 802.11b (greater signal range) and 802.11a (higher speed). To accomplish this objective, it uses OFDM modulation on the 2.4 GHz frequency band.

Why This Matters

The great science fiction writer Arthur C. Clarke once observed that "Any sufficiently advanced technology is indistinguishable from magic." For most of us, the technology that controls high-speed spread spectrum radio could just as easily be a form of magic, because we don't need to understand the things that happen inside a transmitter and a receiver; they're just about invisible when we connect a computer to the Internet. As mentioned earlier in this chapter, you don't need to understand these technical details about how a Wi-Fi transmitter splits your data into tiny pieces and reassembles them into data unless you're a radio circuit designer.

But when you know that there's a well-defined set of rules and methods that make the connection work (even if you don't know all the details), you are in control. You know that it's not magic, and if you think about it, you might also know some of the right questions to ask when the system doesn't work correctly. If knowledge is power, then knowledge about the technology you use every day is the power to control that technology rather than just use it.

Benefits of Wireless

Wireless broadband provides Internet access to mobile devices in addition to allowing network operators to extend their networks beyond the range of their wired connections. For our purposes, two-way radio is the most sensible approach to wireless broadband, but other methods (such as infrared light or visible signaling) are also possible. Connecting your computer to the Internet (or a local network) by radio offers several advantages over connecting the same computer through a wired connection. First, wireless provides convenient access for portable computers; it's not necessary to find a cable or network data outlet. And second, it allows a user to make a connection from more than one location and to maintain a connection as the user moves from place to place. For network managers, a wireless connection makes it possible to distribute access to a network without the need to string wires or cut holes through walls.

In practice, access without cables means that the owner of a laptop or other portable computer can walk into a classroom, a coffee shop, or a library and connect to the Internet by simply turning on the computer and running a communication program. Depending on the type of wireless network you're using, you might also be able to maintain the same connection in a moving vehicle.

When you're installing your own network, it's often easier to use Wi-Fi links to extend your network and your Internet connection to other rooms because a wired system requires a physical path for the cables between the network router or switch and each computer. Unless you can route those cables through a false ceiling or some other existing channel, this almost always means that you must cut holes in your walls for data connectors and feed wires inside the walls and under the floors. A radio signal that passes through those same walls is often a lot neater and easier.

Wireless Data Services

Because radio signals move through the air, you can set up a network connection from any place within range of the network base station's transmitter; it's not necessary to use a telephone line, television cable, or some other dedicated wiring to connect your computer to the network. Just turn on the radio connected to the computer and it will find the network signal. Therefore, a radio (or wireless) network connection is often a lot more convenient than a wired one.

This is not to say that wireless is always the best choice. A wired network is usually more secure than a wireless system because it's a lot more difficult for unauthorized eavesdroppers and other snoops to monitor data as it moves through the network, and a wired link doesn't require as many complex negotiations between the sender and receiver on protocols and so forth. In an environment where your computer never moves away from your desk and there are no physical obstacles between the computer and the network access point, it's often easier to install a data cable between the computer and a modem.

So now we have a bunch of radio transmitters and receivers that all operate on the same frequencies and all use the same kind of modulation. (*Modulation* is the method a radio uses to add some kind of content, such as voice or digital data, to a radio wave.) The next step is to send some network data through those radios. Several different wireless data systems and services are available to connect computers and other devices to local networks and to the Internet, including Wi-Fi, WiMAX, and a handful of services based on the latest generations of cellular mobile telephone technology.

Wi-Fi

The IEEE (Institute of Electrical and Electronics Engineers) has produced a set of standards and specifications for wireless networks under the title *IEEE 802.11* that define the formats and structures of the relatively short-range signals that provide Wi-Fi service. The original 802.11 standard (without any letter at the end) was released in 1997. It covers several types of wireless media: two kinds of radio transmissions and networks that use infrared light. The

802.11b standard provides additional specifications for wireless Ethernet networks. A related document, IEEE 802.11a, describes wireless networks that operate at higher speeds on different radio frequencies. Still other 802.11 radio networking standards with other letters are also available or moving toward public release.

The specifications in widest use today are 802.11a, 802.11b, and 802.11g. They're the de facto standards used by just about every wireless Ethernet LAN that you are likely to encounter in offices and public spaces and in most home networks. It's worth the trouble to keep an eye on the progress of those other standards, but for the moment, 802.11a and 802.11g are the ones to use for short-range wireless networks, especially if you're expecting to connect to networks where you don't control all the hardware yourself.

NOTE *Many first-generation 802.11b Wi-Fi network adapters are still compatible with today's networks, but their manufacturers don't offer the device drivers that are necessary to make them work with the latest operating systems (such as Windows XP or Windows Vista).*

The 802.11n standard is the next one in the pipeline, and when it's released, it will replace both 802.11b and 802.11g because it's faster, more secure, and more reliable. The older standards will still work, so new Wi-Fi equipment will support all three (often along with 802.11a, which uses different radio frequencies) and automatically match your network interface to the signals it detects from each base station.

NOTE *Until the new 802.11n standard is formally approved and released, some manufacturers offer "pre-n" network adapters and access points that include many of the features that will be in the final 802.11n standard. These preliminary versions generally work best on networks that are limited to equipment (adapters and access points) made by a single manufacturer, although they all generally work with any existing 802.11b or 802.11g network. Your best bet is to wait until the final standard is released before you upgrade your system, but if you do buy a pre-n device, the manufacturer will probably offer a free firmware upgrade to the final 802.11n specifications.*

There are two more names in the alphabet soup of wireless LAN standards that you ought to know about: WECA and Wi-Fi. *WECA (Wireless Ethernet Compatibility Alliance)* is an industry group that includes all of the major manufacturers of wireless Ethernet equipment. Their twin missions are to test and certify that the wireless network devices from all of their member companies can operate together in the same network, and to promote 802.11 networks as the worldwide standard for wireless LANs. WECA's marketing geniuses have adopted the more friendly name of Wi-Fi (short for *wireless fidelity*) for the 802.11 specifications.

Once or twice per year, the Wi-Fi Alliance conducts an "interoperability bake-off" where engineers from many hardware manufacturers confirm that their hardware will communicate correctly with equipment from other suppliers. Network equipment that carries a Wi-Fi logo has been certified by the Wi-Fi Alliance to meet the relevant standards and to pass interoperability tests. Figure 2-7 shows one version of the Wi-Fi logo.

Wi-Fi was originally intended to be a wireless extension of a wired LAN, so the distances between Wi-Fi base stations and the computers that communicate through them are limited to about 100 feet (35 meters) indoors or up to 300 feet (100 meters) outdoors, assuming there are no obstructions between the access point and the computer. When 802.11n equipment becomes available, it will support connections between computers and base stations at least as far apart as the older Wi-Fi versions. There are ways to extend the range of a Wi-Fi signal, but those techniques require special equipment and careful installation.

Figure 2-7: A Wi-Fi logo

NOTE *See "Extending the Network" on page 167 for more about long-range Wi-Fi operation.*

Because most Wi-Fi signals have such a limited range, you must find a new access point, or *hot spot*, and set up a new connection every time you move your computer to a new location. And because many Wi-Fi access points don't permit strangers to connect through them, you may have to establish a separate account for each location.

The Wi-Fi networks described in this book follow the 802.11a, b, and g standards, but much of the same information will also apply to the new 802.11n networks when they become available.

Metropolitan Wi-Fi Services

In some metropolitan areas, a large number of interconnected Wi-Fi base stations are being installed by either local government agencies or private businesses to provide wireless service throughout an entire region or in selected neighborhoods as an economical alternative to cable and telephone (DSL) services. The base stations for these services are often mounted on utility poles or rooftops.

These same networks might also provide a variety of special data services to the local government and major subscribers. For example, the local natural gas, electric, and water utilities could add small Wi-Fi adapters to their meters and use the system to send readings once a month. And city buses might have transponders that report their locations to a central tracking system, like the one in Seattle at *http://busview.org/busview_launch.jsp*, as shown in Figure 2-8.

It's not yet clear whether these city-wide Wi-Fi services will be able to overcome possible interference problems and competition from other wireless data alternatives, or whether they will attract enough business to remain viable. But if they do, any computer within the coverage area that has a Wi-Fi adapter should detect the signal and have access to a broadband Internet connection.

Figure 2-8: Wireless technology tracks city buses in Seattle and reports locations on a website.

Cellular Mobile Wireless Services

Several broadband wireless data services are extensions of cellular mobile telephone technology. You might see them described as 3G services because they're based on the third generation of cellular telephone technology. If you have been using a mobile telephone for more than a year or two, you probably remember that the earliest phones were only good for voice calls, but as each new generation was introduced, your mobile carrier offered more and better features. Table 2-2 describes the various generations.

For people who use their computers away from their home or office, the great advantage of a mobile broadband service is that it covers a much wider territory than any Wi-Fi base station; you can connect your computer to the Internet without the need to search for a new hot spot and use a different access account in each new location, and you can even keep the same connection alive in a moving vehicle. Each of the major wireless broadband services offers coverage in most metropolitan areas and much of the countryside between cities.

Table 2-2: Cellular Mobile Telephone Generations

Name	Features
1G	Analog voice communication only
2G	System can handle more calls Digital voice 　Uses less power 　Less background noise Digital data 　Simple text messages 　Email
2.5G	Packet-switched signaling Faster data transfer (up to 144Kbps) Supports relatively slow Internet connections
3G	Even more calls at the same time Much faster data transfer rates (up to 2.4Mbps) Broadband Internet Video and music
4G (not yet available)	Based on Internet technology Packet signaling Very high speed (100Mbps–1Gbps) Will combine telephone, computer, and other technologies

Of course, computer technology has also been improving at the same time, so today's 2.5G and 3G mobile telephones often incorporate enough computing power to allow them to double as pocket-size Internet terminals (as well as cameras and media players). And equally important, from the perspective of this book, broadband data adapters that use 2.5G and 3G technology can attach to a laptop or other portable computer and provide a direct wireless connection to the Internet through the same cellular telephone company that offers mobile telephone service.

Today, most cellular broadband wireless services offer credit card–size adapters that connect to your computer through the PC Card socket on the side of a laptop or into the front or back panel of a desktop computer. In another year or two, many new laptops will come with internal adapters and integrated antennas for both Wi-Fi and 3G wireless or WiMAX that mount directly on the motherboard, just as they contain internal Wi-Fi adapters and dial-up modems today.

NOTE　*Some cellular service providers also offer mobile telephones that can connect a computer to the Internet through a USB cable linked to the phone, but separate PC Card adapters are a lot more convenient and easy to use.*

WiMAX

Worldwide Interoperability for Microwave Access (WiMAX) is yet another method for distributing broadband wireless data over wide geographic areas. It's a *metropolitan area network* service that typically uses one or more base stations that can each provide service to users within a 30-mile radius. The IEEE 802.16 specification contains the technical details of WiMAX networks.

In the United States, the earliest WiMAX services were offered by Clearwire as a wireless alternative to DSL and cable broadband Internet access in fixed locations (such as homes and businesses), but mobile WiMAX access is not far behind. By early 2008, Clearwire plans to offer access to their wireless networks through an adapter on a PC Card. When those adapters become available, WiMAX, 3G cellular data services, and metropolitan Wi-Fi networks will compete for the same commercial niche: wireless access to the Internet through a service that covers an entire metropolitan area.

Each WiMAX service provider uses one or more licensed operating frequencies somewhere between 2 GHz and 11 GHz. A WiMAX link can transfer data (including handshaking and other overhead) at up to 70Mbps, but most commercial WiMAX services are significantly slower than that. And as more and more users share a single WiMAX tower and base station, some users report that their signal quality deteriorates.

Unlike the cellular broadband wireless data services that piggyback on existing mobile telephone networks, WiMAX is a separate radio system that is designed to either supplement or replace the existing broadband Internet distribution systems. In practice, WiMAX competes with both 3G wireless services and with Internet service providers that distribute Internet access to fixed locations through telephone lines and cable television utilities. Home and business subscribers to a WiMAX service usually use either a wired LAN or Wi-Fi to distribute the network within their buildings. Figure 2-9 shows a typical WiMAX network.

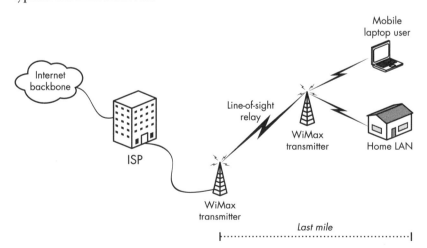

Figure 2-9: WiMAX provides last mile Internet connections to homes and businesses.

What About Bluetooth?

Bluetooth is the other type of wireless networking technology that we ought to describe. Bluetooth uses radio signals to replace the wires and cables that connect a computer or a mobile telephone to peripheral devices, such as a keyboard, a mouse, or a set of speakers. You can also use Bluetooth to transfer data between a computer and a mobile telephone, smartphone, BlackBerry, or other PDA (personal digital assistant).

Bluetooth is an FHSS system that splits the radio signal into tiny pieces. It moves among 79 different frequencies 1,600 times per second in the same unlicensed 2.4 GHz range as 802.11b and 802.11g Wi-Fi services.

Bluetooth is not practical for connecting a computer to the Internet because it's slow (the maximum data transfer rate is only about 700Kbps), and it has a very limited signal range (most often about 33 feet, or 10 meters, or less).

In order to prevent interference between Bluetooth and Wi-Fi signals, many computers that use both technologies (including the widely used Intel Centrino chip set) coordinate the two services. When either module is active, it notifies the other, and the active service takes priority. This coordinated operation is slightly slower than either service operating alone, but the difference is insignificant.

Frequency Allocations

Each type of broadband wireless service uses a specific set of radio frequencies. Some of these frequencies are reserved for the exclusive use of a specific licensed service provider while others are free-for-all bands that are open for anybody to use.

Wi-Fi Services

The 802.11b, 802.11g, and 802.11n Wi-Fi services all operate in a frequency range at or slightly above 2.4 GHz. The 802.11a signal uses a band close to 5.3 GHz. The specific center frequencies of each Wi-Fi channel are listed in Table 2-3.

Unless you're a radio engineer, the important things to know about the different Wi-Fi services are the maximum data transmission rate and the signal range. Table 2-3 shows the important characteristics of each Wi-Fi specification.

The differences between the maximum data speeds and the typical speeds are caused by the handshaking and other nondata information that must attach itself to each data packet. Obviously, there's a tremendous amount of overhead involved in moving information through any kind of Wi-Fi network.

Table 2-3: Wi-Fi Characteristics

Type	Radio Frequency	Signal Range	Maximum Data Speed	Typical Speed
802.11b	2.4 GHz	~30 meters (indoor) ~100 meters (outdoor)	11Mbps	4Mbps
802.11a	5 GHz	~35 meters (indoor) ~110 meters (outdoor)	54Mbps	23Mbps
802.11g	2.4 GHz	~35 meters (indoor) ~110 meters (outdoor)	54Mbps	20Mbps
802.11n (proposed)	2.4 GHz	~70 meters (indoor) ~160 meters (outdoor)	300Mbps	120Mbps

Other Broadband Services

National broadband wireless data service providers use a different variation on spread spectrum technology and a different range of radio frequencies. The broadband wireless services provided by Sprint, AT&T, and Verizon all share the frequencies around 800 MHz and 1,900 MHz used by those companies' digital mobile telephone networks. WiMAX services, such as Clearwire, use signals in the 2.3 to 2.5 GHz and 3.5 GHz bands.

Many new radio frequencies may open up for mobile telephone and data services in the United States after February 17, 2009, when all the existing analog television stations move to new digital channels, and the old VHF channels will close down. The newly vacant radio spectrum will become available for new services, including broadband wireless data.

NOTE   *Don't panic. All your favorite television stations will still be available after the changeover. You will need either an inexpensive converter box or a new digital television set to receive them, but they'll still be there for you.*

The exact frequencies that the WiMAX and broadband wireless data services use are less important to you as a user than the frequencies of Wi-Fi signals because service providers control the base stations and access points. The network interface device in your computer automatically finds the right signal and sets up the connection without forcing you to choose a specific channel.

Choosing a Service

Each type of wireless access to the Internet offers a different combination of cost, coverage areas, reliability, ease of use, and security. Your choice will depend on your particular needs and the availability of signals in the locations where you need wireless Internet access.

For example, if you use your computer in just a few places and all of those places are within range of Wi-Fi hot spots, the built-in Wi-Fi adapter (or an inexpensive plug-in adapter) is probably your best choice. It's likely that Wi-Fi hot spots already exist at your workplace and in the libraries, coffee shops, schools, and conference centers where you regularly spend time, and it's relatively easy and inexpensive to install one or more access points at home. However, you will probably need a separate account to log in to each Wi-Fi network. Some of these Wi-Fi services are free, but others charge for access by the hour, by the day, or by the month; if you need paid accounts at several locations, the total cost can be more than a single account with a cellular service.

Wi-Fi also allows you to add portable computers to an existing LAN at home or in your school or workplace. And if cost is a primary concern, you will probably choose to use free public Wi-Fi hot spots instead of a cellular or WiMAX service that charges a monthly fee.

On the other hand, if you want constant Internet access wherever you go, the cellular data and WiMAX metropolitan area network services are better choices. Both systems provide coverage throughout large geographic regions, and both allow you to maintain a connection while you're moving from one place to another. You can use the same account and the same login and password every time you set up a connection. However, it's important to make sure that there's a usable cellular or WiMAX signal in all the places where you expect to use them *before* you commit to a long-term contract. Most wireless data service providers offer a free or low cost trial period that you can use to test the system.

As WiMAX and cellular data services become more common, many laptop computers and add-on network adapters will operate with both types of wireless services. When the computer detects a high-speed Wi-Fi signal, it will automatically try to establish a connection to that network. But when there is no local Wi-Fi signal, or if you haven't configured your computer to use any of the local signals, it will automatically shift over to your WiMAX or cellular data account and use that service to connect to the Internet.

All three types of wireless Internet services—Wi-Fi, cellular, and WiMAX—offer fast and reliable connections, but each has a different set of strengths and weaknesses. For short-range coverage and for access to local area networks, Wi-Fi is the obvious choice. If you are outside of the service areas of a DSL or cable Internet service, WiMAX is a huge improvement over a slow dial-up service. But when you carry your computer to many locations, a single account with a cellular or WiMAX service will allow you to connect to the Internet without the need to search for a new hot spot and set up a new account.

3

HOW WI-FI WORKS

Wireless Ethernet, better known as Wi-Fi, uses spread-spectrum radio signaling to distribute computer data through local area networks. This chapter describes the technical details of Wi-Fi networking, including the differences among the Wi-Fi standards and the structure of a network. It also includes basic information about Wi-Fi access points (also called *base stations*) and network interface adapters.

Wi-Fi Network Controls

Wi-Fi specifications control the way data moves through the physical layer (the radio link), and it defines a media access control (MAC) layer that handles the interface between the physical layer and the rest of the network structure.

The Physical Layer

In an 802.11 network, the radio transmitter adds a 144-bit preamble to each packet, with 128 bits that the receiver uses to synchronize with the transmitter and a 16-bit start-of-frame field (a *frame* is a packet with additional data added to the beginning or end of the bit string). This is followed by a 48-bit header that contains information about the data transfer speed, the length of the data contained in the packet, and an error-checking sequence. This header is called the PHY preamble because it controls the physical layer (in the ISO model) of the communication link.

Because the header specifies the speed of the data that follows it, the preamble and the header are always transmitted at 1Mbps. Therefore, even if a network link is operating at the full 11Mbps, the effective data transfer speed is considerably slower. In practice, the best you can expect is about 85 percent of the nominal speed, and the other types of overhead in the data packets reduce the actual speed even more.

The 144-bit preamble is a holdover from the older and slower DSSS systems that has stayed in the specification to assure that 802.11 devices are still compatible with the older standards, but it really doesn't accomplish anything useful. There is an optional alternative that uses a shorter 72-bit preamble. In a short preamble, the synchronization field has 56 bits that are combined with the same 16-bit start-of-frame field used in long preambles. The 72-bit preamble is not compatible with very old 802.11 hardware, but that doesn't matter in a modern Wi-Fi network because all the nodes can recognize the short preamble format. In all other respects, a short preamble works just as well as a long one.

It takes the network a maximum of 192 milliseconds to handle a long preamble, compared to 96 milliseconds for a short preamble. In other words, the short preamble cuts the overhead on each packet in half. This makes a significant difference in the actual data transmission speed, especially for things like streaming audio and video and voice over Internet services.

Some manufacturers use the long preamble as the default, and others use the short preamble. It's usually possible to change the preamble length in the configuration software for network adapters and access points.

For most users, preamble length is one of those technical details that you don't have to understand as long as it's the same for all the devices in the network. Fifteen years ago, when telephone modems were the most common way to connect one computer to another, we all had to worry about setting the data bits and stop bits every time we placed a call through a modem. You probably never knew exactly what a stop bit is (it's the amount of time an old mechanical Teletype printer needed to return to the idle state after sending or receiving each byte), but you knew that it had to be the same at both ends. Preamble length is the same kind of obscure setting: It has to be the same on every node in a network, but most people neither know nor care what it means.

The MAC Layer

Within the ISO model, the MAC layer (which is usually understood as a subset of the data link layer) controls the traffic that moves through the radio network. It prevents data collisions and conflicts by using a set of rules called *carrier sense multiple access/collision avoidance (CSMA/CA)*, and it supports the security functions specified in the 802.11 standards. When the network includes more than one access point, the MAC layer associates each network client with the access point that provides the best signal quality.

When more than one node in the network tries to transmit data at the same time, CSMA/CA instructs all but one of the conflicting nodes to back off and try again later, and it allows the surviving node to send its packet. CSMA/CA works like this: When a network node is ready to send a packet, it listens for other signals first. If it doesn't hear anything, it waits for a random (but short) period of time and then listens again. If it still doesn't sense a signal, it transmits a packet. The device that receives the packet evaluates it, and if it's intact, the receiving mode returns an acknowledgment. But if the sending node does not receive the acknowledgment, it assumes that there has been a collision with another packet that scrambled the data, so it waits for another random interval and then tries again.

CSMA/CA also has an optional feature that sets an access point (the bridge between the wireless LAN and the backbone network) as a point coordinator that can grant priority to a network node that is trying to send time-critical data types, such as voice or streaming media.

The MAC layer can support two kinds of authentication to confirm that a network device is authorized to join the network: open authentication and shared key. When you configure your network, all the nodes in the network must use the same kind of authentication. The network supports all of these housekeeping functions in the MAC layer by exchanging (or trying to exchange) a series of control frames before it allows the higher layers to send data. It also sets several options on the network adapter:

- The network supports two power modes: continuous aware mode and power save polling mode. In *continuous aware mode*, the radio receiver is always on and consuming power. In *power save polling mode*, the radio is idle much of the time, but it periodically polls the access point for new messages. As the name suggests, power save polling mode reduces the battery drain on portable devices such as laptop computers and PDAs.

- The network contains the access control that keeps unauthorized users out of the network. A Wi-Fi network can use two forms of access control: the *SSID* (the name of the network) and the *MAC address* (a unique string of characters that identifies each network node). Each network node must have the SSID programmed into it or the access point will not associate with that node. An optional table of MAC addresses can restrict access to radios whose addresses are on the list. It controls the wired equivalent privacy (WEP) or Wi-Fi protected access (WPA) encryption function. WEP encryption can use either a 64-bit or a 128-bit encryption key to encode and decode data as it passes through the radio link; WPA uses a 128-bit key and a 48-bit initialization vector (see Chapter 12 for information about using Wi-Fi encryption).

Other Control Layers

All of the activity specified in the 802.11 standards takes place at the PHY and MAC layers. The higher layers control things like addressing and routing, data integrity, syntax, and the format of the data contained inside each packet. It doesn't make any difference to these layers whether they're moving packets through wires, fiber optic lines, or radio links. Therefore, you can use a wireless network with any kind of LAN or other network protocol. The same radios can handle TCP/IP, Novell NetWare, and all the other network protocols built into Windows, Unix, Macintosh, and other operating systems equally well.

Wi-Fi Network Protocols

The first Wi-Fi method to reach the marketplace was the 802.11b version in 1999, and the faster 802.11a followed about a year later, though the standards were released at the same time. By 2003, the IEEE standards group had developed the newer 802.11g specification that offered the best of both earlier types: It's as fast as 802.11a, and it has the greater signal range of 802.11b. The 802.11g specification is also backward compatible with 802.11b, so an older 802.11b-only network adapter will work (albeit at slower 802.11b speeds) with an 802.11g access point.

NOTE   *There are also specifications designated as 802.11c, d, e and f, but they have to do with things like bridge operation and Quality of Service (QoS). Unless you're manufacturing your own base stations, you'll never have to worry about them.*

The latest Wi-Fi specification is 802.11n. It provides higher speed and better security than any of the earlier versions. You can expect 802.11n access points to also work with 802.11b and 802.11g network adapters.

When you're using a Wi-Fi system to connect to the Internet, it's important to remember that the data transfer speed across the wireless link is less relevant than you might expect. The maximum bandwidth of your incoming Wi-Fi signal can't be greater than the speed of the data that the access point receives. Even if the network's Wi-Fi base station can handle relatively high-speed signaling, it's probably connected to the Internet through a T-1, cable modem, or DSL line that has a maximum speed of 5Mbps or less, so that's the maximum speed that it can relay the signal to you.

Wi-Fi Radio Frequencies

By international agreement, a section of radio spectrum near 2.4 GHz is reserved for unlicensed industrial, scientific, and medical (ISM) services, including spread spectrum wireless data networks. The 802.11b, 802.11g, and 802.11n services all use this band.

Another band of frequencies near 5.3 GHz is reserved for something called the unlicensed national information infrastructure (U-NII). The Federal Communications Commission (FCC) in the United States and similar regulatory bodies in other countries permit wireless networking in both the ISM band and the U-NII band. 802.11a operates in the U-NII band.

However, the exact frequency allocations for Wi-Fi services are slightly different from one part of the world to another; the authorities in different countries have assigned slightly different frequency bands. Table 3-1 shows the 2.4 GHz frequency assignments in several locations.

Table 3-1: Unlicensed 2.4 GHz Spread Spectrum Frequency Assignments

Region	ISM Frequency Band
North America	2.4000–2.4835 GHz
Europe	2.4000–2.4835 GHz
France	2.4465–2.4835 GHz
Spain	2.445–2.475 GHz
Japan	2.471–2.497 GHz

Just about every other country in the world also uses one of these bands. Those minor differences in frequency allocations are not particularly important (unless you plan to transmit across the border between France and Spain or something equally unlikely) because most networks operate entirely within a single country or region, and the normal signal range is usually just a few hundred feet. There's enough overlap among the various national standards to allow the same equipment to operate legally anywhere in the world. The set of channels your equipment can use is typically dictated by the country it was sold in, and it is usually set by the manufacturer.

Wireless Channels

The exact frequency that a particular wireless network uses is determined by its channel. In North America, Wi-Fi devices use 11 802.11b/g channels. Many other countries have authorized 13 channels, but Japan uses 14 channels, and only 4 are available in France. Fortunately, the entire world uses the same set of channel numbers, so channel 9 in New York uses exactly the same frequency as channel 9 in Tokyo or Paris. Table 3-2 shows the channels used in different countries and regions.

Table 3-2: Wireless Ethernet Channel Assignments

Channel	Frequency (GHz)	Used In
1	2.412	United States,[*] EMEA,[†] China, Japan
2	2.417	United States, EMEA, China, Japan
3	2.422	United States, EMEA, Israel, China, Japan
4	2.427	United States, EMEA, Israel, China, Japan
5	2.432	United States, EMEA, Israel, China, Japan
6	2.437	United States, EMEA, Israel, China, Japan
7	2.442	United States, EMEA, Israel, China, Japan
8	2.447	United States, EMEA, Israel, China, Japan
9	2.452	United States, EMEA, Israel, China, Japan
10	2.457	United States, EMEA, France, China, Japan
11	2.462	United States, EMEA, France, China, Japan
12	2.467	EMEA, France, Japan
13	2.472	EMEA, France, Japan
14	2.484	Japan

[*] Canada and some other countries in the Western Hemisphere use the same channel assignments as the United States.

[†] EMEA means *Europe, Middle East, and Africa.* France is part of the EMEA regulatory region, but the French government only permits Wi-Fi usage on channels 10 through 14.

You might have to set your network adapter to a different channel number when you take it abroad (if the adapter doesn't automatically detect a signal), but there's almost always a way to connect, assuming there's a network within range of your adapter. If you're not sure which channels to use in another country, consult the local regulatory authority for specific information. Alternatively, you can use channels 10 and 11, which are legal everywhere except Israel.

Reducing Interference

Note that the frequency specified for each of those channels is actually the center frequency of a 22 MHz channel. Therefore, each channel overlaps with several other channels that are above and below it. The whole 2.4 GHz band only has space for three completely separate channels, so if your network runs on channel 4, for example, and your neighbor is using channel 5 or channel 6, each network will detect the other network's signals as interference. Both networks will work, but the performance (as reflected in the data transfer speed) will not be as good as it would be when the channels are more widely separated from one another.

To minimize this kind of interference, you should try to coordinate channel usage with other nearby network managers (your neighbors running their own home Wi-Fi networks count as network managers). If possible, each network should use channels that are at least 25 MHz or five channel numbers apart. If you're trying to eliminate interference between two networks, use one high channel number and one low number. For three channels, your best choices are channels 1, 6, and 11, as shown in Figure 3-1. For more than three networks, you'll have to put up with some amount of interference, but you can keep it to a minimum by assigning a new channel in the middle of an existing pair.

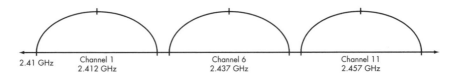

Figure 3-1: Channels 1, 6, and 11 do not interfere with one another.

This all sounds more serious than it is likely to be on the ground. In practice, you can optimize the performance of your network by staying away from a channel that somebody else is using nearby, but even if you and your neighbor are on adjacent channels, your networks will probably work, although your connections might be a bit slower than they'd be on more widely separated channels. Unless your neighbor's network is extremely busy, you're likely to have more problems with interference from other devices using the 2.4 GHz band, such as cordless telephones and microwave ovens.

The 802.11a Wi-Fi specification uses a different range of radio frequencies, as shown in Table 3-3. Each channel is 20 MHz wide, so similar rules about channel separation apply.

Table 3-3: 802.11a Wi-Fi Frequencies

Channel Number	Frequency in GHz	Used In
34	5.17	Japan
36	5.18	North America, Europe, Singapore
38	5.19	Japan
40	5.20	North America, Europe, Singapore
42	5.21	Japan
44	5.22	North America, Europe, Singapore
46	5.23	Japan
48	5.24	North America, Europe, Singapore
52	5.26	North America, Taiwan
56	5.28	North America, Taiwan
60	5.30	North America, Taiwan
64	5.32	North America, Taiwan

Choosing the operating channel is the network operator's responsibility. When you connect to an existing network, your computer or network adapter will automatically detect one or more Wi-Fi signals and allow you to choose the one you want to use. Most Wi-Fi adapters and network interfaces can recognize more than one Wi-Fi protocol and configure the connection for the active signal. So, for example, if your computer finds both an 802.11a signal and an 802.11g signal, you can choose either one without the need to manually change the internal settings.

The 802.11 specifications and various national regulatory agencies (such as the FCC in the United States) have also set limits on the amount of transmitter power and antenna gain that a Wi-Fi device can use. This restriction is intended to limit the distance over which a network link can operate, and therefore it allows more networks to use the same channels without interference. We'll talk about methods for working around those power limits and extending the range of your wireless network without violating the law in Chapter 10.

Wireless Network Devices

After you have defined the data format and the radio links, the next step is to set up a network structure. How do computers use the radios and the data format to actually exchange data?

Wi-Fi networks include two categories of radios: network adapters and access points. A *network adapter* is connected to a computer or some other device, such as a printer, that exchanges data with a wireless network. An *access point* is the base station for a wireless network, and is a bridge between the wireless network and a traditional wired network.

Network Adapters

Wi-Fi network adapters can take several physical forms:

Plug-in PC Cards that fit the PCMCIA sockets in most laptop computers
To bypass the internal shielding in most computers, the built-in antennas and status lights in most wireless PC Card adapters extend about an inch beyond the opening of the card socket. Other PC Card adapters have sockets for external antennas.

Internal network adapters on PCI cards that fit inside a desktop computer
Most PCI adapters are actually PCMCIA sockets that allow a user to plug a PC Card into the back of the computer, but a few are built directly on the PCI expansion cards. As an alternative to a rear panel socket, separate PCMCIA sockets that fit a computer's external front panel drive bays are available from Actiontec and several other manufacturers.

External USB adapters
USB adapters are often a better choice than PC Cards or internal adapters because they're easier to install, and it's almost always easier to move an adapter at the end of a cable to a position with the best possible radio signal path to and from the nearest access point.

Internal wireless adapters built into laptop computers

Internal adapters are modules that plug into the computer's mother-board. They present the same appearance to the operating system as an external PCMCIA card. The antennas for built-in radios are usually hidden inside the computer's fold-over clamshell screen.

Plug-in adapters for PDAs and other handheld devices

PDAs and other handheld devices often have expansion ports that can take one of several types of expansion cards. Typically, they present the same appearance to the operating system as a larger expansion card in a laptop. It is rare for adapters for PDAs and handhelds to have antenna jacks.

Internal network interfaces built into other devices, such as Internet-capable telephone sets and office or household appliances

Today, printers, digital cameras, Internet radios, voice over Internet (VoIP) telephones, home entertainment systems, and many other devices can all use Wi-Fi links to send and receive images, audio, and other forms of data. In the future, sophisticated household appliances will use Wi-Fi to transmit status messages when your clothes are dry or your roast has reached its ideal temperature.

A network adapter should work with any operating system as long as a driver for that adapter is available. In practice, that means you can find Windows drivers for just about everything, but you will have fewer choices if you're using a computer running Mac OS, Linux, or Unix. You can find pointers to sources for Linux and Unix drivers in Chapter 7, and information about using Wi-Fi with a Macintosh in Chapter 8.

Adapters for Multiple Network Types

In some situations, you might want to use different kinds of network connections in different places. For example, when your laptop is running in your office, you will want it to connect to your LAN through a Wi-Fi link so you can use the company's high-speed Internet account and exchange files and messages with other local computers. But when you take the same computer on the road, you want to connect to the Internet through a cellular data service. Therefore, it would be very convenient if your computer could automatically choose the best connection for your current location.

Today, the only way to change network types is to manually choose the software that controls each type of network; you might also have to physically remove one network adapter and insert another one. But the makers of laptop computers and network interface adapters are working on this problem, and several of them will offer a single network adapter and control software in the near future that detects more than one type of wireless service and either offers an onscreen choice or automatically selects the best connection for you.

When you install one of these multiple-service adapters, you can set up your own list of priorities; for example, you might want it to look for your home or office LAN first, and if that's not available, to set up a connection to your cellular data account.

Access Points

Access points are often combined with other network functions. It's quite possible to find a stand-alone access point that just plugs into a wired LAN through a data cable, but there are plenty of other options. Common access point configurations include:

- Simple base stations with a bridge to an Internet port for connection to a LAN

- Base stations that include a switch, hub, or router with one or more wired Ethernet ports along with the wireless access point

- Broadband routers that provide a bridge between a cable modem or DSL port and the wireless access point

- Software access points that use one of the wireless network interface adapters in your computer as the base station

- Residential gateways that support a limited number of operating channels

The physical design of access points varies from one manufacturer to another. Some look like industrial devices that were intended to be placed out of sight on the floor or mounted on an inconspicuous wall, but others (especially the ones targeted at the home network market) have swooshy, "aerodynamic" shapes that appear to have been designed for the top of a coffee table or, more likely, next to a desktop computer. Some have internal antennas, others (like the one in Figure 3-2) have short vertical whips permanently attached, and still others have connectors for external antennas (which may or may not be supplied with the access point). Regardless of its size and shape, every access point includes a radio that sends and receives messages and data between network stations and an Ethernet port that connects to a wired network.

Photo courtesy of Linksys, a division of Cisco Systems, Inc.

Figure 3-2: A typical Wi-Fi access point, this one from Linksys

Building a Network

Wi-Fi networks operate in two modes: ad hoc networks and infrastructure networks. As the name suggests, an ad hoc network is usually temporary. An *ad hoc network* is a self-contained group of stations with no connection to a larger LAN or the Internet. It includes two or more wireless stations with no access point or connection to the rest of the world. Ad hoc networks are also called *peer-to-peer networks* and *independent basic service sets (IBSS)*. Figure 3-3 shows a simple ad hoc network.

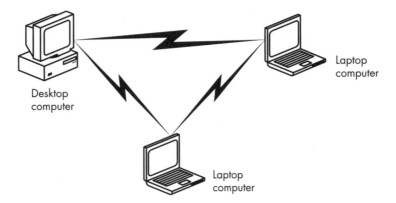

Figure 3-3: An ad hoc wireless network with three stations

Infrastructure networks have one or more access points that are almost always connected to a wired network. Each wireless station exchanges messages and data with the access point, which relays them to other nodes on the wireless network or the wired LAN. Any network that requires a wired connection through an access point to a printer, a fileserver, or an Internet gateway is an infrastructure network. Figure 3-4 shows an infrastructure network.

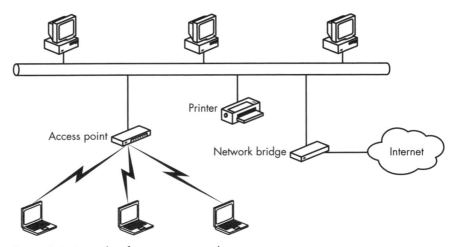

Figure 3-4: A simple infrastructure network

An infrastructure network with just one base station is also called a *basic service set (BSS)*. When the wireless network uses two or more access points, the network structure is an *extended service set (ESS)*. Recall that the technical name for a network ID is the *SSID*. You might also see it called a *BSSID* if the network has just one access point or an *ESSID* when it has two or more access points.

A network with more than one access point (an ESS) creates several new complications. First, the network must include a way for only one base station to handle data from a particular station, even if the station is within range of more than one base station. And if the station is moving during a network session, or if some kind of local interference crops up near the first access point, the network might have to hand off the connection from one access point to another. Wi-Fi networks handle this problem by associating a station with only one access point at a time and ignoring the signals from stations that are not associated. When the signal fades at one access point and improves at another, or when the amount of traffic forces the network to rebalance the load, the network will reassociate the station with a new access point that can provide acceptable service. If you think this sounds a lot like the way a cellular telephone system handles roaming, you're absolutely correct; even the terminology is the same—it's also called *roaming*.

Public and Private Networks

Wi-Fi is an unlicensed radio service, and that means that anybody can set up a base station (licensed radio services typically require an expensive license to operate a radio at a specific location for a fixed number of years). Some of these base stations limit access to a specific set of users, but others allow any computer within range of the radio signal to set up a connection.

When your computer searches for a Wi-Fi signal, it's likely that it will find more than one active network; some of them might be private networks, and others might be accessible to anybody who wants to use them. Public access points, also called *hot spots*, allow any nearby computer to establish a connection; some require paid accounts, but many others, especially in places like schools and libraries, are free (although they might require a login name and password).

As a general rule, most private networks should have one or more security features, such as encryption or MAC address restriction that locks out unauthorized users, but it's not uncommon to find home and business networks that are wide open because the owner never bothered to turn on the security tools. We'll explain how to use MAC address restriction and other security tools in Chapter 12.

Putting It All Together

The radio link, the data structure, and the network architecture are the three essential elements that form the internal plumbing of a Wi-Fi network. Like the components of most other networks (and most plumbing systems, for that matter), these elements should be entirely invisible to the people using the network—if users can send and receive messages, read files, and perform other activities on the network, they should never have to worry about the low-level details.

Of course, this assumes that it always works exactly as it's supposed to work, and users never have to call a network help desk to ask why they can't read their email. Now that you have read this chapter, you probably know more about the way your wireless LAN moves messages from here to there than 95 percent of the people who use Wi-Fi networks. And you have a good chance of understanding the support person who tells you to make sure you're using channel 11, or that you need to change your preamble length, or that your adapter is operating in infrastructure mode.

4

THE HARDWARE YOU NEED
FOR WI-FI

 A wireless local area network (LAN) obviously requires a somewhat different set of hardware components from a traditional wired network. This chapter describes the components that go into a wireless network and offers advice about deciding which components will best meet your needs. As you read the descriptions of features and functions in access points, network adapters, and antennas, remember that the marketplace for wireless networking equipment is both extremely competitive, and rapidly changing. If one manufacturer offers an access point or network adapter with a hot new feature, you can expect that same feature to show up in competing products within a few months or less. Therefore, this chapter does not discuss specific brands or models; by the time you read this, any such recommendation would be wildly out of date.

Everybody Speaks the Same Language (More or Less)

Before we talk about specific features and functions, it may be useful to review the rules—and the realities—about using equipment made by more than one manufacturer in the same wireless network. It can be done, but it's not quite as simple as the people at the Wi-Fi Alliance would have you believe.

Dozens of companies make equipment that qualifies for Wi-Fi certification. To receive that certification, each device must undergo interoperability testing by the Alliance's independent testing lab. If an access point or network adapter carries a Wi-Fi logo, it has passed an extensive series of tests to confirm that it works with previously certified hardware from several other vendors.

Access points and network adapters from different manufacturers may look different on the outside, and each maker provides its own configuration software, but the radio circuits inside are all pretty similar. Adapters that carry many brand names are actually made under contract by other companies, and just about everybody uses one of just a few standard chip sets.

In other words, it's possible to use any combination of Wi-Fi–certified adapters and access points together in the same network as long as they all follow the same specification (e.g., 802.11b, 802.11a, or 802.11g). The critical word in that last sentence is *possible*. In practice, certification really means that a group of technicians who are intimately familiar with the internal workings of Wi-Fi networks can get a mixed-vendor network to operate properly in a carefully run series of tests under tightly controlled laboratory conditions.

Does that mean that a homeowner or the IT person in a small business who has never installed a wireless network can get that same combination of products to work? Oh, probably, but maybe not on the first attempt. It may take a lot of time and aggravation to set all the configuration options to the correct values. It's almost always a safe bet that devices from different makers will have different default settings. For example, some systems use short preambles as the default, and others use long preambles; some configurations request encryption keys as ASCII characters, but others might want them in hexadecimal. You can make all this stuff work together, but it might be a somewhat painful experience.

As a general rule, it's almost always easier to equip your entire network with hardware from a single manufacturer because the configuration settings and options will all be the same, but that's not always possible or even the best choice. You can control the brands of access points in your own network, and you can buy the same brand of external network adapters for your desktop computers, but eventually one of the users in your office network (and you can probably predict who it will be, can't you?) will come to you with a Wi-Fi adapter made by somebody you've never heard of, and they'll expect it to connect to your network. Maybe the adapter showed up at a garage sale or a swap meet, or maybe it came with a shiny new laptop computer. Or maybe it's the one your daughter's school recommended for the on-campus network. And you have little or no control over the make and model of the internal adapters built into a laptop computer or the base station used by a public hot spot. For one reason or another, you'll eventually have to integrate hardware and software from more than one maker into the same network.

The information in this book will help you to understand exactly what you need to do to make everything work together, but when you're building your own Wi-Fi network, you can reduce the number of headaches by using equipment from a single source.

NOTE   *One more point is worth mentioning here: When you buy a Wi-Fi adapter, you generally get what you pay for. In most cases, expensive versions from major manufacturers are a lot more likely to work with a variety of base stations than their less costly generic counterparts. Higher quality radios can also help boost your signal range and make more base stations in an area available to you.*

Network Adapters

A network adapter is the interface between a computer and a network. In a wireless network, the adapter contains a radio transmitter that sends data from the computer to the network and a receiver that detects incoming radio signals that contain data from the network and passes it along to the computer. The computer's operating system treats a wireless adapter just like any other network interface.

If you only plan to use Wi-Fi to connect your computer to the Internet through existing Wi-Fi hot spots in public locations, such as libraries, coffee shops, and so forth, a network adapter (along with the software to support it) is the only new hardware you need to add to your computer. If you want to set up your own home or office network, you'll also need one or more access points.

Built-in Wi-Fi adapters are standard features of new laptop computers. If your laptop already has a wireless interface, there's generally no reason to replace it until a new Wi-Fi specification, such as the 802.11n standard, becomes available—and perhaps not even then if you're satisfied with your existing equipment. So choosing a new adapter is particularly important for owners of desktop computers and older laptops. If you have an older laptop without a built-in adapter, you can add Wi-Fi capability by installing a plug-in adapter on a PC Card or connecting a USB adapter.

Most new Wi-Fi network adapters automatically recognize signals that use all three Wi-Fi specifications (or all four, after 802.11n comes out). When the adapter detects a signal from an access point, it identifies the signal type and uses the same specification to exchange data with that access point.

You should consider several things when you select an interface adapter: the physical package (the form factor), the type of antenna (internal or external? directional or not?), compatibility with the network's access points and other nodes in the network, and compatibility with the computer's operating system. And of course, you should also consider all the standard issues that apply to any piece of computer hardware or software: ease of use, security, quality of technical support, and other users' experiences with the product and the company.

Form Factor

In most cases, the wireless adapter plugs into one of the computer's high-speed I/O ports—either an internal expansion card slot, a socket on a laptop's motherboard, a PCMCIA (PC Card) socket, or a USB port. Network adapters for PDAs usually fit into CompactFlash or SDIO (Secure Digital Input/Output) sockets.

Each type of adapter has its own advantages and drawbacks. The choice of a particular package depends on the computer you will use with the adapter and the way you expect to use it. For example, if you want to connect a laptop computer to the network, an internal adapter or a PC Card is usually the best option because it's easy to install, it doesn't take up much space, and it doesn't force you to carry a special cable. But in a desktop system, a USB adapter is often a better choice.

Internal Adapters

Almost all new laptop computers have an adapter module on a mini-PCI card mounted directly onto the motherboard with one or more antennas inside the clamshell section of the case that also holds the display screen. Even if you choose to save money by ordering a laptop without the adapter, the computer probably has an antenna, so you can install a Wi-Fi module later.

The obvious advantage of an internal adapter is that it doesn't force a user to carry (and possibly forget or lose) yet another accessory item along with the computer. The disadvantage, if there is one, is that it's not practical to move the same adapter to a different computer when it's time to repair or replace the original machine. If the backup unit doesn't have an internal adapter (which is possible because it's probably older than the primary unit), the user or the network manager will either have to provide a separate adapter on a PC Card, connect through a USB cable, or go without wireless access to the local network and the Internet.

A built-in adapter adds about as much to the cost of a new laptop as you would pay for a Wi-Fi adapter on a separate PC Card. It doesn't make sense to replace your current laptop just to get the internal wireless adapter, but when it's time to look for a new computer, it's a feature worth having.

If your computer does have an internal wireless adapter, there's an easy way to disable the adapter when you aren't using it. Most laptops use either a physical on/off switch or a pair of FN keys to turn the internal adapter on and off. If you don't turn it off when it's not in use, the radio unit will drain your computer's battery more quickly than necessary, and it will produce radio signals that can interfere with other users of the same unlicensed 2.4 GHz frequencies. Depending on the software your computer uses, leaving the wireless radio running can also expose you to security risks because your computer may connect to networks without your knowledge.

The internal adapter mounts onto the computer's motherboard with special connectors for the internal antenna. Lenovo calls this a *field replaceable unit (FRU)*; other makers have similar descriptions for parts that are easy to remove and replace. When new adapters that support the 802.11n specification and other adapters that support both Wi-Fi and 3G wireless or WiMAX on a single card become available, it will be possible to remove the existing adapter and install a new one by following instructions supplied by the laptop's manufacturer.

Most laptop manufacturers limit the internal adapters you can use to those certified by the manufacturer, the FCC, and other regulatory agencies. When you buy a new internal adapter, make sure to check both the manual and your computer manufacturer's website to be sure that model adapter works with your model of laptop, or purchase the adapter from the company that made your computer.

PC Cards

If your laptop computer does not have an internal Wi-Fi adapter, you can add one on a PCMCIA card. Just about every maker of Wi-Fi devices has at least one PC Card adapter in its product line.

Wireless adapters on PC Cards are compact and don't add much weight to a portable computer, which are both important features. However, it's important to remove the adapter from the computer when you don't need a network link. Otherwise, the adapter might continue to radiate unwanted signals and possibly allow an intruder to connect to your computer without your knowledge. A Wi-Fi adapter that is not in use also places a small but unnecessary drain on the computer's battery.

PC Card adapters all look pretty much the same because they all have to fit into a computer's PCMCIA socket. However, some adapters have more features and better performance than others. Once again, you generally get what you pay for. As Figure 4-1 shows, they're about the size of a credit card with a multipin connector at one end and a plastic cover for the internal antenna or a connector for an external antenna at the other end.

Photo courtesy of D-Link

Figure 4-1: A D-Link wireless Ethernet adapter with an internal antenna

There are two main types of PC Cards. *PCMCIA*, the original standard, is a slower 16-bit card. Found on older laptops, PCMCIA slots can only support 802.11b speeds. More modern laptops have *CardBus* support, which looks nearly identical to a PCMCIA connector but supports higher speed 32-bit cards such as 802.11a/g/n. Laptops purchased from the late 1990s onward should have CardBus support. Laptops made after 2006 might have a third type of adapter slot, called *ExpressCard*, either as a replacement for the PC Card socket or as an additional feature. This high-speed slot uses a physically different card and is not compatible with previous cards.

Most PC Card adapters include one or two indicator lights on the section of the adapter that extends beyond the end of the PCMCIA slot. One of these indicators lights when the adapter is receiving power from the computer and the other lights when the adapter detects an active radio link from an access point or another node in an ad hoc network.

Many PC Card adapters contain two internal antennas with a diversity system that constantly compares the quality of the incoming signals from each antenna and automatically selects the stronger one. Even though the two antennas inside a PC Card are only an inch or two apart, the improvement over a single antenna can be substantial.

Network adapters on PC Cards usually have built-in omnidirectional diversity antennas, but some manufacturers also offer versions with connectors for external antennas. The choice of an internal versus external antenna is always a trade-off. In most cases, the internal antenna is a lot easier to use with a portable computer because it doesn't force you to carry a separate antenna and cable. But it's much easier to adjust the exact location of an antenna at the end of a cable instead of the side or back of a computer that you must place in a position where you can comfortably see the screen and reach the keyboard. If you want to link to an access point from the extreme edges of a network's coverage area or if you're operating in a location with a lot of interference, a separate high-gain directional antenna can give you better and more reliable network performance than the antennas built into most PC Cards. If your usual PC Card adapter does not have an external antenna input connector, you might want to remove it and use a USB adapter with a high-gain antenna when you're trying to connect from a fringe location.

USB Adapters

If your computer has a USB (Universal Serial Bus) port, as most desktop and laptop computers built since about 1999 do, a wireless USB adapter might be the best way to connect it to your Wi-Fi network. The adapter connects to the computer through a cable or directly into the computer itself, so it's never a problem to move the whole adapter (with its built-in antenna) to the position that provides the best network performance. Even if the optimal location is on top of a bookcase or filing cabinet or on the floor under your computer table, the location of the adapter won't interfere with your ability to use the computer. It's a lot easier to connect a USB adapter to a desktop computer than to use an adapter on an internal expansion card because you don't have to take apart the computer to install a USB device.

USB adapters come in many shapes and sizes depending on the design and marketing philosophies of the manufacturer. Most USB adapters have captive antennas that are often mounted on hinges or swivels that allow a user to make fine adjustments to their positions. Because the antennas on USB adapters are usually larger and easier to manipulate than the antennas in PC Card adapters, you can expect somewhat better signal quality through a

USB device (but remember that you won't notice any improvement over the threshold that provides a full-speed connection).

Figure 4-2 shows a wireless USB adapter with a hinged antenna made by Linksys. Like the adapters on PC Cards, most USB adapters take their power from the computer so they don't require a separate battery or an external power supply.

Other USB Wi-Fi adapters are compact modules similar to flash drives, as shown in Figure 4-3. These adapters are small and easy to throw into your portable computer's bag as an alternative to a PC Card, but they often have lower maximum transmitter power, which translates to less signal range than either a PC Card or a larger USB adapter, so they are more likely to drop an active connection in marginal reception conditions than other adapters.

Photo courtesy of Linksys, a division of Cisco Systems, Inc.

Figure 4-2: Wireless USB adapters are stand-alone devices that connect to the computer through a cable.

Photo courtesy of Linksys, a division of Cisco Systems, Inc.

Figure 4-3: Compact USB Wi-Fi adapters are small and convenient, but they might not reach as far as other adapters.

Expansion Cards for Desktop Computers

Many internal wireless adapters for desktop systems are actually PC Cards mounted in PCMCIA sockets that fit a PCI expansion slot on the computer's motherboard. The adapter fits a slot in one of the mounting plates on the back of the computer. This approach offers several advantages for the manufacturers: They can use the same PC Card adapter that they sell separately for use in laptops combined with a socket that they obtain and re-label from some third party, and the metal housing of the PC Card provides an effective shield that keeps the radio signals away from the inside of the computer.

But it would be difficult to find a worse place to locate the antenna for a wireless adapter. If the adapter has a built-in antenna, you can't easily move it to a different position to improve the signal quality; if the adapter has an antenna socket, the antenna cable (or the antenna itself) is likely to become tangled with the computer's other cables. The card sticks out from the back of the computer cabinet where you can't see the indicator lights. The backs of most desktop computers are often rats' nests of other cables and connectors that can all affect the radio's radiation pattern. And the computer's metal backplane may act as either an obstruction or a source of multipath interference between the adapter and the nearest access point. Of course, it's entirely possible that a PCI adapter will perform flawlessly, right out of the box, in spite of all those potential problems. Don't assume that it won't work until you have actually tried it in your own network, especially when the adapter was supplied with your computer. But when you're adding Wi-Fi to an existing desktop computer, a USB adapter is almost always a better choice because it's more flexible and easier to install.

If you do encounter connection problems, there are a couple of ways to work around them. If the computer has a USB port, removing (or turning off) the internal adapter and installing a wireless USB adapter is the obvious solution. Even if there's no USB port on the outside of the computer, it's possible that the motherboard has a USB port; if it does, you can use an inexpensive cable and bracket to bring the port out to the backplane. For older motherboards that don't have USB ports, you'll need an expansion card with one or more add-in USB ports.

If signal quality is a problem, look for an adapter that has a connector for an external antenna rather than an antenna built into the adapter itself. Adapters with external antenna connectors are available from Buffalo and Proxim Wireless, among others.

If you're committed to using a built-in adapter, you might want to consider installing a PC Card reader or socket that mounts in a spare external drive bay on the front of a desktop or tower computer network and a separate PC Card adapter, rather than a socket, on the backplane. This makes the adapter much easier to reach than it would be at the back of the computer, and it moves the adapter away from the tangle of other cables and plugs behind the computer. The Actiontec PC750 is among the most widely available front-mounting PC Card readers.

NOTE   *When you shop for a PC Card reader, make sure it's designed to work with network adapters and not just with flash cards and other storage devices.*

Internal vs. External Antennas

Most wireless network adapters come with captive omnidirectional antennas. For most users in most situations, these built-in antennas send and receive a strong, clean data stream between an access point and a nearby computer. But if network adapters with built-in antennas don't provide a good enough signal because of distance, obstructions, or interference from other radio signals, an external antenna may be the best way to solve the problem. As a rule of thumb, you can expect an external antenna to provide a signal at least 15 percent stronger than the antenna built into a PC Card adapter; special high-gain directional antennas can offer even better performance. This translates to either faster data exchange or a greater maximum distance between the computer and the access point.

If you identify a dead spot in your coverage area, a network adapter with a connector for an external antenna instead of a built-in antenna may be the right choice for a computer that remains in that location. But it's a lot more cumbersome to set up a separate antenna before you can log in to the network, so PC Cards with built-in antennas are generally the best choice for laptops and other portables.

As an alternative to an external antenna, consider a USB adapter with a built-in antenna. You can place the adapter anywhere within the length of the USB cable and move it around to find the best signal.

Remember that there are two antennas in the link between a base station and a wireless network adapter—one at the access point and one at the computer. A high-gain antenna at either end will have the same impact on the link, so when you're operating your own network, it will be equally effective to replace the standard antenna on either the access point or the network interface. However, a directional antenna will focus most of the signal in one direction, so a directional access point antenna can reduce the quality of links to other network nodes, as shown in Figure 4-4.

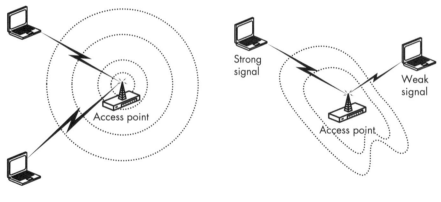

Figure 4-4: Different combinations of directional and non-directional antennas can change the coverage area of a network.

You can find more information about external antennas later in this chapter.

Interoperability

Wi-Fi certification is supposed to assure that network adapters and access points from different manufacturers will work together seamlessly. But there are a few features and configuration options that can make it difficult or impossible to exchange data between certain combinations of hardware. For example, some devices come with 128-bit encryption keys, but others use 64-bit keys. If an access point expects 128 bits, it won't work with the smaller key.

The easiest way to avoid this is to acquire all of your hardware from the same source, and make sure you're not using incompatible models (such as network cards with proprietary "turbo" features). Otherwise, read the specifications carefully, test every new component type with the rest of your network (and one or more public hot spots) as soon as you receive them, and make sure your vendor will accept a return if it isn't compatible.

Adapters and access points that use a prerelease version of the new 802.11n (pre-n) standard are likely to have problems working with devices from other manufacturers because each company is using its best guess about the exact specifications of the new version. So it's best to avoid pre-n equipment unless you have complete control of all the computers that will connect to your network. And even if you do, remember that you may have to upgrade or replace your pre-n devices after the final standard has been adopted. Devices that advertise upgradeability to the final 802.11n standard may be a better choice than devices that do not because it means you will not have to buy new hardware later.

Finding Drivers for Your Adapter

Like every other peripheral device you use with your computer, a wireless network adapter requires specific driver software that contains the controls and interfaces that allow the adapter to exchange data with the computer's central processor. You can safely assume that the software disk supplied with the adapter includes a driver for Microsoft Windows XP and probably for Windows Vista, but that won't do any good if the computer you're trying to link to your network uses Linux or some flavor of Unix. If you're a Macintosh user, Apple's AirPort family of adapters is usually the best choice.

If you don't get the right driver software with your network adapter, you'll have to either find it someplace else or choose a different adapter that supports your operating system. The first place to look is the manufacturer's technical support website, which probably offers a variety of drivers for free download. It you can't find anything there, send a request for information to the manufacturer's technical support center; they might know of a third-party driver for your operating system or invite you to help test a new driver they haven't yet released. If that fails, try an online search for *<adapter make and model> <operating system> driver*.

If you're a Windows user, you must install new drivers when you upgrade from Windows XP (or some earlier version) to Windows Vista. Some drivers are supplied in the Windows Vista package, but many others were not yet available when Vista was released. Again, the best source for new drivers is the adapter manufacturer's website. If your laptop has an internal adapter, look for new drivers on the website maintained by the laptop maker or importer.

Most manufacturers work closely with Microsoft, and when new drivers are available, they often distribute them through the Windows Update website. This is the same site that Microsoft uses to distribute its own updates and patches, but the Automatic Updates feature does not load new drivers unless you specifically request them.

To check for new drivers, follow these steps:

1. Open your Internet Explorer web browser.

2. From the Tools menu, choose **Windows Update**. The Microsoft Update web page will appear.

3. If you haven't used the update tool before, it will offer to load and install the updating software. Go ahead and load it.

4. When the Welcome page shown in Figure 4-5 appears, click the **Custom** button.

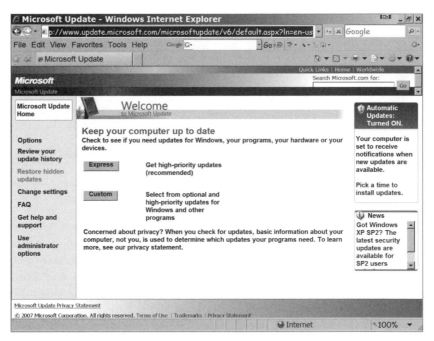

Figure 4-5: Use the Custom button to search for new drivers.

5. The update tool will examine your system and eventually display a list of new updates.

6. In the column at the left side of the web page, look for *Hardware, Optional (n)*, with the number of available updates inside the parentheses. Click the **Hardware** link to see a list of available updates to the network adapter and other devices connected to your computer.

7. Add a checkmark to the box next to each of the updates you want to install. While you're at it, go ahead and look at the *High Priority* and *Software, Optional* lists and select the ones you want to install; they'll probably improve the computer's overall performance.

8. Click the **Review** and **Install** updates link at the top of the list and follow the onscreen instructions to download and install the update software.

9. Restart the computer if the update tool instructs you to do so.

Don't give up if the neither the adapter manufacturer nor Microsoft can help you. Many adapters contain similar internal circuits, so it may be possible to use a driver with an adapter that was originally created for a different brand. For example, the Xircom CWE1100 adapter uses the same drivers as similar adapters from Cisco. See Chapter 7 for Linux and Unix driver sources from user groups and online archives. Without a driver, your adapter is only useful as a paperweight. If you can't find the right driver for your operating system, look for a different adapter. This should not be a problem unless you're using a very old or very cheap adapter, in which case a new one will almost certainly offer more features and better performance than your old clunker.

Ease of Use

Every wireless adapter comes with a utility program that detects nearby Wi-Fi signals and sets the operating mode (infrastructure or ad hoc), the channel number, and all of the other configuration options that must match the settings for the other nodes on the same network.

NOTE *It's always a good idea to look for the most recent software and driver updates on the adapter manufacturer's website. If a web address is not printed on the adapter or in the printed material supplied with it, use Google or some other online search tool to find one.*

As an alternative to the adapter manufacturers' configuration programs, Microsoft includes a generic Wi-Fi program in both Windows XP and Windows Vista, and many laptop makers also provide their own configuration software as part of the customized software package supplied with new computers. So you might have two or three different ways to accomplish the same thing. Figures 4-6, 4-7, and 4-8 show the three programs supplied with a Lenovo ThinkPad laptop.

All three of these programs perform the same job—managing a Wi-Fi connection—but they present the optional settings and status information differently. Some use a single window with all the options in one place while others split things into several separate sections. Some display signal strength and quality as numeric values, but others show the same data in graphic form.

Under ideal conditions, a user would never have to look at the internal workings of the configuration utility because most modern Wi-Fi software automatically matches the adapter's settings to the signal it receives from each access point or ad hoc network. The configuration utility and the status display should both be easy to understand and use. They all contain the same information and options, so the choice comes down to a subjective evaluation: Can you look at the configuration window and understand how to choose a connection? Does the status display tell you at a glance whether or not you have a usable link to the network?

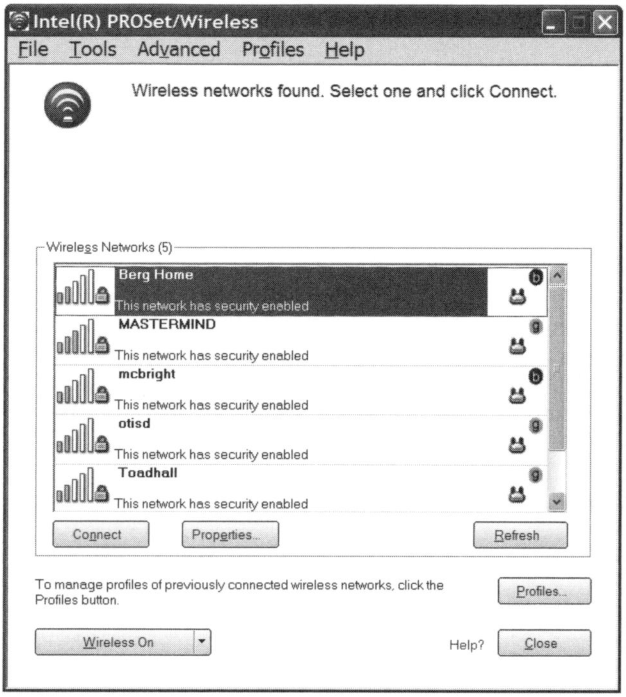

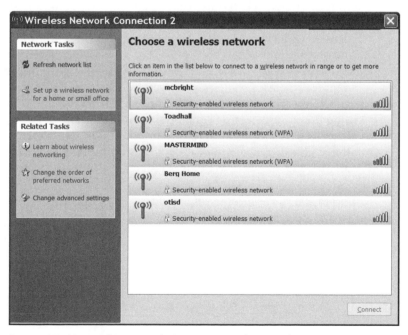

Figure 4-6: Intel's Wi-Fi configuration program is supplied with its mini-PCI Wi-Fi adapters that come in many laptop computers.

Figure 4-7: Microsoft's Network Connection and Network Connection Properties programs in Windows XP control Wi-Fi configuration settings. Similar programs are included in Windows Vista.

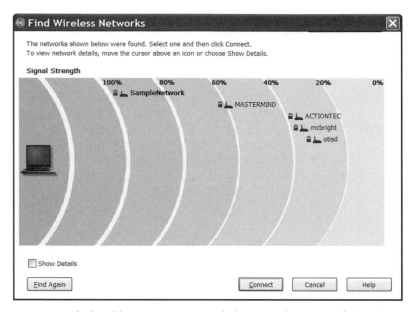

Figure 4-8: ThinkPad laptop computers include yet another way to find and use Wi-Fi networks.

Securing Your Network

The 802.11b specification includes a security scheme called WEP (wired equivalent privacy) that uses either a 64-bit or 128-bit encryption key. Unfortunately, the WEP encryption standard is full of holes, so it's not adequate to truly protect your network against access by unauthorized users. The more recent WPA (Wi-Fi protected access) encryption method is more secure than WEP, but it's not perfect. When you're shopping for a new adapter or access point, look for one that supports WPA encryption.

Chapter 12 contains more detailed information about setting up and using the security features of a wireless network. The best choice, especially if your network has more than one brand of adapters and access points, is almost always to use one of the additional security methods described in Chapter 12 along with WEP or WPA encryption.

Documentation and Technical Support

Every company that makes and sells Wi-Fi hardware offers some kind of technical support for its users. However, the quality and usefulness of that support varies wildly from one vendor to another. If you can't get the information you need from the manufacturer, you should find a different supplier.

At a minimum, an adequate level of technical support should include an accurate and clearly written user's manual, a support center that answers specific questions by telephone and email, a website with answers to frequently asked questions, and a download center that offers the latest versions of device drivers, configuration utilities, and status display software.

Each adapter and access point should come with a detailed user's manual that contains clearly written instructions for installing, configuring, and using the equipment. It's always a good idea to look over the manual before you buy any piece of computer equipment; there's no excuse for a manual with confusing instructions or text that seems to have been badly translated from colloquial Swahili by somebody whose native language was an obscure dialect of Gaelic.

Even the greatest manual ever written won't include the answers to every possible question, so it should also be possible to telephone or send email to a technical support center. It's always nice when tech support has a toll-free telephone number, but it's not essential—you probably paid more for the product to support that "free" service. You should be able to reach a live human technician within a minute or two, or if you call at a busy time, you should be able to leave your telephone number for a callback within a few hours. There is never any excuse for endless time on hold (with or without sappy music), or incomprehensible automated menus that never have the answers to your specific questions.

When you send a question by email, you should receive an acknowledgment within an hour or less, even if it's only an automated "Thanks for your question. We will reply with a complete answer as soon as possible." You should expect an answer to your question no later than the next business day.

And of course, the people who answer your questions should provide information that actually solves your problem. Bad information is worse than no information at all.

Most computer hardware and software companies have technical support websites that contain answers to the most common questions they receive from users. If you have access to the Web when you need a quick answer, that's often the least painful way to find it. The website should also include a download center where you can find copies of the latest drivers and related software for every product that the company has ever sold, including discontinued models.

Reputation

It's almost always helpful to learn about other people's experiences with a wireless adapter (or anything else you might be planning to buy) before you spend your own money. The manufacturer and the dealer who want to sell the product are happy to tell you about all the positive features, but you can't expect them to be completely objective.

Local user groups, published product reviews, and Internet discussions can all be useful sources for information about Wi-Fi equipment. It's not always safe to take every review and every horror story at face value, but when you see or hear a dozen or more reports about a driver that crashed Windows or a PC Card that overheated, you can often assume that there's some kind of pattern emerging. The Practically Networked website (*http://www .practicallynetworked.com/list.asp*) is one good place to look for reviews and users' evaluations of Wi-Fi gear.

At least one major supplier of wireless network equipment has a reputation for bad tech support—long waits for a support technician by telephone and longer waits for replies to email combined with frequently unhelpful answers to questions. In a marketplace with as much competition as the Wi-Fi business, you don't need to put up with a company that doesn't (or can't) provide decent support.

Adapters for Ad Hoc Networks

In an ad hoc network, every network adapter exchanges data with every other node through direct links without an access point acting as a central node. Ad hoc networks are useful for small, isolated networks and direct peer-to-peer file sharing. For example, somebody who uses a laptop computer on the road and a desktop computer in the office can set up an ad hoc network to transfer files between the two. Or two laptop owners might use an ad hoc connection to share files.

Ad hoc wireless networks that connect two or more network nodes without the use of an access point are far less common than infrastructure networks, but they are part of the 802.11 specifications. As such, just about every network interface adapter and wireless configuration program offers an ad hoc network option.

In general, any network adapter with a Wi-Fi logo will work well in an ad hoc network. It's essential that all of the nodes in the network are configured for ad hoc operation, and that all of the other configuration options match as well. Connecting directly to another computer should be no more difficult than connecting to an access point.

The specifications do not provide a standard for 802.11g speeds on an ad hoc network; however, some manufacturers support higher speeds while others adhere to the 11Mbit limitation described in the specification. Generally, if you need the higher speeds of 802.11g for a permanent network, ad hoc isn't the best choice.

Dual-Purpose Adapters

Wi-Fi networking is wildly popular, but it's not the only wireless technology out there. Several other systems are available, including Bluetooth, which provides very short-range connections for computer peripheral devices and accessories such as headphones and keyboards, and the 3G mobile data services that we'll discuss in Chapter 13. Each offers solutions to a somewhat different set of problems, and each fills a different market niche.

Several manufacturers have announced new products that combine a Wi-Fi network interface adapter with an interface for some other wireless service. Some can detect and use both Wi-Fi networking and Bluetooth. Still others might combine access to Wi-Fi LANs with 3G cellular data or WiMAX. The benefits of a combined network interface are obvious—one device is more convenient to carry and install than two, and it provides access to more networks and services. And because the same radio transmitter and receiver handles both services, the potential for interference is also reduced.

An ideal dual-service network adapter would automatically detect radio signals from all compatible networks within range and allow a user to set up an instant connection to any of them regardless of the type of link the network is using. The cost of this combined adapter should be only slightly more than the price of an adapter that only recognizes one networking protocol. Such a perfect wireless networking device may actually appear some time in the next few years.

The latest PDA devices, such as Apple's iPhone, come close to this ideal. When the device is within range of a high-speed Wi-Fi signal, it automatically connects. But when there's no Wi-Fi signal nearby, the device uses a slower 3G network, instead.

The added cost of a dual-mode adapter might be justified if you know that you will be using both of the network services that the adapter supports. Like most other electronic equipment, these adapters will come down in price over time, so there's not much reason to buy one unless you have an immediate need for it.

Access Points

Most wireless network interface adapters perform just one function: They exchange data between a computer and a network. But access points offer a wide variety of features and functions. They're available as simple access points and in combination with hubs, switches and routers for wired connections to nearby computers and other devices. And there's a whole category of wireless access points for home networks called *residential gateways*.

The physical design of an access point is less important than the design of an interface adapter because access points don't have to fit into a computer's card slot or an expansion bay. Some are built into simple rectangular boxes while others are in odd-shaped enclosures that may look more distinctive. The appearance of the package is less important than the features and functions inside, especially when the access point will be placed out of sight in a closet or hidden behind a false ceiling. Regardless of the shape, most access points include mounting plates, brackets, or other hardware for attaching the device to a wall or shelf.

There are a handful of other general features that you might want to look for when you select an access point. If your site survey tells you that you will need high-gain antennas, or if you want to place an antenna outdoors or in some other isolated location, you should use an access point with an external antenna connector instead of a permanently mounted captive antenna. In a high-traffic network where you plan to use more than one radio channel at the same time, a single access point that contains two radio modules can replace two separate access points. And if the best location for your access point is not close to an AC power outlet, choose a model that offers an optional *power over Ethernet* or *active Ethernet* feature.

The best way to choose the type of access point to use in your network is to decide what kind of connections you're likely to need. Are you adding wireless access to an existing wired network? Or do you want to provide some new wired links along with the wireless service? Do you want to use the wireless network to share Internet access? The answers to all of these questions will help you choose the right access point for your network.

Operating Standards

When you are designing a new Wi-Fi network for your home or office, where you can also select the network adapters for each computer that will connect to the network, you can use an access point that supports only one of the Wi-Fi standards. But if you want to provide Wi-Fi access to visitors or to the general public, your base station should support as many standards as possible. Several manufacturers offer dual-band access points or routers that produce both 802.11a and 802.11g signals (an 802.11g access point will also work with an 802.11b adapter). For example, the Linksys router shown in Figure 4-9 provides access using all three standards.

Photo courtesy of Linksys, a division of Cisco Systems, Inc.

Figure 4-9: The Linksys WRT55AG Dual-Band Wireless Router uses both 802.11a and 802.11g signaling.

Pure Wireless LANs

When all the nodes in a LAN exchange data by radio, the access point acts as a hub that provides the central control point for the network as shown in Figure 4-10. Strictly speaking, the access point in this kind of network does not provide access to anything except other wireless nodes. This kind of wireless connection is one of the basic functions of any access point, so you should select the simplest and least expensive model that can provide a usable signal to your coverage area.

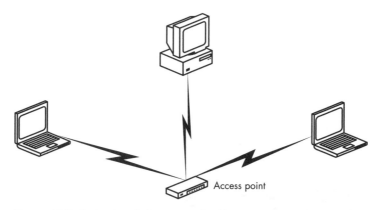

Figure 4-10: A simple wireless network without any external connections

This kind of simple wireless network is possible, but there's not much reason to use an access point in a purely wireless LAN. You can accomplish the same thing in an ad hoc wireless network that creates direct point-to-point links without the need to go through a central hub. About the only time a pure-wireless infrastructure network (with an access point) might make sense would be when you expect to start with wireless links and later expand the network to include a wired Ethernet connection to a fileserver, a shared Internet connection, or more computers and workstations.

Wireless Access to a Wired LAN

Any access point can act as a base station that adds wireless links to an existing wired LAN like the one shown in Figure 4-11. The access point presents the same appearance to the rest of the network as a subsidiary hub or switch that connects wired nodes to the network.

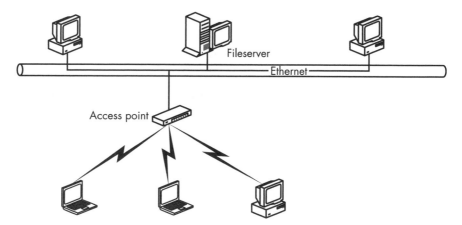

Figure 4-11: A wireless access point connected to a wired Ethernet network

In this kind of hybrid wired and wireless LAN, each device on the network can exchange data with every other network node regardless of how it is connected. It doesn't matter if a particular device is connected to the LAN through a wire or over a radio link, it's all one seamless network.

An access point that acts as a bridge between the wired and wireless sections of the network usually has a single 10Mbps or 100Mbps RJ-45 Ethernet port for connecting a cable from the wired LAN. On higher-end equipment, there's often an additional serial or USB port for a remote terminal that the network manager uses to enter configuration commands and receive status information.

Combining the Access Point with a Wired Hub

In a new LAN that includes both wired connections and wireless links, the best approach may be a single device that combines the functions of a wireless access point with a wired hub or switch, as shown in Figure 4-12. This kind of access point is sometimes described as a broadband router.

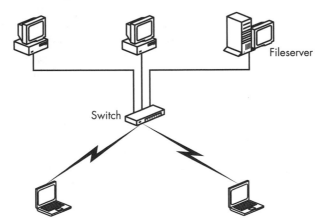

Figure 4-12: A wireless access point combined with a broadband switch controls both the wireless and wired segments of a hybrid network.

A broadband router typically has three kinds of network connections:

- Radio links to computers equipped with wireless Ethernet adapters
- One or more Ethernet ports for wired links to computers with network interface cards
- A broadband wide area network (WAN) port for connecting the router to the network backbone or for stacking the router with additional hubs or switches

Some routers also include a print server that can move documents directly to a network printer.

The major benefits of a combined access point and hub are convenience and economy in a home office or a small business where it's easy to run cables to some of the network computers. A combined unit may also be the quickest way to extend an existing network to both wired and wireless nodes in a remote location.

Broadband Gateways

A broadband gateway is an access point that includes a port for direct connection to a DSL or cable modem that supplies high-speed access to the Internet, as shown in Figure 4-13. Some gateway devices also include several RJ-45 Ethernet ports for wired connections to local computers.

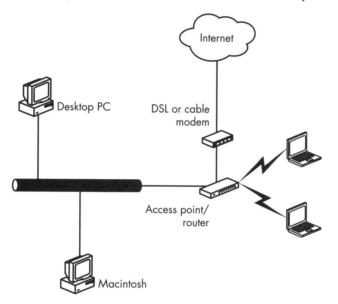

Figure 4-13: An access point combined with a broadband gateway supports a wireless network that shares a high-speed Internet connection.

This approach is most practical in a home network or small business where the service entry for the broadband Internet service runs all the way to the office, rather than stopping at a service entry or a telephone closet, because the access point must be placed in the best possible location to provide wireless network coverage.

Multiple Access Points

A single access point can be completely adequate to support a wireless LAN in an open, relatively small space with a moderate volume of traffic. But when your network must cover a very large area (greater than about 100 feet in diameter), a space obstructed by walls, furniture, or other objects, or interference from other radios, you will probably have to add more access points.

The Wi-Fi specification includes a roaming function that automatically hands off a network link from one access point to another when the signal quality through the new access point is better than the original connection. Most home networks and many networks in very small businesses will need only one access point, so choosing an access point that supports roaming is only a problem for managers of large and complex networks.

After a network client associates with an access point, it automatically surveys all of the other radio channels to determine if some other access point operating on a different channel will provide a stronger or cleaner signal than the one it is currently using. When the client finds a channel that can support a faster link than the current one, it drops the old association and immediately associates with the best available signal source.

Therefore, access points with overlapping coverage areas should be set to different channel numbers. For the least amount of interference from one access point to the next, the channel numbers of any pair of adjacent access points should be at least five channels apart.

In most cases, a network client will not associate with a different access point unless the client moves to a different location while the network link is active or the amount of traffic on the current channel increases. In other words, a hand off can occur when a user carries a laptop or PDA from one place to another and when it becomes necessary for the network to balance the load among all of the available access points.

As Figure 4-14 shows, all of the access points must be connected together through a conventional wired LAN that might also include additional computers and servers that don't require a wireless connection.

In most cases, multiple access points should be placed to provide coverage that overlaps by about 30 percent from one access point to the next. But when your wireless network must support a large number of simultaneous users, the best way to balance the load may be to install two or more access points in the same place with each access point set to a different, non-interfering radio channel.

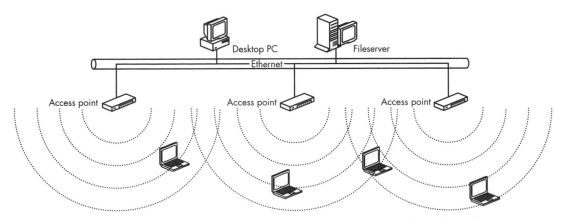

Figure 4-14: Multiple access points on a wired LAN allow wireless users to roam throughout a larger coverage area than any single access point can serve by itself.

Roaming is covered by the Wi-Fi standard, so it should be possible to use different brands of access points in the same network. They're all supposed to work together. But each access point includes a proprietary configuration utility, and each may have a somewhat different design, so a network with only one brand of access point will almost always be easier to configure and use than a mixed network. Building a wireless network is complicated enough; it's always a good idea to eliminate a possible source of confusion.

Enhanced-Performance Access Points

Several manufacturers offer access points and routers with enhancements and special features that can improve the signal quality or performance in difficult settings. For example, you might see devices advertised as *extended range* or *high-speed* access points. Some of these systems improve performance by splitting data into two or more parallel streams and transmitting those streams on more than one channel at the same time.

If one of these enhanced access points comes from a major manufacturer, it will probably perform as advertised, but it's always a good idea to look for independent reviews from magazines and websites before you commit yourself. The improved performance promised by these access points will only occur when you're using a compatible network adapter, which is probably only made by the same manufacturer who built the access point. When you try to connect to an enhanced access point from any other network device, the network performance will be no better than a less expensive access point without the enhanced features.

External Antennas

If you can establish a reliable high-speed data link to any location in your network's coverage area with the antennas built into your network adapters and the captive antennas attached to your access points, there is absolutely no reason to waste any time, money, or energy on external antennas. When you reach the maximum possible speed, better antennas won't move the data any faster.

But when reception conditions are less than perfect, and when you want to push a radio signal as far as you possibly can, a separate antenna can cut through interference, increase data transfer speed, expand the network's coverage area, and establish reliable communication links in places where they would be little more than a rumor if you use adapters and access points with plain vanilla internal antennas.

At first glance, it would appear that the easiest way to improve the quality of a radio signal would be to crank up the power that comes out of the transmitter. Instead of the wimpy 30 milliwatts (0.030 of a watt) produced by most wireless adapters, why not boost it to 10 or 20 watts or more? Wouldn't that produce a much stronger signal?

Sure it would, but the FCC and the other agencies around the world that regulate radio services won't let you do it. More powerful radios would produce stronger signals that would create a lot more interference over wider areas, which would mean that fewer users could share the same piece of the radio spectrum. By comparison, the television station that uses channel 4 in New York City transmits with 100,000 watts of output power, but the nearest station that uses the same channel is in Boston, a few hundred miles away. On the other hand, the radios in a wireless LAN use less than a watt, so the signal is almost inaudible a few hundred feet away.

Since you can't increase the amount of power produced by the radio transmitters, the next best method for improving signal quality is to optimize the performance of the antennas.

Radio antennas come in two types: omnidirectional antennas that transmit and receive in all directions at equal strength and directional antennas that focus their energy and sensitivity in a specific direction. In a wireless LAN, an access point with an omnidirectional antenna is most useful when you want to cover a wide area. A network adapter with an omnidirectional antenna can communicate equally well with any nearby access point. If the coverage area you want to reach with your wireless LAN extends beyond the distance you can cover with internal omnidirectional antennas, you can expect to increase the coverage area by about 15 percent with an external antenna.

In other words, if the signal quality of your link begins to fade at a distance of 100 feet between a network node and the closest access point, you can extend the useful signal range to about 115 feet by using an external omnidirectional antenna on either the access point or the network adapter. If you use external antennas at both ends, you can expect to reach about 132 feet. Of course, that 100-foot value is just an easy-to-calculate example. The actual signal range of a pair of internal antennas might be very different depending on obstructions between the two devices and interference from other radio signals, but the 15 percent improvement rate for each antenna will remain about the same.

The shape of a directional antenna's coverage area and the amount of gain (signal strength from the transmitter and sensitivity to the receiver) depend on the exact design of each antenna. Some directional antennas can provide a moderate amount of gain over a broad pattern (like a floodlight) while others can focus three or four (or more) times as much gain over a much narrower area (like a spotlight).

Directional antennas can provide a huge improvement in signal quality over a tightly focused coverage area, and they can also reduce interference from null areas outside of that coverage pattern. Therefore, they can have several uses in a wireless LAN:

- They can allow a user outside the normal coverage area to join the network.
- They can increase the effective coverage area served by an access point by limiting the coverage to one direction.
- They can reduce or eliminate the effect of off-axis interference from other radio signals.
- They can reduce the amount of interference that a wireless LAN creates for other radios.

Directional antennas come in many shapes and sizes. The next section describes the major types of antennas and offers some suggestions about choosing the best type for your network.

Antenna Characteristics

External antennas come in many shapes and sizes. When you select an antenna, you should consider coverage pattern, gain, form factor, and weatherproofing.

Coverage Pattern

The specification sheet for every antenna includes a diagram that shows the shape of the antenna's coverage pattern. In general, the pattern will be either *omnidirectional* (an antenna that radiates or receives equally well in all directions), *directional* (with the strongest radiation or reception in one direction), or *figure eight* (with strong coverage toward the front and back of the antenna and weak coverage to and from the sides).

Catalog listings and specification sheets for directional antennas usually include an aperture angle, beam width, or capture area expressed in degrees. The aperture angle is the section of a circle that contains the antenna's maximum power coverage or sensitivity. For example, if an antenna has an aperture angle of 45 degrees, the maximum coverage or sensitivity extends outward from the front of the antenna at a 45 degree angle.

Most manufacturers will tell you the beam width in more than one plane. This might be important information when you're planning to place an access point's antenna on a wall, roof, or tower and you want to exchange data with network nodes on the ground.

Gain

The *gain* of an antenna is the ratio of the transmitting power or receiving sensitivity when compared to a standard dipole antenna (a *dipole* is a straight, center-fed, half-wavelength antenna, such as the T-shaped twin-lead antenna supplied with many FM radios and tuners). The gain is usually expressed as dbi (decibels over isotropic). An antenna with a high dbi value has more gain than one with a lower value.

There's often a trade-off between an antenna's beam width and its gain. This occurs because an antenna with a tight aperture angle focuses the same amount of power (or sensitivity) into a smaller area.

Form Factor

A dipole antenna for a 2.4 GHz radio is only about an inch long, but the reflectors and other elements that add gain and directional characteristics might be much longer than that. Many antennas are supplied inside a protective cover that does not affect their performance, but it keeps the actual antenna clean and dry and makes it easier to mount the antenna on a pole or a wall.

Omnidirectional antennas are almost always vertical whips or shafts no more than two or three inches in diameter. Some high-gain omnis can be as much as two or three feet long. For indoor use, especially in rooms with dropped ceilings, a special omnidirectional ceiling mount antenna can be an excellent choice for a wireless network.

Directional antennas can take many shapes, including parabolic dishes and panels that include a reflector behind the active part of the antenna; antennas that resemble a shorter version of a rooftop TV antenna; and patch or panel antennas with several radiating elements, usually within a flat enclosure that resembles a smoke detector or mounted on a swivel that makes it possible to aim the antenna more precisely.

Weatherproofing

Outdoor antennas usually need some kind of protection from rain and snow and from ultraviolet radiation that can deteriorate the materials from which the antenna is constructed. Therefore, many manufacturers offer antennas with sealed elements inside weatherproof enclosures.

A weatherproof enclosure doesn't serve any purpose indoors where the goal should be to make the antenna as unobtrusive as possible. Some antennas are advertised *for indoor/outdoor use,* but the only thing they will do for an indoor installation is increase the cost.

When you mount an antenna outside, remember to consider the damage that could occur if lightning strikes your antenna (or near your antenna). This is especially crucial for antennas mounted on rooftops and poles. Special in-line lightning arrestors are available that can prevent a lightning strike from traveling through the network wires to damage other equipment in your building.

How to Choose an Antenna

It's important to remember that there's no good reason to install an antenna with more gain than you can actually use. If you can establish a clean link with a low-gain antenna, your network won't perform any better or move data any faster just because the access point's antenna is sending and receiving stronger signals. In fact, the overall signal quality might not be as good with a better antenna because it will pick up more noise and interference from other networks and other 2.4 GHz devices.

The standard omnidirectional antenna should be your first choice unless you have a good reason to use something else. If you need a directional antenna, choose one that covers the area you want to reach as efficiently as possible. If you don't need to cover an enormous area, don't waste your money on a high-gain antenna. The least amount of gain necessary to reach all the nodes in your network will work as well or better than a bigger and more expensive antenna that pushes a signal out to places where nobody except unauthorized users will ever receive it.

It's always a good idea to buy your antennas from the same supplier as the radios that you will use with them, in order to prevent unpleasant finger-pointing between two or more vendors when something doesn't work properly. But if your network requires some kind of special antenna that you can't get from the people who make or sell your radios, don't be afraid to go to a specialist dealer.

Rolling Your Own

Some wireless network designers and experimenters have designed a whole class of home brew antennas for 2.4 GHz operation using such cheap and easily obtainable materials as an empty Pringles potato chips canister. We'll describe these antennas in more detail in Chapter 10, which describes long-range point-to-point network links.

Unless you already have a workshop full of tools and test equipment and you're really fond of salted snacks made out of potato flakes, these homemade antennas don't offer any particular advantages over a commercial antenna with well-defined performance characteristics. After you calculate the cost of materials and the value of the time needed to assemble and test a home brew antenna (including the obligatory trip to your local big-box Home Center and Hardware Emporium, where you will spend at least 45 minutes searching for the right mounting brackets), the price of a store-bought antenna doesn't seem to be all that expensive. For example, you can buy a directional antenna with higher gain than the standard Pringles version from HyperGain (*http:// www.hyperlinktech.com/web/antennas*) for about $50.

Where to Use a Directional Antenna

There are three ways to use directional antennas: on an access point, on a network adapter, and on both an access point and a network adapter.

On an Access Point

A directional antenna on an access point will provide a stronger signal to all the network nodes within the access point's coverage area. Therefore, it will reach users who are farther away from the access point and improve the signal quality for users who are closer at the expense of users who are not located within the antenna's coverage pattern.

In a network that requires several access points to provide complete coverage, an access point with a directional antenna at one end of the intended coverage area may be more efficient than an omnidirectional antenna. As Figure 4-15 shows, the directional antenna can concentrate all of the signal in places where it will be used instead of flinging it out equally in all directions. In this example, the directional antenna's coverage angle is about 90 degrees, so it reaches the interior of the building, but it doesn't waste a lot of power on signals to other areas where nobody will want them.

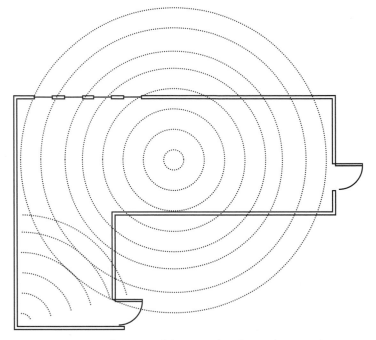

Figure 4-15: A combination of directional and omnidirectional antennas may be the best way to cover a large or odd-shaped area.

Directional antennas can also extend coverage in one direction and direct signals into dead spots and other places where the access points with omnidirectional antennas don't provide adequate signals.

On a Network Adapter

The second option is to place a high-gain directional antenna on a wireless network adapter and point the antenna at an access point with an omni-directional antenna. This might be the best way to add a node to a network through an access point that is also serving other, closer network clients. To eliminate the cost and inconvenience of installing another access point or running an Ethernet cable to a single isolated user, try using a directional antenna on that user's network adapter.

On Both an Access Point and a Network Adapter

A network link that uses directional high-gain antennas at both ends can cover a *lot* of ground. A link from a rooftop to a hilltop location might reach several miles or more if there's a clean line of sight without obstruction from trees or buildings between the two ends. Aiming the two antennas at each other for maximum signal strength can be very critical for long-distance links; turning one antenna (or both) just a few degrees can make the difference between a strong signal and no signal at all. The coverage angles of dish and parabolic antennas can be extremely tight.

As you move the two ends of a radio link apart, two more complications arise. The curvature of the earth and an electromagnetic phenomenon called the Fresnel zone can get in the way, unless the antennas are high enough to avoid them. At 2.4 GHz, the average height of the two antennas must be at least 13 feet above the ground or other obstructions for a 1-mile link. At 5 miles, the minimum height increases to 35 feet, and at 10 miles, the minimum height is 57 feet.

Antennas Are a Whole Other World

Long-range links are almost always solutions to uncommon problems, such as providing access to a place where no other network service is available or adding users in a remote building to a campus or corporate network. Adding a directional antenna that fills a dead spot in an indoor network or a panel antenna that mounts on a roof or an outside wall to cover a parking lot doesn't make your network much more complicated than using access points with omnidirectional antennas. But when you start to think about antennas with complex patterns and very high gain, you're moving beyond what a book about wireless LANs can cover. You need expert help.

Before you can install a big, powerful antenna, you (or somebody working for you) must pay attention to things like wind loading (you don't want the antenna to fall down in a storm), local zoning ordinances (lots of people think antennas are ugly or dangerous or both, so they have rules about where and how you can put them up), and protection from weather and wildlife (you don't want the antenna to ice up in the winter or play host to a family of birds in the spring). And you'll probably want to use an expensive piece of test equipment called a spectrum analyzer to aim the two antennas at each other.

If you don't have experience with this stuff, you'll either need to find help from somebody who does or spend a lot of time experimenting. If that's your idea of fun, have yourself a fine time. You can find more detailed information about long-range point-to-point links in Chapter 10.

It's Time to Buy

This chapter describes the different kinds of wireless network adapters, access points, and antennas that you will need to connect your computer to a Wi-Fi hot spot, construct a new wireless LAN, or add wireless access to your existing wired network. The next step is to make some choices and gather all of the hardware together. You're ready to install the wireless hardware. In the next chapter, you can find step-by-step procedures for installing different kinds of adapters and access points and for running the configuration utility programs that make all those pieces work together in a network.

5

MANAGING YOUR WI-FI CONNECTIONS

 In general, installing a wireless network adapter is easy because most network adapters are plug-and-play devices. As soon as you connect the adapter to your computer, or as soon as you turn on an internal adapter or your computer, the computer automatically detects the device and runs the control software to set up a connection.

This chapter will explain how to set up a Wi-Fi connection for two kinds of users: the home or office user who wants to connect to a fixed access point once and assume that is keeps working every time; and a laptop user who wants to connect to different networks in different locations.

Installing PC Card Adapters

Network adapters on PC Cards plug into the PCMCIA socket on a portable computer or the socket adapter that fits an expansion slot in a desktop computer (yes, that does mean that one kind of adapter sometimes plugs into another kind of adapter). To install the PC Card, just insert it gently but firmly into the socket. When it's properly seated, you should feel the holes on the edge of the card grab the pins inside the socket.

Most wireless PC Card adapters contain internal antennas that extend an inch or more beyond the outer edge of the PCMCIA socket. However, a few adapters come with connectors for external antennas. If you are using an external antenna, place the antenna in the location where you want to operate it, and run the antenna cable from the antenna to the network adapter's antenna connector. *Be gentle.* Often the tiny connectors used by laptop adapters are fragile, and damaging the connectors or cables can lead to loss of signal.

Installing USB Adapters

Most USB wireless adapters are compact devices with one or more internal antennas or with external antennas that are connected to the adapter through a hinge that allows the antenna element to move around, like the one shown in Figure 5-1. Because the adapter connects to the computer through a cable, it's easy to move the whole adapter around when the first position you try doesn't detect an adequate signal from the access point.

Photo courtesy of Linksys, a division of Cisco Systems, Inc.

Figure 5-1: This USB Wi-Fi adapter has a
permanently attached external antenna.

To install a USB adapter, follow these steps:

1. Run a USB cable from the computer to the location where you plan to place the adapter. Note that the two ends of a USB cable have different type of connectors, so make sure the connector at the computer end of the cable mates with the computer's USB port.

2. Plug the cable into the computer's USB port. Plug the other end of the cable into the network adapter. In most cases, Windows will automatically detect the adapter and guide you through the process of loading the driver software.

3. If Windows can't find the device driver for your adapter, look for a driver online, either at the manufacturer's website or at one of the other sites listed later in this chapter, and instruct Windows to use that driver file.

4. Run the configuration program provided with your adapter or use the Wireless Configuration Tool included with Windows XP.

5. Open the signal strength and signal quality display.

6. If the signal quality is not good or excellent (at least three bars out of five), try adjusting the antenna position or moving the adapter for optimal performance.

Installing an Internal Adapter in a Laptop Computer

Most new laptops include a built-in Wi-Fi adapter on a mini-PCI card that mounts directly on the computer's motherboard. If you ordered your computer without an internal Wi-Fi card and decide to install one later, or if you want to replace the existing card with a new and better model (such as a card that includes the new 802.11n specification when such cards become available), you must open up the computer to reach the adapter.

Don't try to take apart a laptop computer without specific instructions for your particular make and model. Laptops are all designed to squeeze as many parts and features as possible into a very small package, and there's usually just one correct way to get to each component. Unless you find and remove exactly the right set of screws and covers in exactly the right order, you probably won't get to the part or socket you want, but you *will* create a whole new set of problems.

Fortunately, most laptop makers offer detailed step-by-step instructions for removing and installing an internal Wi-Fi card in service manuals and online tech support websites. Before you try to open up the computer, it's absolutely necessary to read the full procedure in the manual or online. If there's an online video that shows the procedure, watch the whole thing, and then step through it again (if you have a second computer to watch it on) as you install your new card.

Installing an Internal Adapter in a Desktop System

Adding an internal adapter to a desktop computer is a bit more complicated because it requires opening the case and inserting the adapter into an expansion slot. But it's no different from adding any other expansion card, which most network managers and serious home computer users have probably done more times than they care to think about.

You know the routine: Unplug the power cable. Open the case. Find a vacant expansion slot. Remove the metal backplane cover. Insert the adapter into the slot. Screw it down. Close the case. Plug the power cable back into the computer. Lather. Rinse. Repeat.

Many internal network adapters are actually PC Card adapters with PCMCIA sockets that fit into an expansion slot. Unless the adapter manual tells you otherwise, it's a good idea to remove the PC Card from the socket before you install the socket in your computer. It often takes a bit of twisting and pushing to seat the socket properly in the expansion slot, and the socket is more flexible without the card in place. After you reassemble the computer, insert the adapter into the socket and load the wireless adapter driver.

Loading the Driver Software

Regardless of their physical format, just about all wireless adapters are plug-and-play devices, which means that Windows should automatically recognize the adapter and load the relevant drivers as soon as you install it. However, sometimes you'll need to install a specific software driver manually before your operating system can use the adapter to send and receive data.

Drivers can come from three sources: some are supplied with the operating system or a copy might have been provided on a diskette or a CD with the adapter. But the best source for the most recent version of any driver is the manufacturer's online technical support website. You can also find links to the latest Windows drivers for your adapter from one of these driver directories on the Internet:

http://www.driverzone.com

http://www.driverguide.com

http://www.drivershq.com

http://www.mrdriver.com

http://www.winfiles.com

http://www.windrivers.com

In most cases, the same software disk or download that includes the driver for a wireless network adapter also contains the configuration and control utility program for that adapter. You should install the driver and load the software before you physically install or connect the adapter.

The first time you insert a PC Card in the PCMCIA socket or plug a USB adapter into the computer's USB port, Windows will identify the adapter and run its Found New Hardware Wizard, as shown in Figure 5-2. Assuming you have already loaded the latest version of the driver and the configuration utility, choose the Install the software automatically option. Windows will automatically find and install the driver. If it doesn't find the driver, choose the Install from a list or specific location option to direct Windows to the driver files in a download file or a CD.

NOTE   *Windows Vista presents a different set of screens when it detects new hardware, but the automatic installation is very similar. When in doubt, follow the instructions on your screen.*

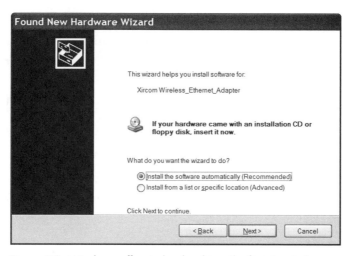

Figure 5-2: Windows offers to load a driver the first time it detects new hardware.

After it installs the driver, Windows will instruct you to restart the computer. Some configuration utilities run automatically whenever a wireless adapter is active; others require a user to start the program from the Start ▶ Programs menu or from an icon in the Windows Desktop. If the configuration program does not open in a program window, it will display a status icon in the System Tray next to the clock.

In Linux and Unix systems, you might have to install your driver manually. Chapter 7 describes Linux and Unix drivers in more detail.

Choosing a Control Program

In Windows your computer has at least two or three different programs that can control your Wi-Fi adapter and configure the wireless connection to a network. One of these programs was included with Windows and another comes with the network adapter. Yet another program might be part of the bundled software supplied by the maker of your laptop computer. All of these programs perform the same tasks, and they all display similar information, but each one arranges the commands and displays differently.

It's worth the time and trouble to try all of the Wi-Fi programs installed on your computer because you will probably find one that is easier to use than any of the others. It's also possible that one program is more sensitive to marginal signals.

The way you use your Wi-Fi control program depends on how you use wireless connections. If you keep the computer in one place most of the time with a Wi-Fi link to the Internet and your home or office network, you should configure the Wi-Fi control program to automatically find and use your own network every time you turn on the computer. On the other hand, if you're mainly using the computer as a portable unit that you move from place to place, the control program should detect and display all the nearby Wi-Fi signals and allow you to choose the one you want to use. We'll cover both scenarios below.

NOTE *When you don't plan to connect your laptop computer to the Internet or a local network, use the hardware or software switch on the computer to completely turn off the radio.*

The Microsoft Wireless Network Connection Utility

Windows includes a Wireless Network Connection utility that supports just about every wireless network adapter. When Windows detects a Wi-Fi adapter, it automatically runs the Wireless Network Connection utility unless you have instructed the computer to use a different control program.

To switch between control programs, you just need to right-click the active Wi-Fi control program in the System Tray. Figure 5-3 shows the pop-up menu command in Windows XP that transfers control to the Intel PROSet/Wireless program.

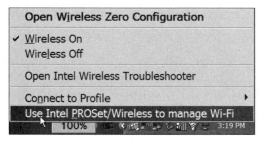

Figure 5-3: Use the pop-up command in the System Tray to shift control to the Intel Wi-Fi control program.

Connecting to an Access Point in Windows XP

To set up a Wi-Fi network connection using the Microsoft program in Windows XP, follow these steps:

1.   From the Windows desktop, double-click the Wireless Network Connection icon in the System Tray (shown in Figure 5-4) at the lower right corner of your screen (to the left of the clock).

Figure 5-4: Windows uses this icon to control the Wireless Network Connection program.

2. The Wireless Network Connection program shown in Figure 5-5 will show one or more nearby Wi-Fi access points. In this example, the program has detected five different networks.

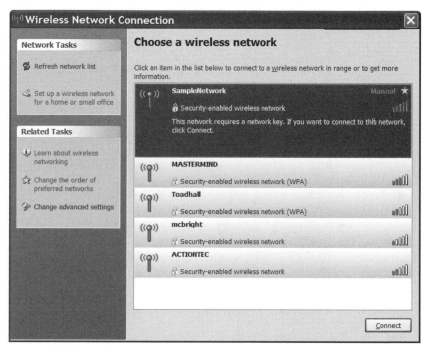

Figure 5-5: The Wireless Network Connection utility displays information about every nearby wireless access point.

3. Like the display on a mobile telephone's screen, the Wireless Network Connection window uses five bars (at the right of each listing) to show the relative strength of each incoming signal. Choose the name of the wireless network you want to join, and click the **Connect** button near the bottom of the window.

4. If you have used this network before, the Wireless Network Connection program will automatically set up the wireless link. If it's the first time you have connected to this network, the program might ask for an encryption key or other security code. If necessary, type the key code provided by the owner of the access point.

5. After the program sets up a wireless link, it identifies the connection in the list of networks, as shown in Figure 5-6. In this example, the computer is connected to the SampleNetwork access point.

When your network connection is up and running, you can close the Wireless Network Connection window.

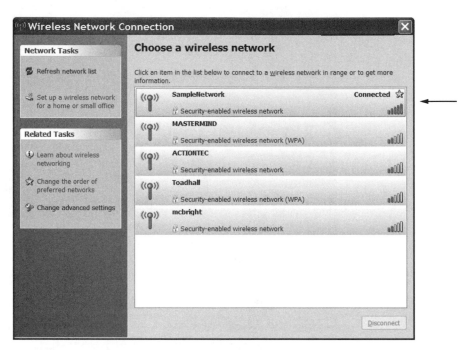

Figure 5-6: The connected flag in the SampleNetwork listing tells you that your computer is connected to that network. The star indicates that this is a preferred network.

Connecting to an Access Point in Windows Vista

Setting up a Wi-Fi connection in Vista works in a similar manner to XP, but the screens are different. Follow these steps to establish a wireless link:

1. If it's not already on, turn on the wireless adapter in your laptop or plug the adapter into a USB port. The Network Connections icon shown in Figure 5-7 will appear in the Notification Area (the System Tray).

Figure 5-7: Click the Network Connections icon to open a Wi-Fi connection.

2. Click the Network Connections icon to open the information window shown in Figure 5-8.

Figure 5-8: The Network Connections information window lets you know if one or more wireless networks are within range.

3. Choose the **Connect to a Network** option. The Select a Network To Connect To window shown in Figure 5-9 will appear.

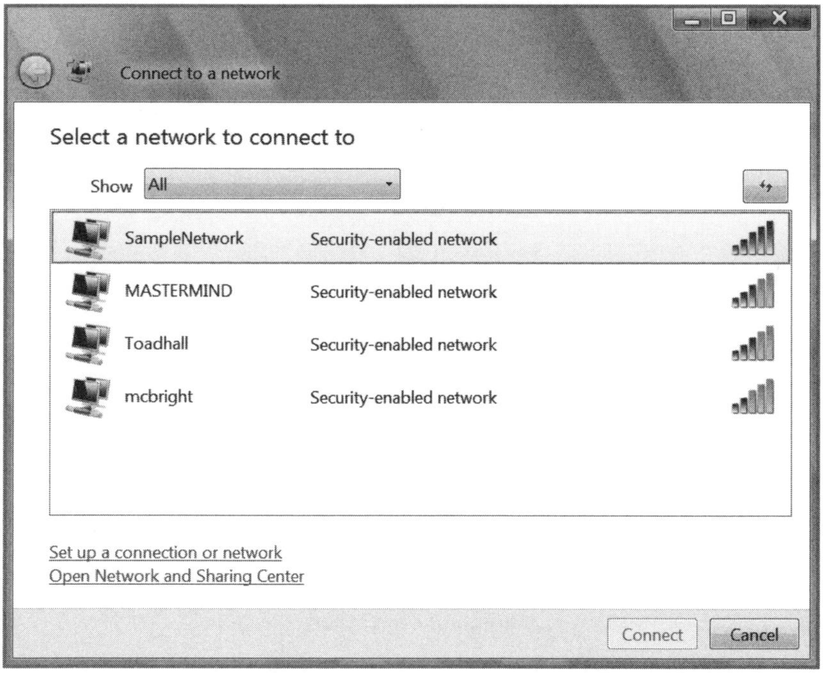

Connect to a network

Select a network to connect to

Show All

	SampleNetwork	Security-enabled network	
	MASTERMIND	Security-enabled network	
	Toadhall	Security-enabled network	
	mcbright	Security-enabled network	

Set up a connection or network
Open Network and Sharing Center

Connect   Cancel

Figure 5-9: The Select a Network To Connect To window displays a list of all nearby wireless networks.

4. Select the name of the network you want to use and click the **Connect** button at the bottom of the window. If the network is encrypted and a security window appears, type the correct security key for this network. If the network is not protected by encryption, Windows will make the connection immediately.

5. Move your mouse cursor over the Network Connections icon in the System Tray. If the pop-up window shows *Access: Local Only*, click the icon and choose the **Network and Sharing Center** option to open the window shown in Figure 5-10.

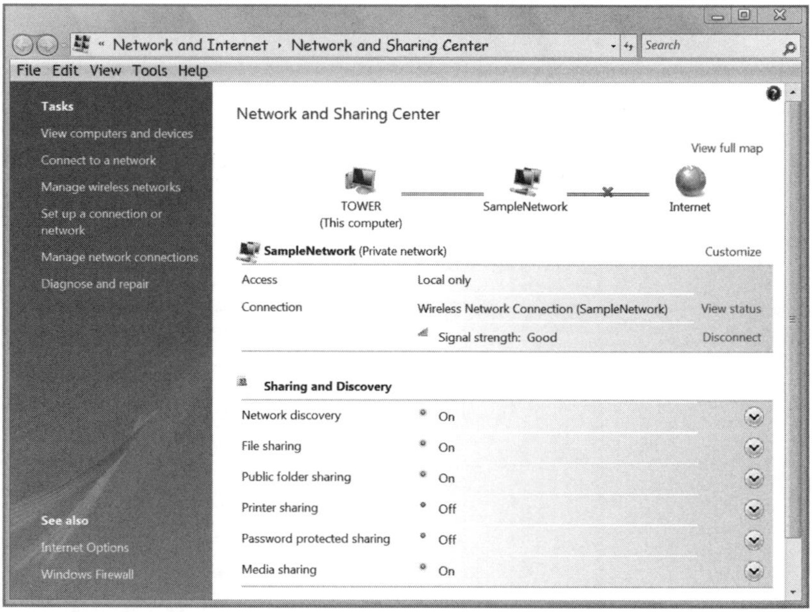

Figure 5-10: The Network and Sharing Center window shows the current status of your network connection.

6. To connect your computer to the Internet, click the red *X* in the diagram between the local network and the Internet. Windows will examine your connection and establish a link to the Internet.

Making an Automatic Connection

Most of us use a limited number of access points and network services to connect our computers to the Internet. When you're using a wireless link to connect to your home or office network, or if most of your connections are at the coffee shop, the library, or the airport club that you visit frequently, you should set the control program to find and use those access points whenever they detect their signals. Windows calls these *preferred networks*.

Setting Up a Preferred Network in Windows XP

To create a preferred network profile, follow these steps:

1. Take your computer to the location where you want to connect to a Wi-Fi network.

2. If the computer has a built-in Wi-Fi adapter, turn the adapter on. If the computer uses an external adapter, plug the adapter into a PC Card socket or connect it to a USB port. The Wireless Network Connection program should detect one or more nearby networks and display them in a list.

3. Double-click the name of the network you want to set as your preferred network. If the network is encrypted, the program will ask for a network key, as shown in Figure 5-11. Type the network key in both fields and click **Connect** to join the network. If the network is not encrypted, the program will connect your computer to the network immediately. Either way, it will add this network to your list of preferred networks.

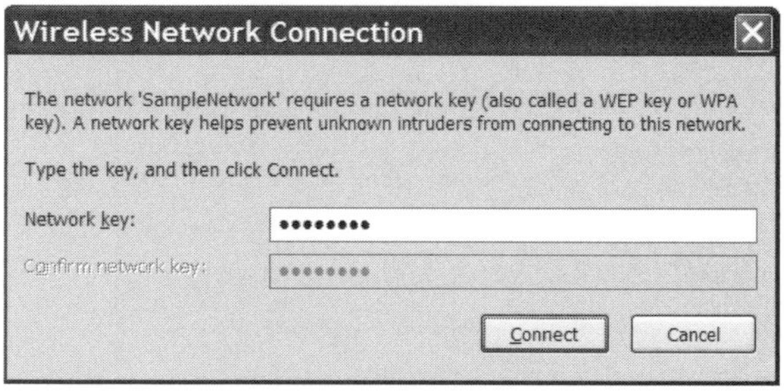

Figure 5-11: When the Wi-Fi control program detects an encrypted network, it will ask for the network key.

The next time you turn on your computer when you're within range of this network, the Wireless Network Connection program will automatically make the connection without the need to choose it from a list.

If you have identified two or more preferred networks (for making connections in different locations), the program will connect in the order that they appear in the list in the Wireless Network Connection Properties dialog box.

NOTE   *Windows uses the SSID (the name of each network) to identify a preferred network. Therefore, it will automatically connect to any network that has that SSID. This can be convenient when you use your computer in more than one coffee shop owned by the same chain, but it could be a problem if your preferred network's owner hasn't changed the default SSID on an access point.*

In most cases, the order of the networks on your list of preferred networks won't make any difference because they will be physically separated from one another—one might be at home, a second at the library, and yet another in a coffee shop. But if two or more preferred networks have overlapping coverage areas, you might want to change the order of the items in the list. To change the order, follow these steps:

1. From the Wireless Network Connection window, click the **Change Advanced Settings** option in the list of Related Tasks at the left side of the window.

2. In the Properties window, choose the **Wireless Networks** tab to open the dialog box shown in Figure 5-12.

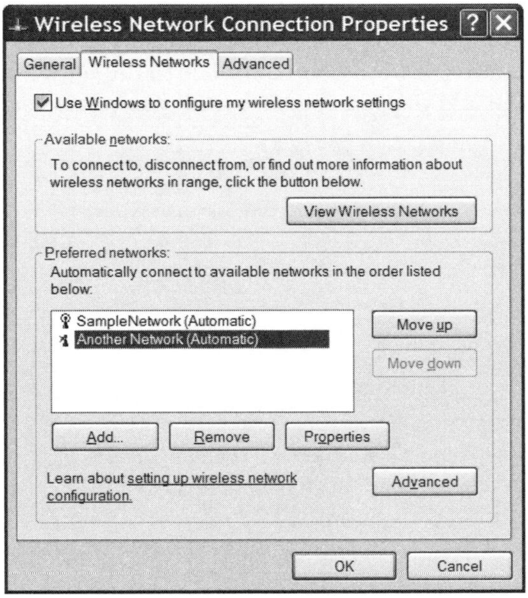

Figure 5-12: Use the Move Up and Move Down buttons to change the order of items in the list of Preferred Networks.

3. In the list of Preferred Networks, choose one of the items and use the Move Up and Move Down buttons to change its position on the list. Repeat until all the items on the list are in the order you want.

Setting Up a Preferred Network in Windows Vista

In Windows Vista, to make the current Wi-Fi connection the default connection that will automatically open whenever your computer is within range of that network's signal, follow these steps:

1. Right-click the Network Connections icon in the System Tray and choose **Connect to a Network** from the pop-up menu.

2. Right-click the name of the network that you want to set as the default and choose **Properties** from the pop-up menu. Choose the **Connection** tab to open the window shown in Figure 5-13.

Figure 5-13: Use the options in the Connection tab to set a default network.

3. Choose the Connect automatically when this network is in range option, and click the **OK** button at the bottom of the window.

4. Close all the open windows.

Disconnecting from an Access Point

To disconnect your computer from a wireless network, follow these steps:

1. Right-click the Wireless Network Connection icon in the System Tray.

2. Choose **View Available Wireless Networks** from the pop-up menu. The Wireless Network Connection window will appear.

3. Click the name of the network that is currently connected.

4. Click the **Disconnect** button.

Viewing Technical Details

In almost all cases, the Wireless Network Connection utility automatically detects nearby access points and sets up a Wi-Fi connection for you without any need to pay attention to technical details like the preamble length or the amount of power that the radio transmitter is using. But when you have a problem, or when you or your technical support advisor wants to troubleshoot a flaky connection, follow these steps to open the Properties window for your wireless network adapter:

1. From the Wireless Network Connections window, click the **Change Advanced Settings** item in the list of Related Tasks.

2. In the Wireless Network Connection Properties window, click the **Configure** button next to the name of your wireless network adapter to see the window shown in Figure 5-14, where you can view or change some of the more obscure configuration settings. As you scroll down the Property list, the text in the Description box will tell you what each item means.

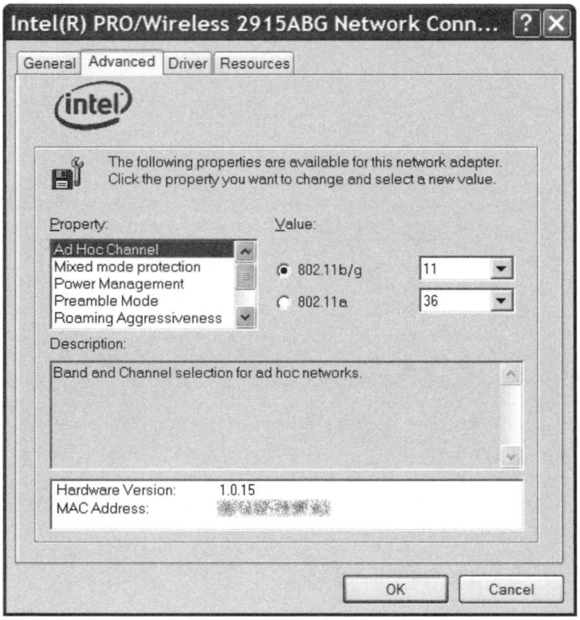

Figure 5-14: The Advanced tab of the Network Connection Properties window controls several rarely-used configuration settings.

The Intel PROSet/Wireless Program

If your computer came with an Intel mini-PCI Wi-Fi adapter, a version of the PROSet/Wireless control and configuration program was probably preloaded on the system along with Windows and the laptop maker's proprietary software.

The PROSet program does the same thing as the Microsoft Wireless Network Connection program, but it displays the controls differently, and it provides a lot more information about the signals it exchanges with an access point. You don't need any of that information to set up and use a Wi-Fi connection—the adapter and software automatically detect the channel number and the Wi-Fi mode that each access point uses—but it can be extremely useful when you (or your technical support) want to troubleshoot your system.

Figure 5-15 shows the PROSet/Wireless program's main screen with a list of nearby access points detected by the computer's Wi-Fi adapter. The list of nearby access points shows the signal strength and the Wi-Fi mode each access point is using and whether or not the signal is encrypted. To connect to a network, click the name, and click the **Connect** button under the list.

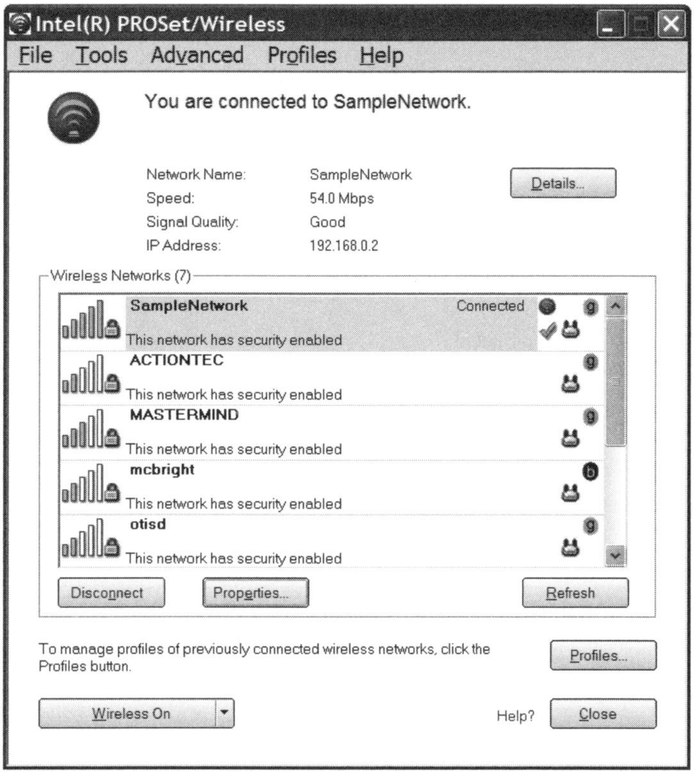

Figure 5-15: The main screen of the Intel PROSet control program is similar to the Microsoft Program.

When you connect to a network, the PROSet/Wireless program will automatically create a new profile for this network and add it to your list of known wireless networks. The program treats the list of profiles just like the Windows program handles its list of Preferred Networks; it will automatically use a stored profile to set up a connection whenever it detects one of the networks on the Profile list.

So far, the Intel program looks like it works just like the Microsoft utility. But notice that this window has several buttons that aren't on the Microsoft screen. The important ones are Properties, under the list of detected networks, and Details, near the top of the window (the Details button is only visible when a connection is active).

The Properties screen, shown in Figure 5-16, provides information about the network and each of the network's access points. If the host network uses more than one access point, the Properties screen shows information about each of them. In this case, it tells us (among other things) that the Sample-Network access point is using channel 1.

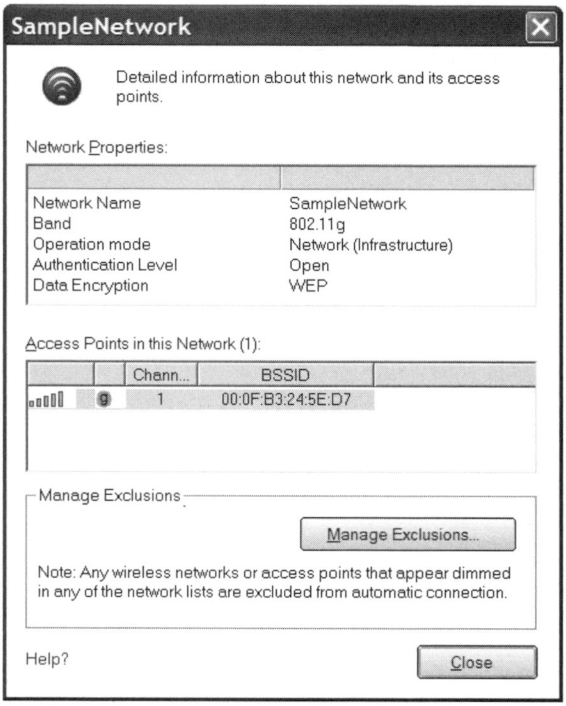

Figure 5-16: The Intel program's Properties window provides information about the incoming signal from an access point.

The Details button opens the Connection Details window shown in Figure 5-17 when a Wi-Fi connection to a network is active. This window shows even more technical details about the adapter and the connection, including the channel, the radio frequency, the MAC addresses of both the adapter and the access point, and the amount of power the adapter's radio transmitter is using (some of these details require scrolling down the list of details). You won't use any of this information very often, but when there's a problem with your connection, it can be very valuable.

Other Wi-Fi Adapters and Control Programs

If you're using a different brand of mini-PCI adapter, a Wi-Fi adapter on a PC Card, or a USB adapter, the control software supplied with that adapter probably has a completely different layout and a different set of controls and data display from either the Microsoft or Intel programs. The programs supplied by many laptop computer makers are also quite different. Each of these programs accomplishes essentially the same thing as the Microsoft and Intel programs.

Connection Details   ☒

Profile Name: SampleNetwork

Network Name: SampleNetwork

Signal Quality: Good

Signal Strength: ▫▪▪▪▪▪

IPv4 Address: 192.168.0.2   [Repair]

Adapter MAC Address	░░░░░░░░░░
Band	802.11g
Supported Data Rates	1, 2, 5.5, 6, 9, 11, 12, 18, 24, 36, 4...
Radio Frequency	2.412 GHz
Channel Number	1
Network Authentication	Open
Data Encryption	WEP
802.1X Authentication Type	None
802.1X Authentication Protocol	None

Help?   [Close]

*Figure 5-17: The Intel Connection Details window
offers a more or less complete technical description
of the active Wi-Fi connection.*

As you saw in the last chapter, Lenovo ThinkPad laptop computers come with their own Wi-Fi program, shown here again in Figure 5-18. In this case, the program shows the relative signal strengths of several access points through a graphic display instead of the five bars. There's another screen in the ThinkPad software (behind the Show Details option) that shows technical details.

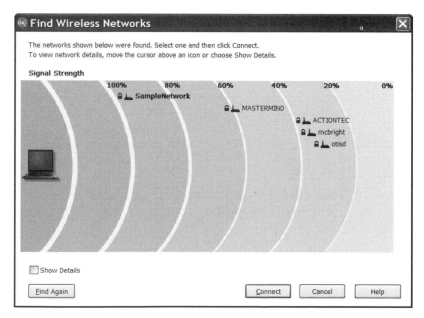

*Figure 5-18: The ThinkPad wireless control program shows the relative strength of
each nearby access point's signal.*

The layout may be quite different, but the commands and controls work in a similar manner to the two programs described in this chapter. If you can't make sense of your own adapter's control program, either consult the manual supplied with the adapter, or switch to the Windows Wireless Connections program.

Status Information

Each Wi-Fi control program provides a somewhat different set of information. Your status display may contain one or more of the following items.

Signal strength

Signal strength is the amount of power in the radio signal that the adapter received during the most recent scan. Most programs use the familiar five bars display to show signal strength, but some might offer the measured strength in *dBm* (decibels below 1 milliwatt). In practice, the signal strength value is most useful as a relative measurement to show how the signal changes in different locations.

Mode

The *mode* is the Wi-Fi specification that the access point is using. It will be either 802.11b, 802.11a, 802.11g, or 802.11n. Some control programs show the mode simply as *a, b, g,* or *n*.

Channel

This field shows the radio channel number that the adapter is currently using.

Signal quality

Signal quality is the quality of the data packets the adapter received during the most recent scan. A 100 percent reading indicates that 100 percent of the received packets are good.

Overall quality

Overall quality is a calculated value based on the signal strength and signal quality. It is usually expressed as excellent, good, fair, or poor.

Link speed or data rate

The *link speed* is the nominal data transfer speed that the adapter and the associated access point are currently using.

Association

This field confirms that the adapter has established an association with a wireless LAN.

MAC

This field identifies the network adapter's unique MAC (media access control) address. The MAC address is loaded by the manufacturer, and it's usually printed on the outside of the adapter. If your laptop has an internal Wi-Fi adapter, the MAC address is probably also on a sticker located on the bottom of the computer.

SSID

The SSID is the name of the network with which this device is currently associated. All nodes and access points in a wireless LAN must use the same SSID.

Network type

If the network uses one or more access points, the network type is *infrastructure*. If it's a peer-to-peer network, the type is *ad hoc*.

Encryption

This field shows whether the adapter is currently using WEP or WPA encryption.

Activity

The activity display shows the number of outbound and inbound packets that the adapter has sent and received.

Changing Your Adapter's Configuration Settings

In most cases, your Wi-Fi adapter's default settings will do everything you need to connect your computer to a nearby network. But if you're dealing with an unusual situation, it's always possible to use the adapter's configuration tool to make changes. Because the specific settings for each make and model of adapter are slightly different, the configuration program is supplied with the adapter. The configuration settings will remain the same even if you connect to a different network.

For example, Figure 5-19 shows the configuration tool for the Intel mini-PCI adapter supplied with a ThinkPad laptop. To change one of the adapter's properties, scroll down the list of properties and highlight the item you want to change, then choose the new setting from the drop-down Value menu, which changes for each item in the list of Properties.

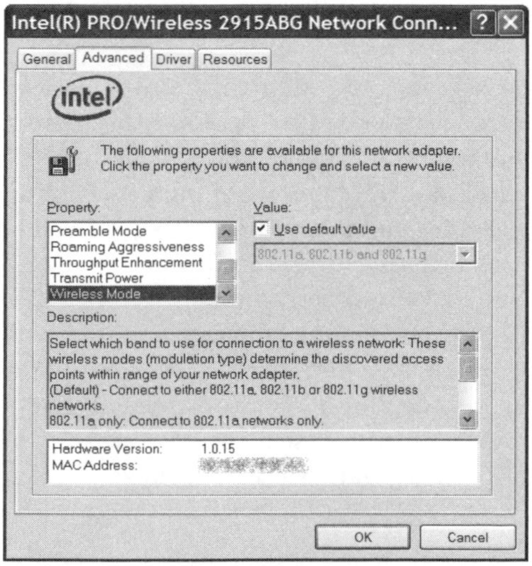

Figure 5-19: The Intel Properties window is a typical Wi-Fi configuration tool.

Configuring a Network Connection

The easiest way to configure a whole network full of adapters is to start by configuring the access point and then noting the wireless configuration settings that you must match in the individual adapters. If you expect your users to configure their own adapters, you will want to prepare a standard information sheet or card that lists these settings:

- The network's name (the SSID)
- Network type (infrastructure or ad hoc)
- DHCP (automatic address assignment) on or off
- If DHCP is off, the IP address and subnet assigned to this user's computer
- Type of encryption (none, WEP 40/64-bit or 128-bit, or WPA)
- WEP or WPA encryption key (or a telephone number of the help desk that can provide it)
- Preamble length
- URL, login, and password for access to the network (if necessary)

No matter how clear you make the written instructions, some people will have trouble connecting to the network without help. So your instruction sheet should also include the name or telephone number of the people who can help set up an adapter and talk a confused user through the configuration process.

If most of your users have the same kind of adapter, you might want to include screen captures of that adapter's configuration window and the Windows Network Settings window with step-by-step instructions for opening those windows.

The Mobile Life: Moving from One Network to Another

If you use your portable computer on more than one wireless network, you may want to prepare your own cheat sheet for configuring your network adapter to work with each network that you regularly use: home, office, coffee shop, airport, and so forth. Some configuration utilities offer multiple preset configuration profiles, but if yours does not, you will have to set all the options each time you move to a different network.

The Wireless Network Connection utility in Windows XP includes an Automatic Wireless Configuration feature that detects every wireless network within range and automatically configures your wireless adapter. This can save a lot of time and trouble, but if Windows doesn't detect a network that ought to be there, it won't hurt to use a sniffer tool such as NetStumbler (*http://www.netstumbler.com*) to perform your own search for nearby access points.

To use the automatic wireless configuration feature in Windows XP, follow these steps:

1. Make the Windows Wireless Connections tool the active Wi-Fi control program.
2. Open the Wireless Network Properties window by either clicking the network icon in the System Tray next to the clock or opening Start ▶ Settings ▶ Network Connections, right-clicking the icon for the wireless network connection, and selecting **Properties** from the drop-down menu.
3. Select the **Wireless Networks** tab.
4. Enable or disable automatic configuration by selecting the **Use Windows to configure my wireless network settings** option.
5. Click the **Advanced** button to open the window shown in Figure 5-20, where you can set the type of networks that Windows will automatically detect.

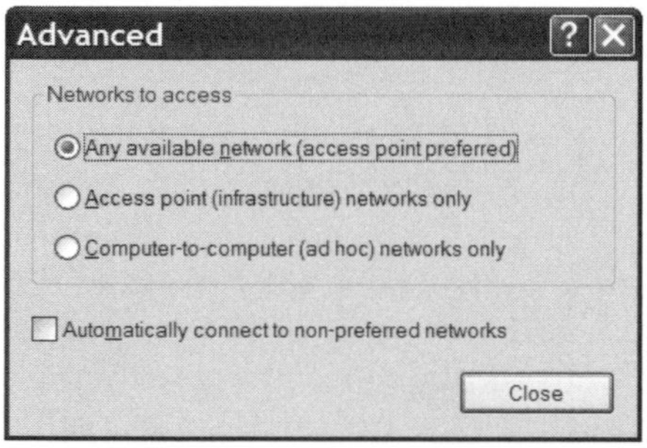

Figure 5-20: The Advanced window specifies the networks that Windows will automatically detect.

6. Choose the type of network that you want your computer to detect. To instruct Windows to detect and connect to any nearby network, even if it's not in the Preferred Networks list, select the **Automatically connect to non-preferred networks** option. If you plan to use your computer with public Wi-Fi hot spots, make this option active.
7. Click the **Close** and **OK** buttons to save your choices and close the open configuration windows.

Beyond Windows

Every adapter manufacturer provides software for the most popular versions of Microsoft Windows, but that's not the only operating system you can use with a wireless network adapter—if you can find the right drivers. Drivers for less common operating systems may be available from the adapter manufacturer's technical support websites or from user groups devoted to the operating system in question.

For Macintosh users, your best bet is to use Apple AirPort adapters and the software provided with them, which are fully compatible with other Wi-Fi networks. But some other adapters will also work with a Mac, if you have the right drivers. Chapter 8 explains how to use AirPort software with a Macintosh.

If you have some other make of PC Card or USB wireless adapter, don't give up hope. Cisco and other manufacturers also offer Mac OS drivers and configuration software. Check the adapter maker's website for the latest versions, or run a web search for *Macintosh* plus the make and model of your adapter.

Drivers for some adapters are also available for Linux, FreeBSD, NetBSD, and other varieties of Unix, either directly from the manufacturer (for example, both Proxim Wireless and Cisco offer Linux drivers through their websites) or through user groups. Some recent releases of several flavors of Unix and Linux include drivers for several widely-used Wi-Fi chip sets. Chapter 7 contains more detailed information about using Linux and Unix on a Wi-Fi network.

Signal Strength vs. Signal Quality

Most wireless utilities show signal strength and quality in bar graphs, or as a percentage value, but they don't tell you what a signal at 100 percent strength is 100 percent *of*. It's important to understand that signal strength and signal quality are not the same thing; a wireless adapter does not have to receive a signal at full strength to move data at the maximum possible speed. As long as the receiver can capture a clean signal, the network's performance should be acceptable. But even a strong signal can suffer if the receiver also picks up interference from other wireless networks or from other devices that use the same radio frequencies, such as wireless telephones and microwave ovens.

And even if the data transfer speed is slower than the maximum possible rate, it might not make any real difference. For example, if you're using a Wi-Fi network to connect your computer to the Internet through a DSL line (at about 1.5Mbps or less), it won't matter if your local wireless network speed drops from 11Mbps down to 2Mbps; that's still a lot more bandwidth than you need because the slower DSL line is the slowest part of the overall connection. On the other hand, when you use the same networks for computer-to-computer file transfers, a faster wireless link will make a noticeable difference.

The spread spectrum radio signal used in a Wi-Fi network is not the same as an FM radio signal, but the interference and signal quality problems are similar. If you live in or near a big city, you can probably receive a dozen or more FM radio stations on your kitchen radio. Some of these stations might have transmitters close to your house, and others transmit from the other side of town or even farther away. But as long as your radio can capture a station at a minimum useful level, the radio reproduces the music reasonably well; the signal from the little teakettle college radio station a mile away sounds just as good as the big commercial station with a much more powerful transmitter up in the hills (this is a technical discussion—programming is a whole other question). On the other hand, if you're out on the fringes of the station's coverage area, or if there's another nearby station using the same frequency, the sound of the station you want to hear might be noisy and hard to understand. In the same way, the overall quality of a wireless network link is affected by both signal strength and the presence or absence of unwanted noise.

The technical definition of *noise* in an information channel is *any unwanted energy or information.* The only thing you want your network adapter to receive is the digital signal that came from the access point you want to use; so everything else that shows up at the receiver is noise. This can include interference from other wireless data networks and other radios using the same frequencies (such as cordless telephones, microwave ovens, and medical electronics) and interference from natural sources such as lightning. Up to a point, the digital technology and spread spectrum radio system used in an 802.11b network can do a pretty good job of ignoring interference, but when the noise is just as strong as the signal you want, the network will apply its error correction features until it can confirm that an intelligible signal has made it from the transmitter to the receiver.

A stream of noise or another pair of radios trying to use the same channel at the same time can reduce a link's data transfer speed, but so can a weak signal. As the distance between the transmitter and the receiver increases, the amount of energy that the receiver detects will decrease until the signal is simply too weak for the receiver to decode the data. And if there are physical obstructions that absorb some of the radiated energy between the transmitter and the receiver, the useful signal range will be even shorter. That's why Wi-Fi reception is better outdoors than indoors.

It's possible to use a high-gain antenna to increase the signal strength, and you can raise the antenna to the top of a tower or a tall building to increase the useful distance that it will travel, but at some point the signal strength will be too weak to be useful. That's why most wireless network utility programs show separate readings for signal strength and signal quality. When a problem does occur, you can use the two measurements to help identify the source of the problem: If the signal is strong but the quality is low, the problem is probably caused by some kind of interference, but if both signal quality and signal strength are low, it's likely that you're too far away from the nearest access point or there's some kind of obstruction between you and the access point.

Any time the network fails to transmit a data packet successfully, the device at the receiving end instructs the transmitting device to send the same packet again. This can happen when there is noise or interference on the link (radio or wired), when other users are trying to use the same channel at the same time, or when a radio signal is too weak for the receiver to decode the data contained in the packet. One or two repeated packets in a data stream won't make any real difference, but when it becomes necessary to send almost every packet several times before the receiver accepts it, the actual data transfer speed will be half or less of the nominal speed. A pair of Wi-Fi radios might try to compensate for a poor signal by dropping the transmission speed (this is the same kind of approach as speaking slowly and distinctly over a noisy telephone line), but the effect is often the same: It takes longer to receive the data.

Slow data transfer is not always caused by the radio portion of the network; it can also happen when there's heavy traffic on a server or some kind of noise on the wired portion of the network.

So several problems can all produce the same symptoms. When the data speed appears to slow down, the cause could be in:

- The radio link or signal quality
- The server
- Someplace else in the network—your local network's access point might be connected to a noisy land line

To isolate the source of the problem, run your Wi-Fi status program or a signal monitor program like NetStumbler on the client computer. If the signal strength is low, try moving to a different location away from obstructions between your computer and the access point. If the signal strength is adequate but signal quality is poor, the network adapter is probably receiving noise along with the network data; look for a signal from an access point that uses a different channel number. If you can, move your network to other channel numbers as far away as possible from the other networks near you to find a segment of the spectrum that has fewer competing signals. And if both signal strength and signal quality are adequate but the data transfer speed is slow, the cause is probably in the server or someplace else in the network.

6

WI-FI FOR WINDOWS

In an ideal world, it would be possible to plug a wireless network adapter into a computer, fire it up, and connect to the network right away. No fuss, no bother (and no need for a book like this one). That's the way Windows ought to work; when Windows identifies a network adapter during startup, it should automatically place a Network icon on the desktop and configure all of the settings your computer needs to make a connection.

But nothing is ever that simple. Before you can start to move data across a wireless network, you will probably have to tell Windows exactly how and where to find the network and how to connect to the Internet through the wireless LAN. This chapter explains the general principles involved in making Windows work with a wireless LAN and the specific procedures you will need to configure the networking tools and features in different versions of Windows. This is tedious, nitpicky stuff, but it will eliminate a lot of grief when your network connection doesn't work properly.

In Windows XP and Windows Vista, all of this configuration activity is supposed to happen automatically if your network adapter contains firmware compatible with Microsoft's automatic configuration tool. Most of the latest Wi-Fi adapters come with drivers that work with the Windows XP tools, but you might have to download an updated version to use your adapter with Vista. If your computer does not automatically recognize an adapter, look for device driver software on the manufacturer's website.

NOTE *Unfortunately, device drivers for Windows Vista are not available for many older Wi-Fi adapters, especially the ones that only use the 802.11b standard. The manufacturers might call these* end of life *or* legacy *products, but it comes down to the same thing: They have stopped supporting them. You're out of luck if you want to use one of these adapters with Vista; your only option is to buy a new adapter.*

If you have experience setting up Windows networks, you shouldn't have much trouble with wireless. As far as Windows is concerned, a wireless adapter is just one more type of network interface that exchanges data with applications and the operating system. Up through Windows 2000, the "wireless" stuff happens someplace else; in XP, there's a separate tab for wireless-specific settings, as shown in Figure 6-1. Configuring Windows for wireless is a matter of making this particular computer aware that it's connected to a network and setting the addresses of the network servers and services.

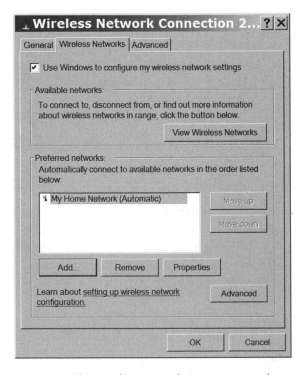

Figure 6-1: The Wireless Network Connection window includes a Wireless Networks tab.

Windows Network Configuration in General

Different versions of Windows use somewhat different configuration tools, but they all accomplish the same thing: The computer's IP address, subnet mask, and gateway address settings must all match the values that the rest of the network requires. It's entirely possible to set these values without understanding what they mean, but it's always helpful to know something about how the network actually works.

The installation manual for the wireless access point on your LAN router should tell you which IP addresses or other settings to use when you're configuring your network. If you can't find the information in the printed material that came with your hardware, ask your network manager or Internet technical support center for help.

IP Addresses

The numeric Internet protocol (IP) address of a network client is the formal identity that the other computers in the same network use to reach that device. Every computer on a network must have a different address.

The agencies that administer the Internet have established a complex numbering system with a unique address for every device connected to the Internet. Numeric IP addresses always appear as four groups of numbers between 0 and 255, so the total universe of IP addresses runs from 0.0.0.0 to 255.255.255.255. These numbers are sometimes called *octets* because they use eight binary digits (binary 11111111 equals decimal 255).

A numeric IP address can identify a single computer, or it can be a gateway to a LAN (or a larger network) with two or more computers connected to it through a router. In some networks, all the computers (and other devices such as printers) on a LAN can share one public interface through a mechanism known as Network Address Translation (NAT).

Each local computer must also have a unique numeric IP address within the LAN (an internal address). In a network using NAT, the router or other gateway that connects the LAN to the Internet translates between internal and external IP addresses.

To prevent conflicts between local IP addresses and Internet addresses, several ranges of numbers have been reserved for use by local networks as internal IP addresses. These addresses will never be found on the Internet, and they can be used on multiple local networks at the same time (so long as the networks don't have to talk to each other directly), but if you're maintaining several networks, it might help you keep your sanity to use different ranges, anyway. The private network address are:

10.0.0.0 to 10.255.255.255

172.16.0.0 to 172.31.255.255

192.168.0.0 to 192.168.255.255

Assigning Addresses

In some networks, a Dynamic Host Configuration Protocol (DHCP) server assigns a different IP address to every client device on the network. The server assigns an address to each client device whenever the client joins the network, so the same client might have a different local address from one session to another; that's why it's called *dynamic host configuration.*

The DHCP server is usually in the router that controls all the devices in the network. In a pure wireless network, that's probably in an access point; in a mixed network that has both wireless and wired links, the DHCP server is likely to be in the Internet gateway. Figure 6-2 shows the server in a typical network.

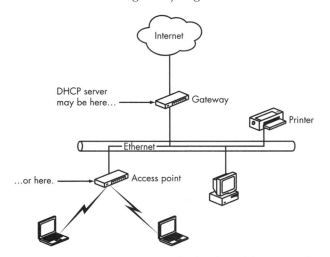

Figure 6-2: A DHCP server provides local IP addresses to all the devices in a LAN.

When a DHCP server is active, all of the network client computers on the LAN should instruct Windows (and other network operating systems) to obtain an IP address automatically. If a network does not use a DHCP server, the network manager must assign a permanent address to each client. If your network manager assigns addresses manually, keep a copy of the address in a text file with a backup copy on paper. If you are the network manager, keep two or more copies of your own list of addresses as you assign them.

The manual for your access point should specify the correct range of addresses for client devices and explain how to assign them. If you use DHCP, the server will assign them automatically. If you don't use DHCP, you must use a different address within the specified range for each device on your network (in other words, you must make sure that two or more devices don't use the same IP address).

With most DHCP servers, it's also possible to assign the same address to each client every time, which can be very helpful. How to configure this depends on your DHCP server, but it usually requires knowing either:

- The name of the client (sent by most operating systems in the DHCP request), which is an arbitrary human-readable name, usually the same as the system name Windows is configured to use for filesharing.

- The MAC address of the client, which is a 12-character address that is unique to every network card. The easiest way to get this address is to either look at the network device properties on the client system or at the connection logs on the access point or DHCP server.

The Subnet Mask

The *subnet mask* is a string of four numbers that specifies which parts of the IP address identify the network or the local subnetwork (the subnet) and which parts identify individual computers and other devices on the network. Each of the four numbers is usually either 255 or 0. For example, if the subnet mask is 255.255.255.0 (the most common value), then all the numeric IP addresses in the network must be *XXX.XXX.XXX.ZZZ*, where *XXX.XXX.XXX* is the same for all addresses, and *ZZZ* is different in each address.

The subnet mask must be identical for all of the access points and wireless clients served by those access points. In small and medium-sized networks, the subnet mask is almost always 255.255.255.0.

Gateways

The *gateway* is the wireless access point, router, or other device that acts as the interface between the computers on a LAN and other devices or networks that are not part of the local network. Any time a computer that is not part of the local network tries to communicate with a device on the network, it must move data through the gateway.

The gateway address (sometimes called the *default gateway*) is the numeric IP address of the gateway server. In a wireless network, the gateway address setting in each network client must be the same as the IP address used by the access point. If a wireless network has more than one access point, all the access points in the network must use the same gateway address.

If an access point doubles as a hub or router, the gateway address that the access point uses for wired and wireless clients is not the same as the gateway address that it uses to communicate with a LAN or Internet server. When you configure a network client, remember to use the access point's LAN IP address as the default gateway, and not the address of the WAN gateway.

Domain Name Servers

A *Domain Name Server* is a computer that converts domain names such as *nostarch.com* or *hard-cider.com* to the numeric IP addresses of the computers or other devices that use those addresses. Some DHCP servers provide a DNS address automatically, but others require a manual entry. If you are not using DHCP, you must specify at least one DNS address.

Most networks and Internet service providers use two or more DNS servers, in order to provide an automatic backup when the primary server is offline. Your network manager or your Internet service provider should give you the addresses of your network's DNS servers. As a last resort, if you can't find the addresses for your own network's DNS servers, you can use one or more of the public DNS servers listed at *http://www.tech-faq.com/public-dns-servers.shtml* or the OpenDNS Tier 2 servers listed at *http://www.opennic.unrated.net/public_servers.html.* Choose the servers closest to your own location for the best performance.

Some access points and network gateways also request a DNS address. The list in the access point or gateway should be identical to the list of DNS servers on each client.

File and Printer Sharing

When filesharing is active, other network users can read and write files to and from your computer. Printer sharing allows other users to send files and documents to a printer connected to the shared printer. In Microsoft networking, a folder that contains files that are available to other users is called a *share.*

The access level of a shared file or folder specifies whether other users can read a file but not change it, or if they have permission to add, remove, or change the contents of a file.

Network Interface Adapter Options

If you can't find a setting or option in the configuration utility, look in the Properties window for your wireless adapter. The driver for each type of network interface adapter includes a set of options that control the specific features of that adapter, such as the name that the client will use on the network, the data transfer speed, the operating mode, and the power saving mode. Figure 6-3 shows a typical list of adapter properties.

To open the Properties window in Windows XP, go to the Windows Control Panel, select the System icon, choose the **Hardware** tab, and then click the **Device Manager** tab. In Windows Vista, open the Control Panel, choose **System**, and click **Device Manager** in the list of Tasks at the left side of the System window. Open the list of Network Adapters and double-click the entry for your wireless adapter. The list of options is under the Advanced tab.

Many of the same adapter options also appear in the configuration utility supplied with the adapter and in the Wireless Configuration Utility in Windows XP. When you change an option in one place, that change should also appear in the other location the next time you open it.

Naming Your Computer

The network uses a numeric IP address to find and identify your computer, but the human users of the network will want a name that is easier to recognize and remember than one of those strings of numbers and dots. Most users won't know or care that 192.168.0.34 is the computer in their office, and 192.168.0.37 is the laptop in the kitchen. So you (or the network manager) must assign a name to each computer in the network. This name will appear in all of the directories and lists of computers that can be reached through your network, as shown in Figure 6-4. Each computer must have a unique name with a maximum length of 15 characters and spaces.

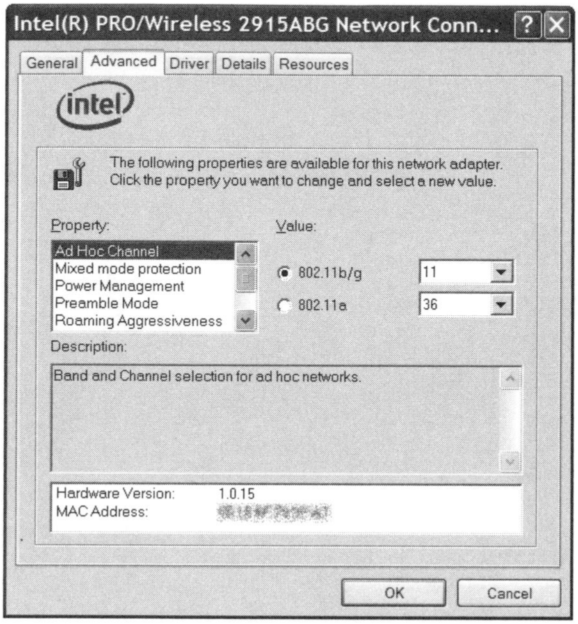

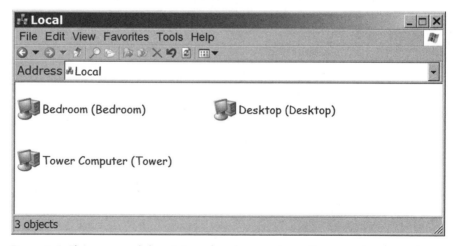

Figure 6-3: The Advanced network connection tab controls
many configuration settings.

The Computer Description field is not required, but it can provide
more detailed information to other users about a network client than the
15-character Computer Name limit allows.

Figure 6-4: The name and description of each computer on the network appears in a
network window.

Windows also provides a space to assign each computer on the network
to a workgroup. In a small LAN, you will probably want to assign all of the
computers to a single workgroup. Therefore, the workgroup name setting
must be identical on every computer in the network.

There are at least two different ways to assign a name to your computer and join a workgroup. When you set up your network in Windows XP or Vista, the Network Setup Wizard includes screens where you can assign a name and description and identify the workgroup; unfortunately the workgroup name reverts to a default (such as MSHOME for home networks), so it's essential to change it to your own workgroup's name any time you run the wizard.

After the network has been set up, you can change the name of a computer or assign it to a different workgroup in XP by opening Control Panel ▶ System ▶ Computer Name. In Vista, use Control Panel ▶ System and Maintenance ▶ System ▶ See the name of this computer ▶ Change Settings.

In some wireless networks, the name of the workgroup must be the same as the SSID used by the access point, especially when the network configuration utility doesn't display a list of nearby networks. If you're having trouble connecting, try changing the workgroup name to the SSID of the network you want to join.

Configuring Windows

Microsoft includes specific support for wireless networking in Windows XP and Windows Vista that is supposed to integrate wireless configuration with other Windows configuration settings. In theory, this should make it easier to set up and use wireless networks, but it's still not a simple plug-and-play process.

The goal is automatic wireless configuration: Windows should automatically detect your wireless network adaptor and search for accessible wireless network signals. When it detects a nearby network, Windows should allow a user to join the network with just a few mouse clicks. And if you replace your adapters with a different brand, you won't have to learn a new set of commands and controls.

That's the goal, but there are still a few obscure configuration settings buried in the Device Manager rather than the wireless configuration tool, so it might be necessary to use the configuration tool supplied with your network adapter for the less obvious network configuration settings and options.

Do You Have the Latest Firmware?

Just about every manufacturer of network adapters offers the latest upgrades on its website as free downloads. While you're at it, use the Windows Update link in Internet Explorer's Tools menu to make sure you have the very latest version of Windows, including all the available updates, patches, and service packs.

Using the Windows Wireless Tools

Some vendors have integrated the Windows Wireless Properties controls with their own programs, and others have turned the whole process over to the Windows utility. For example, the Adapter Settings command in the Intel PROSet/Wireless control screen (shown in Figure 6-5) links to the Windows Network Connection Properties window (the one shown in Figure 6-3).

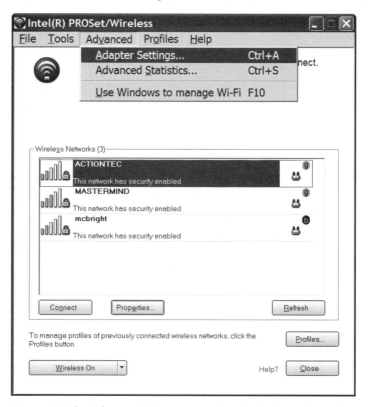

Figure 6-5: The Adapter Settings command in the Intel control window links to the Windows Wireless Network Properties window.

Other adapters allow you to choose between their own control programs and the Windows tools. In addition, some popular laptop computer makers include yet another Wi-Fi control program as part of their proprietary software packages. All of these programs probably do the same things, so the correct choice is the one you like best. Try each of them, and use the one that seems easiest to understand and use.

The following sections explain how to use the Windows wireless configuration tools.

Making a Connection

To connect your computer to a Wi-Fi network, double-click the network icon in the System Tray next to the clock. In some systems, like the one shown in Figure 6-6, you might see two or more separate wireless icons—one for each control program. In this example, the Microsoft icon is on the left, the Lenovo icon is in the middle, and the Intel logo is on the right.

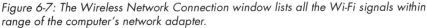

Figure 6-6: Click a wireless network
icon to set up a Wi-Fi connection.

NOTE *The images in this section are all from Windows XP. The windows and dialog boxes in Windows Vista are similar but not identical.*

The Wireless Network Connection window shown in Figure 6-7 will open.

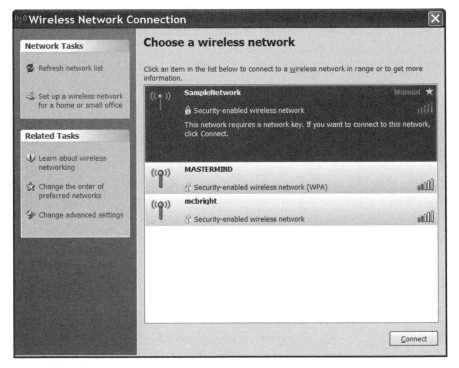

Figure 6-7: The Wireless Network Connection window lists all the Wi-Fi signals within range of the computer's network adapter.

Select the network you want to join and click the **Connect** button near the bottom of the window. In this example, SampleNetwork is the strongest nearby signal (five bars).

The Wireless Network Connection Status window shows the current state of your wireless link, including the connection status, the amount of time the current link has been active, the data transfer speed, the signal quality, and the number of bytes the adapter has sent and received since the adapter connected itself to the network. To view the Status window, right-click the wireless icon and choose **Status** from the pop-up menu. Figure 6-8 shows the status window.

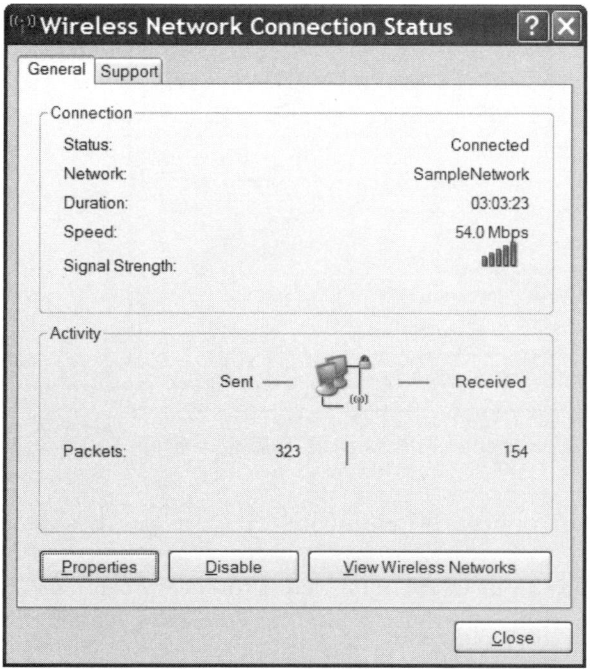

Figure 6-8: The Wireless Network Connection Status window in Windows XP

In most cases, the Connection tool will automatically configure your computer to exchange data with the network. If it doesn't, you might have to change one or more settings. If you're trying to connect to your own network, consult the manual that was supplied with your Wi-Fi access point. If you're connecting to a public network, look for printed or online configuration or setup instructions supplied by the Wi-Fi service provider.

To change the most common network settings, click the **Properties** button at the bottom of the Wireless Network Connection Status window. To turn off the radio link, click the **Disable** button.

Network Configuration Settings

The Wireless Network Connection Properties window is similar to the properties windows for wired network connections, with an additional tab for Wireless Networks, as shown in Figure 6-9.

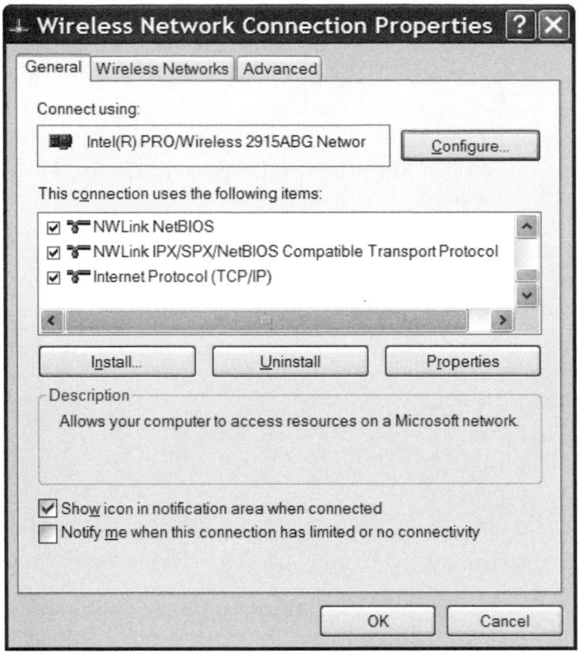

Figure 6-9: Select Internet Protocol (TCP/IP) to set network options.

To configure your wireless connection, follow these steps:

1. In the list of installed items, select **Internet Protocol (TCP/IP)** and click the **Properties** button. An Internet Protocol (TCP/IP) Properties window like the one in Figure 6-10 will appear.

2. If the DHCP server in your access point or some other network device is active, select the Obtain an IP address automatically and Obtain DNS server address automatically options. If you are not using a DHCP server, select the Use the following IP address option, and type the IP address assigned to this computer in the IP address field. Public networks almost always use a DHCP server to make it as easy as possible for users to connect; try the Obtain an IP address automatically option first.

3. The Subnet Mask field is in the same Internet Protocol (TCP/IP) Properties tab that also controls the IP address. If you are not using a DHCP server on your network, type the same subnet mask as the one used by the access point. If you don't know the subnet mask value, try 255.255.255.0.

4. If you are not using a DHCP server, type the wireless access point's LAN IP address in the Default Gateway field. You can obtain the address from your network manager or from the access point's manual.

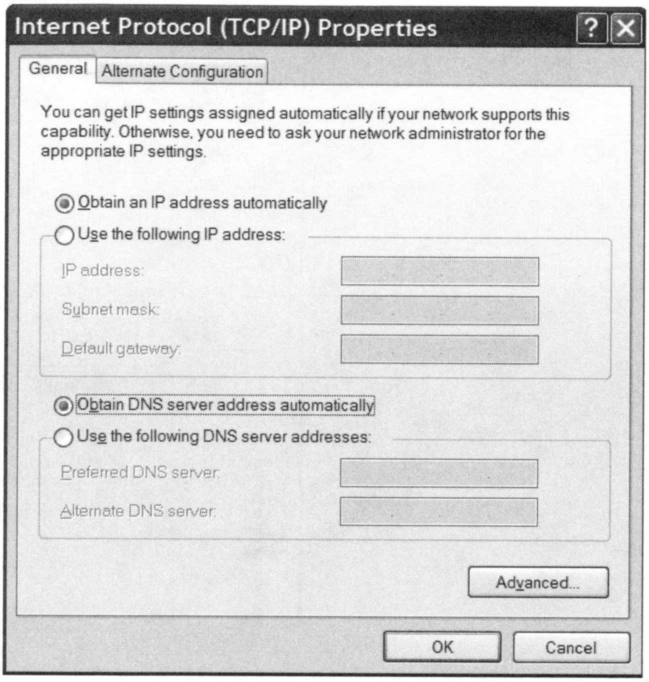

Figure 6-10: The Internet Protocol (TCP/IP) Properties window controls network connection options.

5. If a DHCP server assigns DNS addresses to network clients, choose the Obtain DNS server address automatically option. If the network uses a static domain name server, choose the Use the following DNS server addresses option and type the DNS addresses supplied by your network manager or Internet service provider.

6. Click the **OK** button to save your settings and close this window.

File and Printer Sharing

To make the contents of a folder or an entire drive available to other network users, right-click the folder or drive's icon and choose the **Sharing and Security** option (in Windows XP) or the **Share** option (in Windows Vista) from the drop-down menu to view the dialog boxes shown in Figure 6-11.

To permit access to this folder or drive to users on this computer in XP, choose the Share this folder on the network option. In Vista, click the **Advanced Sharing** button and choose Share this folder. To permit other users on the network to edit or delete files, choose the Allow network users to change my files option.

When you permit sharing in Windows XP, the icon for the shared item changes. A shared folder or drive has an icon with a hand "serving" the item to the network.

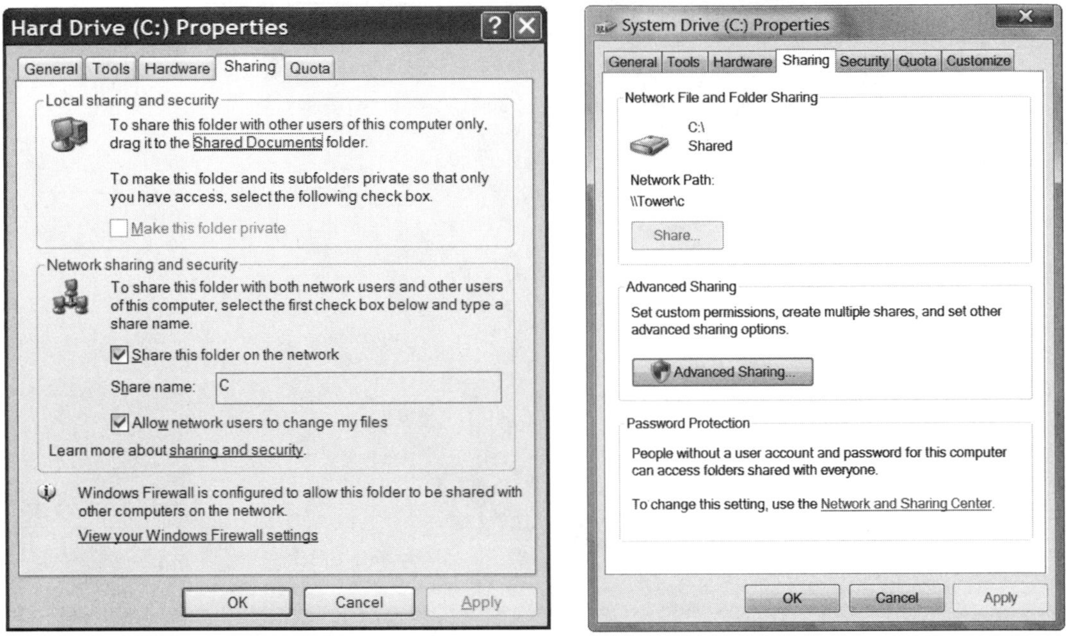

Figure 6-11: Click the Sharing tab to change the file and folder sharing characteristics of a folder or drive.

Network Interface Adapter Options

To change the network interface adapter options, follow these steps:

1. Double-click the Windows Wi-Fi icon in the System Tray to open the Wireless Network Connection window.

2. Choose the **Change advanced settings** item in the list of Related Tasks at the left of the Connection window. The Wireless Network Connection Properties window will open.

3. From the Connection Properties window, click the **Configure** button. The Adapter Properties window will appear.

4. Click the **Advanced** tab. A list of properties like the one in Figure 6-12 will appear. The specific details and wording of the options are somewhat different for each make and model of network adapter.

5. Highlight each of the items in the list of properties to see the current setting in the Value field. Some values are text fields and others are drop-down menus. To change the current value in a text field, select the current text and type the new value. To change a value in a menu, open the drop-down menu and select the new value you want to use.

6. Click the **OK** button to save your changes and close the window. Click the **OK** button in the Network window to return to the desktop.

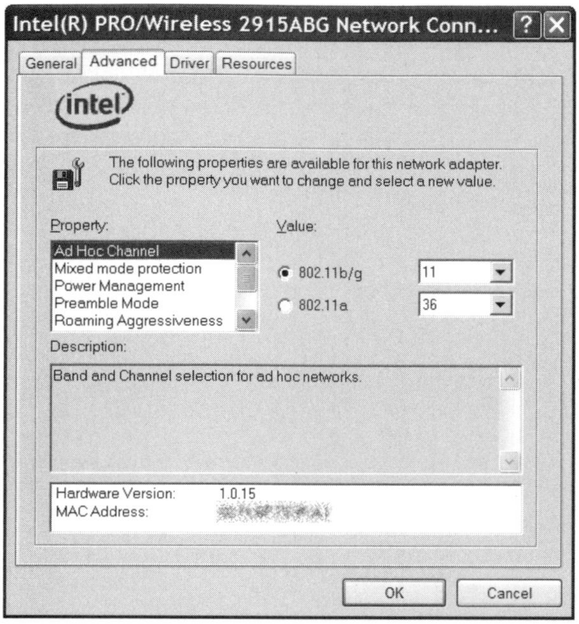

Figure 6-12: Click the Advanced tab in the adapter's
Properties window to configure your network adapter.

Some wireless network adapters do not accept any option settings through windows. If you don't see an Advanced tab in the Adapter Properties window, use the configuration utility program supplied with the adapter to change the adapter settings.

Naming Your Computer

To set or change the name assigned to your computer in Windows XP, click the **Computer Name** tab of the System Properties window. Follow these steps to change the settings:

1. From the Control Panel , double-click the System icon. In Windows XP, the System Properties window will appear. In Vista, the View Basic Information About Your Computer window will open; under the Computer Name, Domain and Workgroup Settings heading, click **Change Settings**.

2. Click the **Computer Name** tab. The dialog box shown in Figure 6-13 will appear.

3. Type the name that identifies this computer on the network in the Computer Description field.

4. Click the **Change** button. The Computer Name Changes window in Figure 6-14 will open.

5. Click the **OK** button to save your changes and close the window.

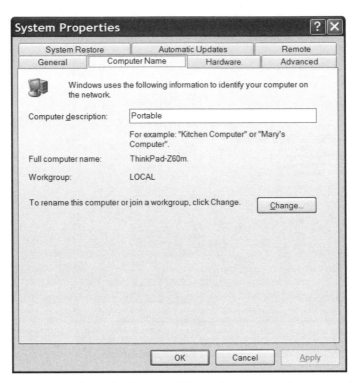

Figure 6-13: Open the Computer Name tab to change the computer's name and the network's SSID.

Selecting a Network

If your computer is within range of more than one network, you must choose the one you want to use. The Wireless Properties utility includes a list of Preferred Networks, but it doesn't limit you to the networks on that list.

The list of networks in the Wireless Network Connection window shows the SSIDs of all the networks that will accept a link from your wireless adapter. If the adapter detects just one network, Windows will automatically try to connect to that network. When a network adapter detects more than one network, it compares the SSID of each network to the names in the Preferred Networks list and automatically connects you to the network with the highest priority. You can change the order in which Windows searches for networks by clicking **Change the Order of Preferred Networks** in the Connection window with the Move Up and Move Down buttons in the Properties Window.

If your adapter detects a network that's not on your Preferred list, it will set up a connection *if* the nonpreferred option in the Advanced window is active. Click the **Advanced** button in the Properties window to open that window.

Of course, it's possible that the computer will make the wrong choice; if it detects two or more networks, it might not automatically connect to the network you want. When that happens, select the name of the correct network

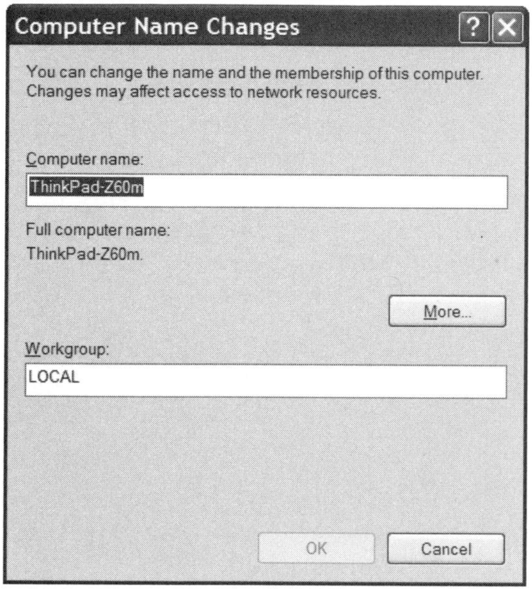

Figure 6-14: Use the Computer Name Changes window to set the computer's name and SSID.

in the Available Networks list and click the **Configure** button. This will open another window with more information about that network, and it will set up a connection with that network.

Connecting to an Encrypted Network

The listing for each Wi-Fi network in the Wireless Network Connection window will tell you whether that network uses encryption, and if so, which type of encryption it uses. The first time you try to connect to an encrypted network, Windows will ask for the network key for that network. After you have established a connection, Windows will store the key and try to use it whenever you connect to the same network.

Troubleshooting the Connection

Whether you're using Windows XP or some earlier version of the operating system, it ought to be possible to set up a link to a wireless network. If the automatic connection function doesn't work, don't assume that you've done something wrong—more likely, you're a victim of somebody's bad design. Here are some things to check:

- Is the SSID used by your computer exactly the same as the SSID of the network you want to join?

- Is encryption turned on or off? If it's on, are you using the correct encryption key? Is encryption set to 64-bit or 128-bit?

- Does the access point use MAC address filtering? Is your wireless adapter on the list of qualified users?
- Does the workgroup name match the SSID?
- Does your access point use a DHCP server? If not, are the IP address, subnet mask, and default gateway settings correct?
- Is the preamble length setting correct? To change the preamble length, open the adapter's Properties window (the one shown in Figure 6-12) and choose **Preamble Mode** or **Preamble Length** from the Properties menu.

7

WI-FI FOR LINUX AND UNIX

Wi-Fi networking is not limited to computers that use a Windows operating system. Computers running Linux, Unix, and Mac OS X can all support Wi-Fi, if you can find the driver software for your network adapter. A TCP/IP network doesn't care what kind of operating system the computers connected to the network are using. It's just receiving bits and bytes from a computer port and moving them around. All of the most popular versions and distributions of both Linux and Unix (including Mac OS X) include wireless networking configuration and control tools that perform the same functions as the Windows utilities described in Chapter 6. This chapter contains information about connecting your Unix- and Linux-based computer to a Wi-Fi network, and it describes some utilities and other tools that can make things easier.

If you're not already using Unix or Linux, connecting to a wireless network is not a good enough reason to start. There are some Linux and Unix tools for measuring the performance of a Wi-Fi network and for cracking wireless encryption that aren't available for Windows, but unless you're a network manager, you probably don't have any real need for them.

This chapter is written for Unix and Linux users who already have enough experience to set up and use one of those operating systems on a laptop or desktop computer. If you need more help using your Unix or Linux clients, you should ask for help from your neighborhood guru or find a more general how to use Linux or Unix book, such as *Ubuntu for Non-Geeks, 2nd Edition* by Rickford Grant (2007, No Starch Press) or *Absolute FreeBSD, 2nd Edition* by Michael W. Lucas (2008, No Starch Press).

Many Linux and Unix distributions for desktop and laptop computers (rather than servers), including Ubuntu, openSUSE, and PC-BSD (among others) include drivers and control software that support many common Wi-Fi adapters, so a computer running one of those distributions will probably detect and connect to a nearby wireless signal automatically. If you're using one of those distributions with a supported adapter, you can just turn on the computer, plug in the adapter, and go. But if your distribution doesn't include Wi-Fi drivers and utilities, or if you have a less common adapter, you'll have to find the driver and control software separately. You can find pointers to many sources for those drivers later in this chapter.

If you're not satisfied with the Wi-Fi control program supplied with your Linux or Unix distribution, or if your distribution doesn't include a Wi-Fi program, you can choose from several other Wi-Fi control programs that perform the same actions as the built-in control programs but present them differently. There's a list of these programs later in this chapter.

NOTE   *If you're operating a Unix or Linux network server, it's better to locate the server in the same room and use Ethernet cables to connect the server to the network router, instead of wireless links. As a general rule, Wi-Fi is not the best way to connect a server to a LAN because the data transfer speed of a Wi-Fi link is almost always slower and more susceptible to interference than a wired connection.*

Drivers, Back Seat and Otherwise

Before we go any deeper into connecting devices to wireless networks, let's take some time to review exactly what a driver does and why drivers are important. Later in this chapter, you can find advice about finding the right drivers for different kinds of wireless network adapters and how to use them to connect Unix and Linux computers to a wireless network.

A device driver is the software interface between a computer's operating system and the inputs and outputs of a peripheral device connected to the computer. The driver contains the instructions that translate incoming commands and data from the device into a form that the operating system can understand, and it translates outbound instructions from the operating system into specific device controls. It handles memory management and timing, and it specifies the input/output (I/O) port and the interrupts that the device will use to communicate with the operating system. Figure 7-1 shows the relationship between a computer and a very generic device driver.

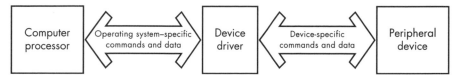

Figure 7-1: A device driver is the data and control interface between a computer and a peripheral device.

Every peripheral device, including a wireless network adapter, requires a driver that converts standard instructions from the computer to controls that handle the specific features and functions of that device. Without the driver, the device won't operate. A device without the right driver is useful only as a paperweight or a doorstop.

So, for example, the driver for a keyboard tells the computer which I/O port carries data to and from the keyboard, converts keystrokes into input data, and turns the Caps Lock, Num Lock, and Scroll Lock lights on or off. A printer driver includes the specific controls that make the difference between an impact printer and a laser printer. A driver for an input or output device will specify whether the device uses a serial or parallel port, a USB port, a PCMCIA socket, or one of the internal expansion slots on the computer's motherboard. And the driver for a wireless network adapter specifies things like the channel number that the radio will use to send and receive data, the amount of power the radio will transmit, and the data transmission speed that the adapter will use to transfer data.

The drivers for Wi-Fi adapters handle the physical layers of TCP/IP communication—just the information the adapters need to set up and use radio links to a network, while other layers handle data formatting and content. This assures that the adapter can handle many data formats and the data can pass through many different adapter types.

Drivers also make it possible for the same piece of hardware to work with different operating systems. A driver converts the input and output signals produced by the operating system to and from commands in the device's "native language." Drivers written for different operating systems that control the same device start with instructions in different forms, and convert those instructions into the same set of device controls. Therefore, your computer requires device drivers written specifically for that operating system.

It might be useful to think of a driver as the instruction manual for a device. Manuals written in English, Dutch, and Malay all contain the same set of instructions, but they are provided in languages that different users will understand. Computer device drivers are similar, except the languages are operating systems instead of human speech.

The device driver is a separate program from the configuration utility, but many software designers combine the two in a single installation. The configuration utility provides a set of commands and displays that send and receive data in both directions through the driver to the network adapter.

Where to Find Drivers

You need a driver for your computer's operating system before you can use your wireless network adapter. If you're lucky, or if you have done some careful shopping, the right driver is either on the CD supplied with the adapter, or it's bundled with the operating system. For Linux and Unix systems, most drivers are already built into the core, or kernel, of the operating system.

Many wireless adapters are actually private-label products that were made by somebody whose name does not appear anywhere on the package or the device itself. So it's often necessary to do some detective work to identify the right driver for a particular adapter. Proxim and Atheros are particularly active in the private-label adapter business. The adapter manufacturers might not want to tell you whose hardware is lurking inside their boxes, but the people who develop third-party Linux drivers have often figured out which brands work with which drivers.

The first place to look for a Linux or Unix adapter is in the operating system core itself. Generally speaking, the most stable and well-supported drivers will have been merged into the kernel development process. Most distributions will turn on all the stable drivers by default, but it might be necessary to recompile your kernel in some situations.

If you have a choice, it's better to pick an adapter that is already supported by your operating system. Some manufacturers provide the necessary specifications to write complete drivers, or they have written and contributed drivers themselves. Other manufacturers offer no official support for Linux and BSD, but dedicated individuals have written drivers by painstakingly reverse engineering the official drivers from other platforms. The final option for users trying to get an adapter functioning is to use a *wrapper* framework, which takes a Windows device driver and wraps it in code that makes it act like a driver for Linux or Unix.

Adapter manufacturers who have produced their own Linux and Unix drivers, or who have worked with the open source community to provide official specifications, have generally done a good job of supporting devices and making drivers available to users. Several major vendors, however, provide no such support or assistance. If you already have an adapter that will not support Linux or Unix, you will probably have to move from the relatively sane world of commercial software to the wide-open universe of user groups, email lists, and community websites. Communities of users are out there, made up of people who are anxious to improve the performance and compatibility of their favorite operating systems. Within these communities, dozens of open source developers have created device drivers and wireless configuration utilities.

Linux Drivers

More than a hundred different brands of wireless network adapters carry Wi-Fi certification labels, but almost all of them use one of just a handful of internal chip sets. If you can't find a Linux or Unix driver for a specific card, you can often use a generic driver for the adapter's chip set.

As Linux becomes more popular, a growing number of companies will provide their own Linux drivers for their wireless network adapters. If you can't find a Linux driver from your adapter maker, you can probably use one of the drivers supplied in Linux distribution packages, or you can download a separate driver from the chip set provider or a third-party developer.

One very good place to find Linux drivers is the Linux Wireless LAN Support website at *http://linux-wless.passys.nl.* As Figure 7-2 shows, this site provides a search tool that you can use to identify the chip set in your adapter and find a direct link to a driver.

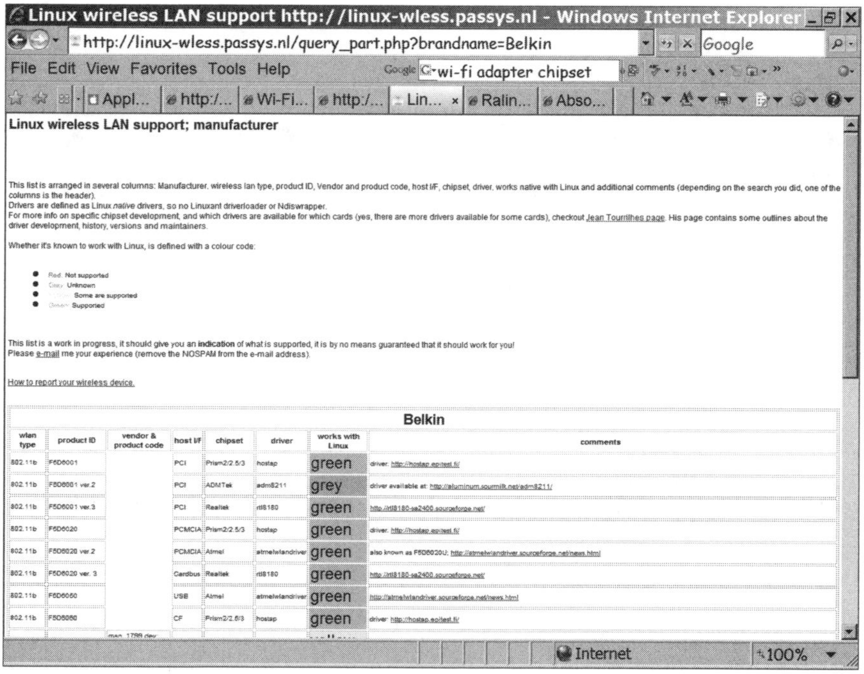

Figure 7-2: The Linux Wireless LAN Support website provides a wealth of useful information about Wi-Fi adapters and drivers.

To find a driver for your adapter, use one of the search menus on the first page of the Linux Wireless LAN Support site to open either a list of adapters made by each manufacturer or a list of interfaces sorted by the type of interface that the adapter uses to connect to your computer (most often either PCMCIA or USB). The listing for each make and model or each chip set includes a direct link to a driver for that device.

If you can't find a driver for your adapter on one of those lists, your best bet is to ask for help. The Linux community is famous for assisting new users. Somebody who knows which driver will work with your Whoopie-Matic Lightning Bolt Wireless Adapter has probably posted pointers to exactly the information you need in a Linux newsgroup. The comp.os.linux.networking newsgroup is the best place to ask questions about finding drivers for wireless network adapters. Before posting your own questions, it's always a good idea to scan the newsgroup's archives for previous answers that will solve your problem. Look in the comp.os.linux section of *groups.google.com* for a searchable archive of old questions and answers.

If none of those sources can tell you where to find a Linux driver for a specific make and model of adapter, the next step is to identify the chip set inside the adapter and find a driver for that chip set. Some adapters come with data sheets or manuals that identify the chip set, but if yours does not, open a console and try one of these commands:

- If the adapter connects to the computer through a USB port, use lsusb.
- If the adapter is a 32-bit PC Card (a CardBus card), use lspci.
- If the adapter is an older 16-bit PC Card, use pccardctl ident.
- If the adapter is mounted inside a desktop computer on a PCI card, use lspci.

After you connect the adapter, look at the kernel messages via dmesg to see if additional information is available.

As a last resort, you can almost always identify the chip set by entering the FCC ID code from the adapter's label into the Federal Communications Commission's FCC Equipment Authorization System Generic Search form at *https://gullfoss2.fcc.gov/oetcf/eas/reports/GenericSearch.cfm*. This web page provides links to a database with copies of the paperwork that the manufacturer filed with its application for type approval, usually including a technical description and one or more circuit diagrams. A few minutes reading those documents should tell you who made the adapter's chip set, which should be enough to let you find the applicable driver at the Linux Wireless LAN Support website.

If you can't find a driver for your adapter in the Linux Wireless LAN Support list or any other source, there are two other last resort alternatives that convert Windows drivers to Linux. The first is a free program called NDISwrapper that wraps Linux support around the manufacturer's Windows driver. For more information and a free download, go to the project's home page at *http://ndiswrapper.sourceforge.net*. The other option is a similar commercial program, DriverLoader, created by Linuxant. For more information about DriverLoader and a free 30-day trial download, go to *http://www.linuxant.com/driverloader*.

NOTE   *Before you spend a lot of time trying to find and install a compatible third-party driver for your old or obscure Wi-Fi adapter, consider replacing it with an inexpensive new adapter that works out of the box with your Linux version. You will probably see better performance and experience less aggravation than with your old adapter.*

Unix Drivers

Wi-Fi drivers and network software for Unix systems are less common than the ones for Linux, but there's enough support out there to connect computers running many major versions of Unix to a wireless network. The major BSD versions—FreeBSD, NetBSD, and OpenBSD—all include integrated drivers for the most widely-used Wi-Fi chip sets. Solaris and other Unix versions don't support as many chip sets as the BSD versions, but they do include a few drivers in their distribution packages or distribute them through their respective user communities.

It's even more important with Unix than with Linux to find a driver *before* you buy an adapter because drivers for some chip sets simply don't exist for every version of Unix. Adapters that use the most common chip sets are often supported, but you might not have as much luck with a more obscure adapter.

Some Unix distributions (especially the ones that are targeted at desktops and laptops rather than servers, such as PC-BSD, found at *http://www.pcbsd.org*) include plug-and-play support for many common Wi-Fi adapters and chip sets. If your Unix distribution does not support your adapter, you will have to find and install a separate driver. To identify the right Unix driver, follow these steps:

1. Use the lists at *http://linux-wless.passys.nl* to identify the chip set in your Wi-Fi adapter.

2. Look in the list at *http://en.wikipedia.org/wiki/Comparison_of_open_source _wireless_drivers* for links to the correct driver for your Unix version and chip set.

If you can't find a driver for your adapter and version of Unix, try a web search for *<name of Unix type> <name of chip set> driver*, or ask in the users' forum for your Unix version. For information about using Wi-Fi with Solaris, start at *http://www.opensolaris.org/os/community/laptop/wireless*.

Wi-Fi Control Programs

The Wi-Fi configuration and control programs supplied with Ubuntu, SUSE, PC-BSD, and other distributions are all you really need to set up your computer for a Wi-Fi connection. The adapter attached to your computer detects nearby wireless networks and either connects automatically or offers a list and allows you to choose the network you want to use. No muss and a minimum of fuss.

But some other distributions don't include bundled Wi-Fi software, so you must find and install one of the add-on programs. Some of these are designed for the GNOME or KDE desktop, and others are more generic.

Using Built-in Software

The wireless networking software included with many Unix and Linux distributions is easy to use: If the system doesn't automatically set up a link, just open the Network or Network Devices tool and select the Wireless option. For example, follow these steps to set up a wireless connection in Ubuntu Linux:

1. If it's not already turned on, turn on the Wi-Fi adapter or connect it to your computer.

2. Choose **System ▸ Administration ▸ Network** to open the Network Settings window shown in Figure 7-3.

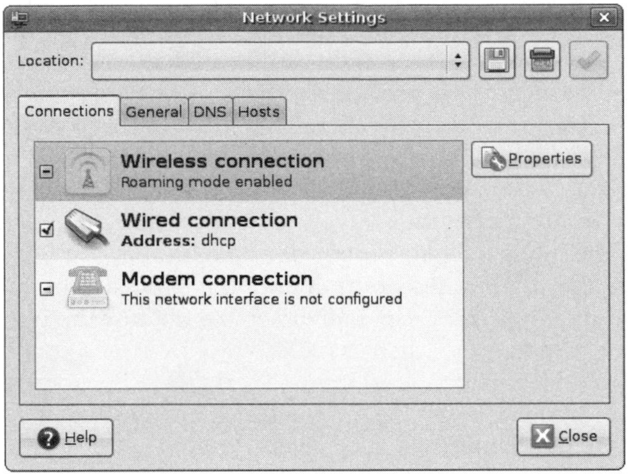

Figure 7-3: The Network Settings window displays both wired and wireless network connections.

3. Select the **Wireless Connection** item in the **Connections** tab, and click the **Properties** button. The Settings window shown in Figure 7-4 will appear.

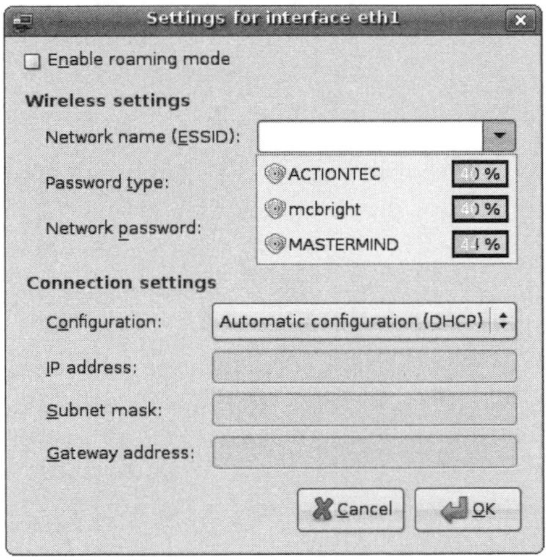

Figure 7-4: The Wireless Settings window controls Wi-Fi connections.

4. Remove the checkmark from the Enable roaming mode option.

5. Open the drop-down Network Name menu to view a list of Wi-Fi networks detected by your network adapter.

6. Choose the network you want to use.

7. If the network is encrypted, choose the type of encryption and type the password.

8. Choose the connection type (static or DHCP) from the drop-down Configuration menu.

9. If the network does not use DHCP to assign an IP address, type the IP address, Subnet Mask, and Gateway Address in the respective fields.

10. Click the **OK** button to save your settings and close the window.

Other distributions use slightly different programs, but they're all very similar. Look in your desktop's Network Settings or Control Center menu for a Wireless Networks section where you can turn the wireless adapter on or off, choose a network, and enter a WEP or WPA password.

Add-on Wi-Fi Programs

If your own distribution (of either Linux or Unix) doesn't include a Wi-Fi control program, or if you want a different arrangement of features and controls, you have several choices, as shown in Figures 7-5 through 7-10. Some of these programs are only available for Linux, but like the GNOME and KDE desktops that many of these programs use, many of them will work with Linux and several versions of Unix.

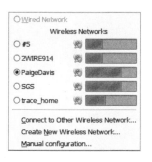

Figure 7-5: NetworkManager is the default Wi-Fi control program for several distributions, including Ubuntu. A KDE version of the program—KNetworkManager—is also available (http://gnome.org/projects/Network-Manager, http://en.opensuse.org/Projects/KNetworkManager).

Figure 7-6: wpa-supplicant's GUI provides WPA client support (http://hostap.epitest.fi/wpa_supplicant).

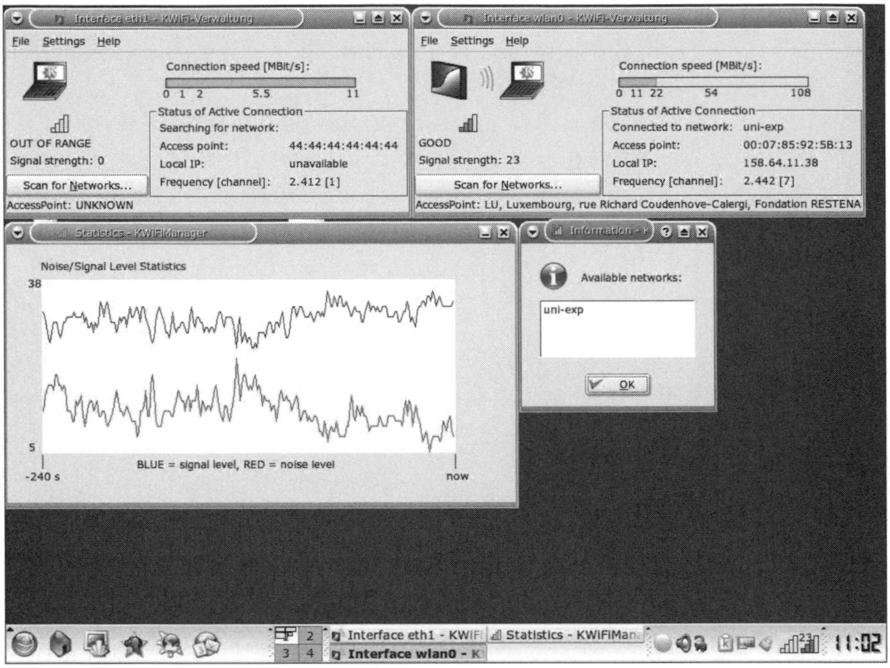

Figure 7-7: The KWiFi Manager program for KDE desktops (http://kwifimanager
.sourceforge.net)

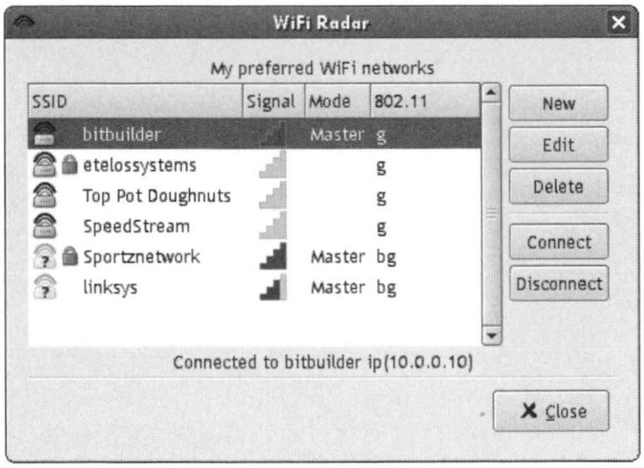

Figure 7-8: The WiFi Radar program window
(http://wifi-radar.systemimager.org)

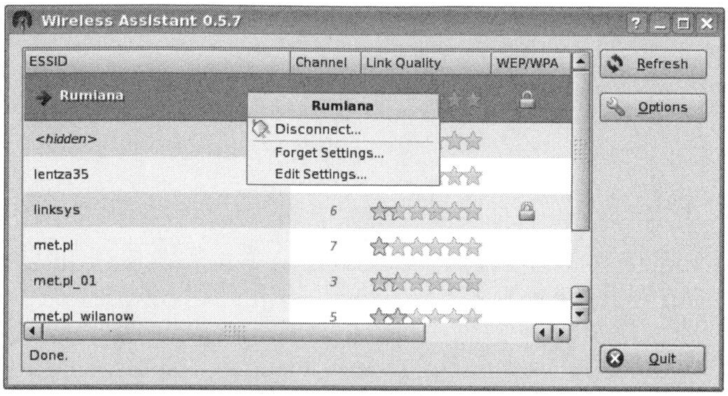

Figure 7-9: The Wireless Assistant display window
(http://wlassistant.sourceforge.net)

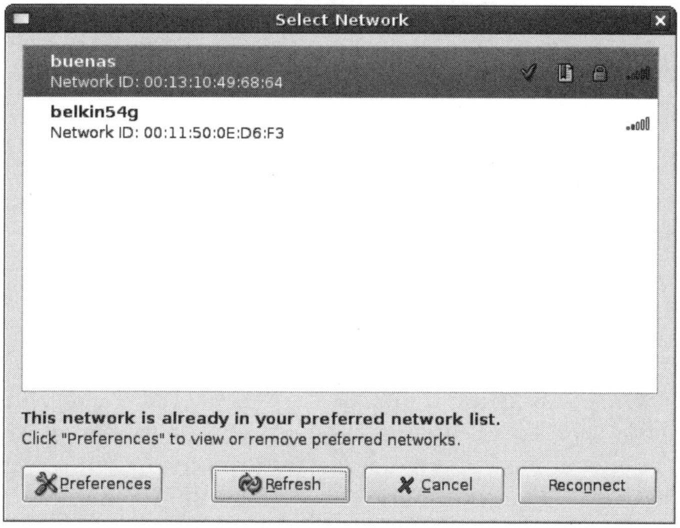

Figure 7-10: The GTKWifi Wireless Connection Manager
(http://sourceforge.net/projects/gtkwifi)

Looking Under the Hood

Many of these packages are based on the Wireless Extensions for Linux API that are included in most recent Linux releases, and the Wireless Tools programs that use the wireless extensions. The combined documentation for both Wireless Extensions and Wireless Tools is online at *http://www.hpl .hp.com/personal/Jean_Tourrilhes/Linux/Linux.Wireless.Extensions.html*.

As other wireless software for Linux appears, the *Wireless Tools for Linux* document (*http://www.hpl.hp.com/personal/Jean_Tourrilhes/Linux/Tools.html*) will probably be one of the best places to learn about it.

If a driver supports wireless extensions (and all Linux drivers do), the user can change the network configuration with any tool that provides an interface with the wireless extensions API, or the command-line tools iwconfig, iwlist, and iwpriv.

Wireless Tools

Wireless Tools is a set of programs that manipulate the wireless extensions. You can find instructions for downloading the most recent version from *http://www.hpl.hp.com/personal/Jean_Tourrilhes/Linux/Tools.html*. The Wireless Tools are command-line programs, but they also provide a foundation for other programs that add a graphical user interface (GUI) to their controls and statistics.

Wireless Tools contains a */proc* entry and three programs: iwconfig, iwspy, and iwpriv.

/proc/net/wireless

The */proc* entry is a listing in the */proc* pseudo-filesystem that shows some statistical information about the wireless interface. */proc* entries act as files, so the command cat /proc/net/wireless will display wireless statistics:

```
>cat /proc/net/wireless
Inter-|sta|  Quality        |Discarded packets
face  |tus|link level noise| nwid crypt  misc
 eth2: f0   15.  24.   4      181    0     0
```

The status listing shows the current state of the network device. The Quality values show the signal quality of the link, the signal level at the receiver, and the amount of noise at the receiver when no signal is present. The Discarded packets values show the number of packets discarded due to an invalid network ID (nwid) because the adapter was not able to decrypt the contents of the packets.

iwconfig

The iwconfig program controls the wireless adapter's configuration options. In an 802.11b network, it includes these parameters:

channel   The channel number that the adapter will use.

nwid   The network identification. In an 802.11b network, the nwid is the same as the SSID.

name   The name of the type of wireless network or protocol in use on this network. This may be the type of adapter or a generic name such as *802.11b*.

enc   The encryption key currently in use.

The command iwconfig, with no argument, produces a list of current iwconfig and /proc/net/wireless values.

iwspy

The iwspy program sets and displays the local computer's IP address and the MAC address.

iwpriv

The iwpriv program provides additional support for device-specific extensions.

Programs Based on the Wireless Tools

Obviously, the Wireless Tools programs are more of a framework for software developers than easy-to-use resources for end users. They do the actual work for the programs described in the next couple of sections, so it's useful to know that they exist and what they do. In actual operation, programs like NetworkManager are a lot easier to use for everyone except the most hard-core command-line geeks.

netcfg

netcfg is a network configuration tool for the GNOME environment. It allows a user to create and manage connection profiles and change network settings in real time. The netcfg home page is at *http://netcfg.sourceforge.net.*

wavemon

wavemon uses ncurses to monitor and configure wireless adapter settings. It includes an Overview screen with all the important information from Wireless Tools in graphic form, a *level alarm* that triggers when signal strength drops below a preset level, and a full-screen history display that shows changes in signal level, noise level, and signal quality over time. There's also a configuration tool that uses menus for easy set up.

For more information about wavemon and links to the most recent version of the program, see *http://www.janmorgenstern.de/projects-software.html.*

Status Display Programs

Several programs import the information from the /proc/net/wireless listings into graphic displays. The major difference among these programs appears to be the display format.

WMWave

WMWave (Figure 7-11) is a dockapp that shows link quality, signal level, and noise level in a small onscreen window. It's available at *http://wmwave.sourceforge.net.*

Figure 7-11: WMWave shows the characteristics of an active Wi-Fi connection.

GKrellMwireless

The Gkrellm monitor stack is a graphic display of system information that can use themes to match the appearance of many window managers. The Gkrellm plug-in adds information about wireless network connections to the monitor stack. For general information about GKrellMwireless, go to the main website at *http://gkrellm.luon.net/index.phtml*. For details about the wireless plug-in, go to *http://gkrellm.luon.net/gkrellmwireless.phtml*.

xwipower

The xwipower utility shows wireless signal strength in an onscreen icon and also includes a bar graph that tracks signal strength over time (Figure 7-12). The signal strength icon shows a set of bar graphs that correspond to the strength of the received signal. The icon displays a message in Japanese when the adapter fails to detect a signal (roughly translated, it means *outside of signal area*).

Figure 7-12: xwipower shows the strength of a wireless signal as an onscreen icon.

The same icon also shows the current battery level. When the tiny battery in the icon is solid, the battery is fully charged or the computer is using external power. The battery icon appears as an outline when the battery level drops below 10 percent.

xwipower works in Linux, FreeBSD, and NetBSD. It's available for download at *http://www.freebsd.org/cgi/cvsweb.cgi/ports/sysutils/xwipower*.

Remote Monitoring

The /proc/net/wireless entry looks like a file, so it's possible to retrieve status information about remote network clients through the network. Steven Hanley's Signal Level Server and Clients programs present this information in a graphic display. For details and downloads, go to *http://svana.org/sjh/wireless*.

Configuring an Access Point

Most configuration utilities for wireless access points use either a web-based interface, an internal command-line interface from a remote terminal, or both. So it should not make any difference what operating system you use on the host computer that connects to the access point. The access point's commands, controls, and status displays will be the same on any system.

The exception is the Apple AirPort Base Station access point, which presents a different set of problems. The internal software supplied with the AirPort Base Station assumes that you're configuring it from a Macintosh using the AirPort Setup Assistant and the AirPort Utility. In practice, that's usually a safe bet because just about everybody who uses an AirPort Base Station is also using at least one Macintosh computer.

There's really not much reason to use anything but a Mac to configure your AirPort Base Station, but it can be done. To set up an AirPort Base Station from a Linux host, you need a Linux configuration program. At this time, only one program, the AirPort Base Station Configurator, appears to fit this description. Separate versions for the two versions of the AirPort Base Station (*Snow* and *Graphite*) are available from *http://wireless.ictp.trieste.it/school_2003/soft/java_configurator/APconfigurator.html*.

Because it was written as a Java application, the AirPort Configurator program will run on any computer with Java Runtime Environment (JRE) in place. This includes Windows, Solaris, and Linux platforms. You can obtain a copy of JRE from *http://java.sun.com/javase/downloads/index.jsp*.

Wi-Fi for Unix

The number of wireless options for people who use various flavors of Unix is limited, but they do exist.

Configuration Tools

Each BSD Unix version also includes configuration programs that control the settings and options of the adapters that use the an and wi drivers. Some of the commands have slightly different names, but the functions are essentially the same. Table 7-1 lists the configuration commands for different versions of BSD Unix.

Table 7-1: Unix Configuration Programs

Unix Type	wi Configuration	an Configuration
FreeBSD	wiconfig	Driver not used
NetBSD	wiconfig	ifconfig and ifmedia
OpenBSD	wicontrol	ancontrol
Solaris	Wiconfig	Driver not used

As Wi-Fi networks become more common, more versions of Unix will support wireless services. As always, the official and unofficial mailing lists, newsgroups, and websites dedicated to each version will have the news of new drivers and network support as soon as they become available and people start discussing them.

wiconfig and wicontrol

The configuration programs for the wi driver can set all the network and adapter options. The syntax for the wiconfig and wicontrol commands are identical in all three Unix versions that contain them.

The syntax for `wiconfig` and `wicontrol` in an 802.11 network is:

```
wicontrol OR wiconfig [interface] [-o] [-e 0|1] [-k key [-v 1|2|3|4]]
[-t tx rate] [-n network name] [-s station name] [-p port type]
[-m MAC address] [-d max datalength] [-r RTS threshold]
[-f frequency] [-A 0|1] [-M 0|1] [-P 0|1] [-T 1|2|3|4]
```

The `interface` argument identifies the logical interface name of the network adapter. The names are typically `wi0`, `wi1`, and so forth. Assuming you have just one wireless adapter in the computer, it will show up as `wi0`.

To view the network adapter's current settings, type the command (either `wiconfig` or `wicontrol`) and the interface name with no other flags. The WEP encryption key will only appear if you have root access to the system.

- The -o option displays the statistics counters for this interface.

- The -e option enables or disables WEP encryption. Type -e 0 to turn off encryption or -e 1 to turn it on. The default is encryption disabled.

- The -k key [-v 1/2/3/4] option sets the WEP encryption keys. If the command omits the -v setting, the command will set the first key.

- The -T 1/2/3/4 option identifies the WEP key that the adapter will use to encrypt outbound packets.

- The -t tx rate option sets the transmission rate. The tx rate values are:

1	1Mbps
2	2Mbps
3	Automatic rate select (default value)
4	4Mbps
5	6Mbps
11	11Mbps

- The -n network name option sets the name (SSID) of the network that this client will join. The default setting is an empty string, which will instruct the client to associate with the first access point it finds. The -p option must be set to BSS mode for this option to work.

- The -s station name option sets the name that will identify this client on the network.

- The -p port type option identifies the operating mode that this network client will use. Use -p 1 for infrastructure mode or -p 2 for ad hoc operation.

- The -m MAC address option changes the MAC address of the network adapter. There is rarely a good reason to change the factory-assigned MAC address.

- The -d max_data_length option changes the maximum frame size in bytes. The default is 2304.
- The -r RTS threshold option sets the RTS/CTS threshold in bytes. The default is 2347.
- The -f frequency option sets the adapter's operating channel number. In infrastructure mode, most network adapters automatically scan through all available channels to search for an access point, so this option should be omitted unless you want to select a specific channel in an environment where more than one signal is present.
- The -M option enables or disables the option that reduces interference from microwave ovens. Use 0 to disable this option or 1 to enable it.
- The -P 0/1 option enables or disables power management.

This all looks a lot more complicated than it really is. In practice, if the kernel recognizes the card, and if the adapter settings match the settings for the access point and other adapters in the same network, you should be able to connect without any trouble. If the kernel doesn't find the card, rebuild the kernel.

When you set up a new connection, it's easier to enter each option as a separate command than to try to run a whole string at one time. Here are the commands that you will use most often:

wiconfig -p 1 Set the network client to operate in infrastructure mode with one or more access points

wiconfig -s Sally's Laptop Identify the network node as "Sally's Laptop"

wiconfig -e 1 Turn on WEP encryption

wiconfig -k [WEP key] Set the WEP encryption key

Along with the wireless settings, it's also necessary to set the standard network configuration options that apply to any TCP/IP connection. The ifconfig command handles these settings in most Unix versions.

After you have configured your wireless network adapter and your network connection, they will operate just like any other network connection. You can run network utilities like ping, web browsers, email clients, and other applications, and you can connect to network resources just as you would over a wired connection.

8

WI-FI FOR MAC

Apple's AirPort family of wireless networking products is the logical choice for Macintosh users who want to create a wireless network to connect their computers and for those who want to connect their Macs to an existing wireless network. Because Apple controls both ends of the network link—the access point and the network client—an AirPort network is a lot easier to set up than a generic Wi-Fi network. The AirPort Extreme (Apple's name for its access point) automatically loads its Internet configuration settings from an existing Macintosh connection and transfers those settings to all the other computers on the same network.

Apple is a member of the Wireless Ethernet Compatibility Alliance (WECA), and both the AirPort Extreme and the AirPort Extreme Card carry Wi-Fi certification. Therefore, a Macintosh with an AirPort card can join any Wi-Fi network almost as easily as it can join an AirPort network. A mixed-platform wireless network that includes Macs, Windows-based PCs, and Unix or Linux machines can use one or more AirPort Extremes as access points.

Apple uses different names for some of the features and functions in its wireless networks, but the general rules for designing, configuring, and using an AirPort network are the same as the rules for setting up generic wireless networks. The only difference between an AirPort network and any other Wi-Fi network is some of the terminology and the software that moves configuration data from a network client to the base station.

This chapter explains how to set up and use a wireless AirPort network on Macintosh computers, how to add a Macintosh with an AirPort Extreme Card to an existing Wi-Fi network that does not use an AirPort Extreme access point, and how to add a computer running Windows to an AirPort network.

AirPort Components

The AirPort product family includes three components: wireless network adapters called the AirPort and the AirPort Extreme Card, and an access point called the AirPort Extreme.

The *AirPort Extreme Card* is an internal Wi-Fi adapter that fits inside many Macintosh models. New MacBook and MacBook Pro laptop computers and many desktop Macs include a built-in AirPort Extreme Card as standard equipment; if your computer does not include one, you can either install it inside your computer or use a third-party USB Wi-Fi adapter with the OrangeWare driver described in "Using Non-Apple Adapters with a Mac" on page 138.

The AirPort Extreme is a stand-alone access point that manages the wireless network. The latest version includes an Ethernet WAN port, three 10/100Base-T Ethernet ports, and a USB port along with the wireless access point. Figure 8-1 shows an AirPort Extreme Base Station.

Photos courtesy of Apple

Figure 8-1: Apple's AirPort Extreme access point has been optimized for use with Macintosh computers.

As shown in Table 8-1, AirPort Extreme has a status light on the case that displays its current operating status.

Table 8-1: AirPort Extreme Status Lights

Color	Status
Dark	AirPort Extreme is not connected to a power outlet
Flashing green	AirPort Extreme is starting (one second)
Steady green	AirPort Extreme is operating
Flashing amber	AirPort Extreme can't connect to a wired network
Steady amber	Startup sequence in process
Alternating amber and green	Startup problem—AirPort Extreme will restart

Along with the AirPort hardware, Apple provides several software tools:

- The AirPort Setup Assistant is an automated configuration tool that automates the process of setting up most network installations.
- The AirPort Utility provides direct access to configuration options for setting and changing more complex network options. A separate version of AirPort Utility is available for Windows.
- The AirPort Status Menu is a simple tool for monitoring and controlling network activity from the menu bar in the main Macintosh screen.

Setting Up an AirPort Network

Most AirPort users can use the AirPort Setup Assistant to create and configure their networks without the need to worry about complex configuration options. But when local conditions require direct control of advanced settings, and when the network manager wants to monitor the network's operation, the AirPort Utility offers more complete control of all network settings.

Using the Setup Assistant to create a network is fast and easy: Just configure a client, click a few buttons, and let the software make all the decisions for you. The Setup Assistant automatically loads all the settings and fires up the network for you.

Installing the Hardware

Many recent Macintosh models come with built-in AirPort adapters and AirPort software bundled with the operating system. If you are using an older Macintosh that does not already have an AirPort adapter, you must install the AirPort Extreme Base Station before you try to run the AirPort Setup Assistant.

To install an AirPort Extreme, follow these steps:

1. Place the AirPort Extreme Base Station in the location where you plan to operate it. Like any other wireless network access point, a single AirPort Extreme should be close to the center of the area you want to reach with your network. If you are installing more than one unit in order to cover a large area, spread them evenly through the entire space.

2. Run a cable between the Base Station's Internet WAN port and an existing wired Ethernet hub or a broadband Internet gateway router, such as a DSL modem or a cable modem. If you do not have access to a wired LAN or a broadband Internet service, or if you want to use a telephone line as backup to your broadband connection, run a USB cable from the Base Station's USB port to a modem for the telephone line.

3. If you want to connect one or more nearby computers or other network devices to the network through cables, run CAT5 or CAT5E cables from those devices to the Ethernet ports on the Base Station.

4. Plug the power cable into the Base Station's power outlet and an AC outlet.

The Base Station's antennas are built into the enclosure, so it's not possible to move them without moving the entire unit. After running the AirPort Setup Assistant, if you discover that the signal level is not adequate for reliable data exchange with all of your computers and other network clients, it might be necessary to move the Base Station to a different location for better signal coverage. H-Squared (*http://www.h-sq.com*) makes an optional Air Mount bracket that can hold the AirPort Extreme on a wall, ceiling, or other vertical or horizontal surface, but you'll still have to allow for access to the power and Ethernet cables.

Running the AirPort Setup Assistant

Follow these steps to use the AirPort Setup Assistant with Mac OS X (version 10.4 or later) or to configure your computer's connection to a Base Station:

1. Confirm that the AirPort Extreme is connected to either a telephone line, a broadband connection, or both, and that power is connected to the access point. The indicator light on the AirPort Extreme should light.

2. Open the Utilities folder in the Applications folder. A list of nearby Wi-Fi networks like the one in Figure 8-2 will appear.

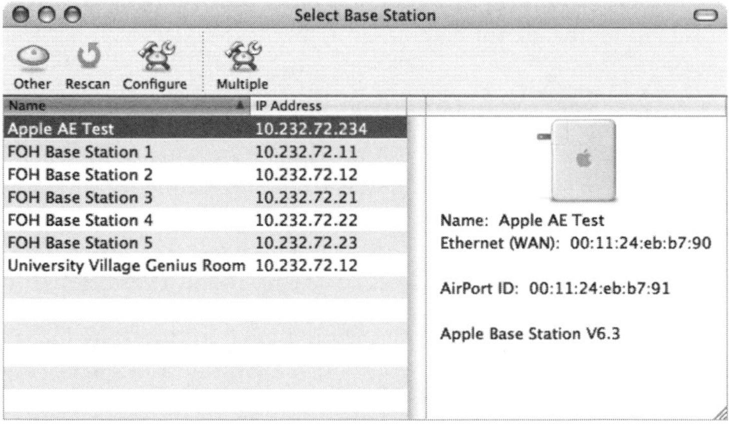

Figure 8-2: Use the AirPort Application to choose or configure a Base Station.

3. Choose your AirPort Extreme access point from the list, and click **Configure** at the top of the window.

4. Step through the onscreen instructions to configure the access point.

The AirPort Utility

The AirPort Utility (called the AirPort Admin Utility in OS X versions 10.4 and earlier) is Apple's tool for configuring a Base Station. Figure 8-3 shows the AirPort Utility window.

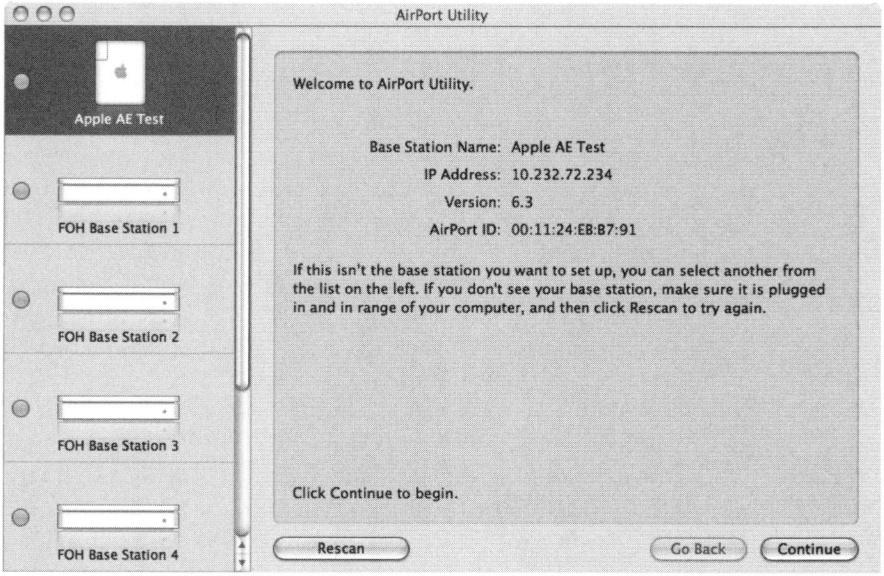

Figure 8-3: The AirPort Utility controls the local computer's wireless network connection.

To set up a Base Station, choose that network from the list of Base Stations and click **Continue**.

The AirPort Status Icon

The AirPort Status icon appears at the top of the Macintosh screen whenever the AirPort Extreme Application is active. Click this icon to open a menu with commands to switch between networks, monitor the signal strength of the active network, and turn the wireless adapter on or off.

Using an AirPort Network

When the AirPort network is up and running, a Macintosh treats the computers connected to the network through wireless links just like any other network resource. File transfers, Internet access, remote printers, and other services show up on directories the same way they would appear if they were connected through Ethernet cables.

For most users, the only indication that a wireless connection is active will be the flashing lights in the menu bar at the top of their screens that light and go dark as the quality of the wireless signal changes due to interference and network activity. Unless a networked computer is on the edge of the Base Station's coverage area or is receiving a lot of interference, the connections to the local network and the Internet should be just about as fast and clean as they would be through a wired network.

Connecting Macintosh Clients to Other Networks

Apple hopes that most Macintosh users will use their AirPort Cards to connect their computers through an AirPort Extreme to other Macs. But that's not the only possible way to use a wireless network with a Macintosh. Because the Setup Assistant automates the process, it's easier to connect Macs to an AirPort Extreme network than it is to build a mixed-platform wireless network that can use access points, network adapters, and configuration software from different sources. AirPort Extreme Cards do meet the Wi-Fi specification for interoperability, so they can also communicate with Wi-Fi access points made by many other manufacturers (and in ad hoc networks with other Wi-Fi adapters). Therefore, it is not a problem to use a Macintosh computer in a new or existing wireless network that also includes network clients that run Windows or other operating systems.

For example, PowerBook and MacBook owners who carry their computers to offices and public spaces served by Wi-Fi hot spots can connect to those networks just as easily as the owners of Windows-based laptop computers, and a wireless network in an office or household can provide service to both Macs and PCs without any changes to the network configuration.

Using Non-Apple Adapters with a Mac

Most Macintosh owners will probably want to use an AirPort Extreme Card rather than some other brand of network adapter because the AirPort software is so closely integrated with Mac OS networking functions, but it's also possible to install a different brand of USB-based wireless network adapter if you can find driver and control software for the Mac OS version used by your computer. In many cases, the Wi-Fi adapters from other makers cost considerably less than similar Apple products.

The Apple AirPort Extreme adapter uses a Broadcom bcm43xx chip set (for older models) or the Atheros chip set (for newer models on Intel-based Macs), so the driver and control software may work with other brands that contain the same chip set. You can use the search tool at *http://linux-wless .passys.nl* to find specific makes and models. The same tool will tell you the chip set in most other adapter makes and models.

For adapters that use the Atheros chip set (including many adapters made by 3Com, D-Link, NETGEAR, Fujitsu, IBM, Linksys, NEC, Samsung, and Sony; see the list at *http://www.orangeware.com/endusers/wirelessformac .html*), the OrangeWare Wireless Driver for Mac offers performance that

OrangeWare claims is faster and more flexible than the Apple software. The OrangeWare driver is available for a free 10-minute trial at *http://www.orangeware.com/endusers/wirelessformac.html*; if it works with your existing hardware, the added cost is less than the cost of a new AirPort Extreme Card.

For adapters using PRISM chip sets, look for a driver at *http://wirelessdriver.sourceforge.net.*

For adapters with Ralink chip sets, download drivers and support software from *http://www.ralinktech.com/ralink/Home/Support/Macintosh.html.*

If you're using an older PowerBook with a PCMCIA socket or a desktop Mac with one or more PCI expansion slots, and (like me) you have one or more old Wi-Fi adapters that only recognize 802.11b networks, the driver software from IOXperts (*http://www.ioxperts.com*) can add support for many (now obsolete) Wi-Fi adapters. You could probably find a very inexpensive compatible adapter through eBay or a surplus dealer, but don't waste your money; you're better off spending a little more on a new adapter that also works with one of the other drivers in this section using the newer and faster 802.11g and 802.11n standards.

Connecting an AirPort Card to a Non-AirPort Access Point

When a Macintosh with an AirPort Card is within range of a signal from a non-AirPort access point, the AirPort Card should detect the network signal and display the access point's SSID in the AirPort application's Choose Network menus and the AirPort Control Strip. When a user selects that network from the menu, the AirPort Card should associate itself with that access point just as it would associate with an AirPort Extreme. The Control Strip and the AirPort application will show the quality of the signal from the access point in their graphic displays the same way they show a connection to an Apple Base Station.

In most large business networks and public wireless services, the network manager has probably prepared a "how to connect to our network" document for employees and visitors who want to use their portable computers and other devices on the wireless LAN. This document might be a printed information sheet or brochure or an online web page. Either way, it will include some specific settings that users must change in their configuration utility programs. The configuration program for an AirPort adapter is the AirPort Utility, but Apple has chosen to use different names for some of the settings, including *Network Name* for the SSID and *AirPort ID* for the network adapter's MAC address. Fortunately, the AirPort utilities will detect the network name and ID automatically, so it's not necessary to manually change them.

If the wireless network uses a DHCP server in the access point or someplace else in the network to assign IP addresses to network clients, open the Internet tab of the AirPort Utility and set the Configure TCP/IP option to accept DHCP addresses.

If the network does not use DHCP, the network manager will provide a list of configuration settings assigned to this client. To configure an AirPort client to connect to the network, set the Configure TCP/IP option to Manually and enter these addresses in the Internet tab of the AirPort Utility. Copy the IP Address, Subnet Mask, DNS Servers, and Domain Name provided by the network manager directly to the fields in the Admin Utility. The setting that AirPort calls a *Router Address* is known to the rest of the world as the network gateway. Use the Gateway address supplied by the network manager in the AirPort Utility's Router Address Field.

Connecting Other Wi-Fi Clients to an AirPort Network

Just because a wireless LAN uses an AirPort Extreme as its access point does not mean that the network is limited to AirPort clients. Every client computer on an AirPort network does not have to be a Macintosh. There is absolutely no difference between an AirPort network and any other Wi-Fi network, so a computer that uses some other brand of network adapter and a different operating system will have no trouble detecting an AirPort network.

An AirPort Extreme appears to the network adapters in computers that use other operating systems as a standard Wi-Fi access point. The adapter will use the AirPort network to exchange data with other computers and as a gateway to the Internet. From the adapter's point of view, connecting to an AirPort Extreme is just like connecting to any other brand of access point.

Detecting the radio signal is one thing, but configuring a network client to use the network is a bit more difficult because Apple uses different names for some of the standard network configuration settings. If you don't know how to translate between AirPort and Wi-Fi terminology, you may have trouble getting the network to work properly. Do not panic. We're here to help. It's not as bad as it seems when you have the translation keys that are revealed in the next few pages.

Network Properties

In Windows, the Network Properties window contains the settings and options that a computer must use to connect to a TCP/IP network. On a Macintosh, the same information is in the AirPort Utility.

If the AirPort Utility is set to use DHCP to configure TCP/IP, the configuration utility on the client must also be set to accept DHCP (in Windows, select the Obtain An IP Address Automatically and the Obtain DNS Server options).

If the AirPort Utility is set to configure TCP/IP manually, the owner of a Windows client must enter these TCP/IP Properties settings:

IP Address   Use the IP address provided by the LAN manager or ISP.

Subnet Mask   Copy the address from the AirPort Utility's Internet tab. If you don't know the address, try 255.255.255.0.

DNS Servers   Copy the DNS server addresses from the Admin Utility's Internet tab.

Host   Copy the Network Name from the Admin Utility's AirPort tab.

Domain Copy the Domain name (if any) from the Admin Utility's Internet tab.

Gateway Copy the Router Address from the Admin Utility's Internet tab.

Configuring an AirPort Extreme from Windows

Apple's AirPort Extreme access point is more expensive than many other products that will do the same thing without the special Macintosh configuration program. So it's likely that most people and most businesses that use an AirPort Extreme will have one or more Macintoshes in their networks. Therefore, the Macintosh Admin Utility is generally the best choice for setting up an AirPort Extreme network.

However, Apple also offers free software that you can use to set up and run an AirPort Extreme network from a computer running Windows. The AirPort Express Assistant, shown in Figure 8-4, is part of the free AirPort for Windows package, available for download from *http://www.apple.com/support/downloads/airport42forwindows.html*.

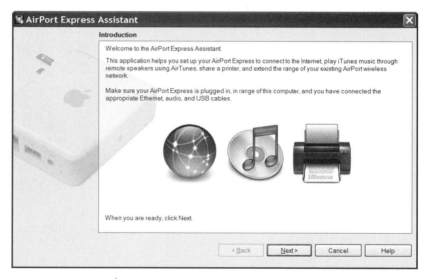

Figure 8-4: The AirPort Express Assistant for Windows provides a step-by-step process for setting up an AirPort Extreme network.

Is AirPort the Answer?

Because Apple could control both ends of its AirPort design—the access point and the network clients—it has come up with a system that automates the configuration hassles that confront many other Wi-Fi networks. And once you know the secret handshake (in the form of AirPort's oddball names for some standard features and functions), your Windows and Linux/Unix computers with other manufacturers' network adapters will also work perfectly well on an AirPort network.

An AirPort network is indeed the obvious choice for a wireless network in a business or household where most of the computers are Macintoshes. For the rest of us, the AirPort Extreme is a completely adequate access point, but it's considerably more expensive than many other brands, so some other type of access point can generally provide similar performance at lower cost.

Keep in mind that AirPort Extreme is not your only choice if your PowerBook or desktop Mac didn't come with a built-in Wi-Fi adapter. Other makers' PC Cards and USB Wi-Fi adapters, combined with third-party drivers and control software, will allow you to add your Macintosh to a Wi-Fi network just as well as the more expensive Apple products do.

9

INSTALLING AND CONFIGURING
WI-FI ACCESS POINTS

 Many Wi-Fi users never install or maintain an access point—they connect to public hot spots in coffee shops and libraries and maybe in the workplace, where there's a network manager to worry about providing a signal to their computers. But if you want to use Wi-Fi in your own small business or home network, you'll have to know something about access points.

An *access point*, or *base station*, in a wireless network is the central transmitter and receiver that exchanges data by radio with individual computers and other network clients. Multiple access points can increase the size of the area served by the network and support a larger number of network clients, but every Wi-Fi network must include at least one access point. The number and location of your network's access points defines its coverage and capacity.

When you decide to install a wireless network, you have at least two options: You can unpack all the boxes, hook up the radios to your computers, and try to make it all work, or you can do some advance planning and think about the best locations for each component before you start playing with hardware. This chapter is for those conscientious and methodical people who plan first and install things later. It's also for the rest of us who tried to fire up a network without any planning, and now we want to learn how to do the job properly.

The first thing to do when you start planning your wireless LAN—or for that matter, any LAN—is to spend some time thinking about exactly how you expect to use the network. Are all of the computers in your network in fixed locations with easy access to cable runs? Are you thinking about wireless because it's the best way to add computers and users to your network or just because it's the flavor of the month?

For example, I live in a one-story house with an unfinished basement. I could use wireless to extend my home network from the front room to the kitchen (and I did, when I was testing equipment for this book), but it's almost as easy to use a gateway router and the built-in Ethernet interface adapters in my computers and string cable through the basement rafters instead. On the other hand, if I wanted to use my laptop computer on the front porch or the back yard as well as the kitchen, or if I lived in a two-story house or an apartment where I couldn't get inside the ceilings or under the floors, then it could make sense to install an access point in the front room and a wireless network card in the laptop so I could carry it from place to place.

You can apply the same kind of analysis to a business network. As long as all the computers are stationary and you have an easy way to run cables (such as a false ceiling or cable conduits in the walls and floors), a wired network is usually the better choice. But if the salespeople all carry portables when they call on customers, or the engineers want to use their laptop machines in meetings or over lunch, or if there's some other good reason to extend the network beyond the reach of cables, it's probably time to add wireless access.

In most cases, the wireless network should be a supplement to the wired connections rather than a completely wireless operation. At least one computer should probably connect to the network through cables; a wired connection is often easier to use when you're changing the access point's wireless configuration settings.

Installing Access Points

As Chapter 3 explained, many access points are combined with other devices, such as network routers, broadband Internet routers, and traditional Ethernet hubs. At a bare minimum, every access point must include a radio transmitter and receiver, one or two captive antennas or connectors for external antennas, and (usually) an Ethernet port for connecting the access point to a wired network. The access point should also contain some kind of internal configuration software that displays the current settings and accepts commands to make changes.

Because each make and model of access point comes in a different package with different inputs, outputs, and controls, you will want to follow the specific installation and configuration instructions supplied with your device. Unfortunately, the manufacturers' manuals don't always give you all the information you need. This section offers a general procedure for installing a generic access point, with occasional side comments about features and functions that don't exist in every product. It is intended to supplement the installation procedure provided in your own access point's manual.

Here are the general steps for installing an access point:

1. If necessary, assemble the access point. The user's manual for your access point should contain specific instructions for the make and model you are using.

2. Based on the information in your site survey, place the access point in the location where you plan to operate it.

3. If the access point has a captive antenna on a swivel or other mechanism that allows you to move it around, adjust the antenna to a position as close to vertical as possible. If you are placing the antenna at or near the ceiling, place the antenna so that it points straight down, if possible. If the antenna is closer to the floor, point it straight up. If you can't adjust the antenna's position, don't worry about it; the access point should work almost as well in its fixed position.

4. If the access point has a connector for an external antenna, install the antenna and run a cable from the antenna to the access point. Keep this cable as short as possible without stretching it or turning any sharp corners.

5. Connect power to the access point. Most access points are supplied with "wall wart" DC power adapters, but some have AC power cords. Either way, connect the power cable to the access point first, then plug the cable or power supply into an AC outlet. Take a moment to label the power adapter or plug to indicate that it connects to the access point—many times there is no branding to identify which device it goes to.

6. An access point does not draw a lot of power, so it's not necessary to use a dedicated AC power source, but if you use an uninterruptible power supply or a surge protector to protect your computers, you should also protect your access point.

7. If you are using a Power over Ethernet (PoE) system to provide power to the access point, follow the PoE instructions supplied with your access point to make the connection. Most PoE systems use the 802.3af power standard; however, there are other power standards as well. Make sure that the access point matches your power equipment.

8. Connect an Ethernet cable between the LAN connector on your access point and the nearest network router, hub, switch, or other network point of presence.

9. Consult the manual to find out how to connect a control cable to the access point. Some access points use a serial cable from a nearby computer, and others connect through the network. You will use this connection to set the access point's configuration.

10. If the access point uses a serial connection, it might be easier to take a laptop computer to a temporary location near the access point, where you can see the LED indicators light and go dark as you run the configuration routine, rather than running a longer cable to an existing computer.

11. Turn on the access point's power switch. You will probably see an LED indicator light. It could take a few minutes before the access point's internal processor is ready to operate. The access point's manual should explain the functions of the LED indicators.

After the physical installation is complete, the next step is to configure the access point. If you are using the same brand of access point and wireless interface adapters, the default settings are probably the same, so you might be able to install an adapter into a nearby computer and test the network right away.

Configuring the Access Point Through a Browser

Most access points accept configuration commands through a dedicated local numeric IP address. In other words, you can gain access to the configuration program by typing the access point's numeric address into your web browser. You can find the access point's default IP address in the manual supplied with the hardware or from the manufacturer's technical support web pages.

You can typically use Microsoft Internet Explorer, Firefox, Safari, or any other graphical web browser to view and change access point settings. Because of this, the configuration program will run through a computer running any operating system. Rarely, an access point might require a specific configuration tool or a specific browser.

The first time you turn on the access point, it will use the default settings that were set at the factory. Unless you change some of these settings, it might be possible for unauthorized users to gain access to your network and for network users (authorized or not) to make changes that should be made only by the network manager. At an absolute minimum, you should change the configuration program's password.

Once again, the specific configuration procedure is different for each type of access point, but the general principles are similar. Use this procedure as a supplement to the information in the access point manual:

1. Confirm that the access point is connected to the LAN.

2. From a computer connected to the LAN, open the web browser of your choice.

3. In the browser's Address field, type the default numeric IP address for the access point, as specified in the access point manual, and then press the ENTER key.

4. If the software requires a password, the browser should find and open the access point's password window. Type the login name and password.

5. You should see the top-level configuration page. Figure 9-1 shows a typical configuration page, this one for the Actiontec combined Wi-Fi access point and DSL modem supplied by Qwest to its DSL subscribers.

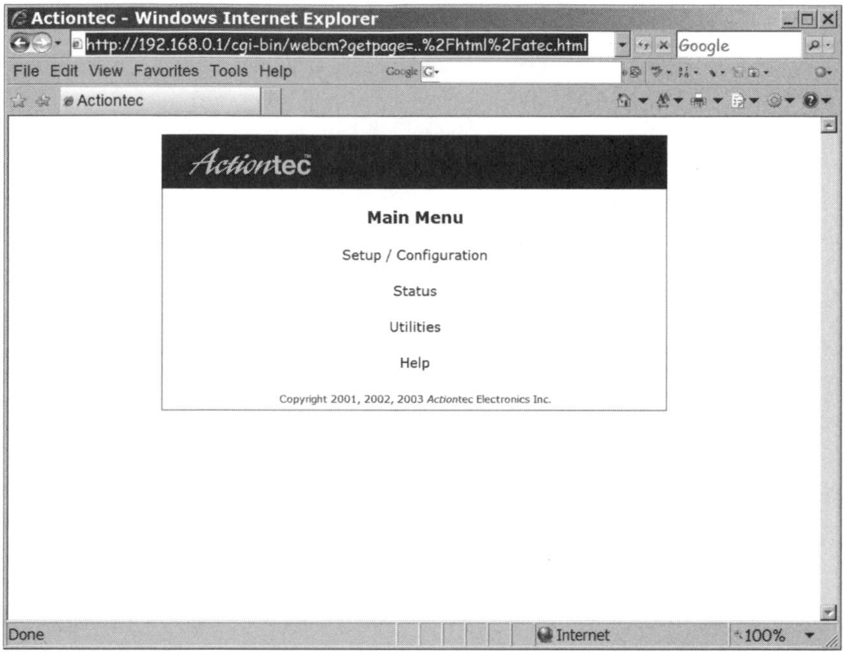

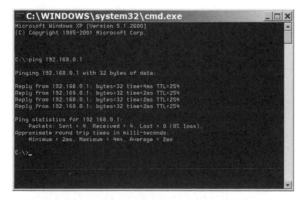

Figure 9-1: The configuration menu screen for an Actiontec access point. Configuration screens for other access points display similar information, but they arrange it differently.

If you get an "unable to connect" message instead of a login window or a top-level menu when you try to open the configuration utility, send a ping request to the access point. In Windows, enter **Start ▶ Run ▶ cmd** to open a command window, and type `ping IP address`, using the access point's numeric IP address. If the network recognizes the address, you should see a response like the one in Figure 9-2. If the program reports "host unreachable," a conflict probably exists between the Dynamic Host Configuration Protocol (DHCP) server on your LAN and the default address for the access point. The next section explains how to deal with this problem.

Figure 9-2: A successful ping request returns a series of timed echoes from the target device.

DHCP and Other Distractions

DHCP automatically assigns an IP address to each computer on a network. Because DHCP eliminates the need to manually assign a separate address to each computer, it can save a lot of time and trouble, but when the network hub or switch and the wireless access point both try to act as DHCP servers, or when a client device expects a specific address but the DHCP server assigns an address on the fly, trying to set up the network can become ugly.

Conflicting DHCP servers can cause problems when you add an access point to a LAN. Some standalone access points expect to receive requests for access to the web-based configuration screens at a specific numeric IP address. When that access point is connected to a hub that is acting as a DHCP server, however, the server assigns a different IP address to the access point. So when a user tries to connect to the IP address listed in the access point manual, nothing happens (or the browser reports "unable to find this address," which is about the same thing).

It's important to remember that a LAN can have only one DHCP server. If the LAN includes another DHCP server (usually in a router) that assigns numeric addresses, it's best to disable the DHCP function in the access point and allow the main server to handle address assignments for the entire network, including both wired and wireless nodes. As a general rule, the active DHCP server should be in the device closest to your Internet connection—usually the DSL modem or cable modem or other Internet access device.

This is one case where a generic description of the problem is less useful than the specific procedure provided with your particular access point. The hardware manual should contain setup instructions that cover both the access point's configuration utility and the Windows networking settings that apply to each client machine. Find the manual, and try to follow those instructions as closely as possible. When you do come up with a combination of access point configuration settings and Windows networking settings that actually works (and it's a safe bet that such a combination does exist), note those settings on paper and store them with the manual. You will need them later to add more computers and access points to the same network.

DNS Addresses

The Internet uses Domain Name System (DNS) to convert between numeric IP addresses and plain-language addresses. If your computer can't find an active DNS server, your web browser, email program, and other tools won't work because they won't know where to find other computers on the Internet. When DHCP is active, most access points provide DNS service to the computers that receive IP addresses from the DHCP server. Therefore, you must specify one or more DNS server addresses when you configure an access point. You can obtain DNS addresses from your network manager or ISP or from a list of public name servers such as the ones at *http://www.opennic.unrated .net/public_servers.html* (use the Tier 2 servers) or *http://www.resolvingnameserver .com/freerns.html.*

Configuration Commands and Settings

Each manufacturer's configuration utility handles them differently, but every access point should include the same basic set of options. As you set up your wireless network, you might want to change some of these options from the default values.

Many web-based configuration utilities use tabs or menus to split the list of options into several screens. If the location of a particular command is not obvious from the layout of the top-level screen, either try opening lower-level screens until you find the one you want or look in the access point manual for specific navigation instructions. In general, the configuration utility should include the following options.

Passwords

The setup program will also ask you for a password or passphrase. This is the code that your users will enter to connect to an encrypted access point.

Every access point's configuration software requires a password before it will allow you to make changes. When you unpack and install an access point, it uses the manufacturer's generic password. Because these passwords are well known to hackers and crackers who could change the password and lock you out of your own network, you *must* reset the password as soon as you install the network.

NOTE   *If you forget or lose an access point's password, you can return it to the default password by using the physical Reset control on the access point. Consult your access point's manual for specific information (if you don't have the manual, look for a downloadable copy on the manufacturer's website). If you reset the access point, you will have to reconfigure all of its settings and options.*

LAN IP Address

The LAN IP address field displays the numeric IP address currently used by the access point within the local network. This could be a default address assigned at the factory, an address automatically assigned by the LAN's DHCP server, or an address assigned manually by the network manager. If your wireless network has two or more access points, each one should have a different IP address.

Subnet Mask

The Subnet Mask field identifies the subnetwork that includes the access point and the wireless clients that connect to the LAN through the access point. The address of the subnetwork is assigned by the network manager. If your LAN does not include a subnetwork, use the default value of 255.255.255.0.

Wireless Network ID (SSID)

The *Service Set Identification (SSID)* is the name of the wireless network that includes this access point. When a wireless client attempts to connect to a network, it searches for an access point with the same SSID as the one in its own configuration settings. If it finds a signal with a different SSID, it rejects the association and continues to scan for the correct SSID.

Therefore, the SSID serves two purposes: It acts as the first line of defense against unauthorized access to a wireless network, and in an environment where more than one wireless LAN is operating, it associates each client with the correct network. However, the SSID by itself is not a particularly effective security tool because some network adapters will accept an SSID of *ANY*, which will allow the client to associate with the first access point it finds, regardless of the access point's SSID. Also, every time a user connects to the access point, it transmits the SSID, even if the access point is configured to hide or cloak the SSID.

A network adapter will assume that all the access points with the same SSID are part of the same network. This can work in your favor when you set up a network with more than one access point (use the same SSID for all of them), but it also means that it's essential to change the default SSID supplied with your access point to a unique name to make sure your users don't connect to the wrong access point by mistake.

Channel

The Channel setting is the radio channel number that the access point will use to exchange data with the client devices in the wireless LAN. Each access point operates on a single channel, but most network adapters scan across all the channels to find the best available signal with the same SSID. You can assume that nearby client devices will find your access point, regardless of the channel setting, as long as both devices use the same operating mode. If one of your users tries to use a network adapter with a preset channel, however, the channel settings for the access point and the client must match.

In a noisy environment, some channels might perform better than others because other networks and other 2.4 GHz devices could generate interference on some frequencies but not on others. If other wireless networks are operating nearby, you can often reduce interference and improve performance by using channel numbers that don't overlap. If that's not possible, use channels as far apart from one another as possible.

If your network includes more than one access point, you should set adjacent access points to different channels. To avoid overlap between signals, remember to use channels that are at least five channel numbers apart, such as channels 1, 6, and 11.

Mode

Most new access points support several different Wi-Fi specifications (or modes), including 802.11b, 802.11g, and usually 802.11a. Access points made after the 802.11n standard is approved will also include that mode along with the others. When the access point detects a signal from a network adapter, it automatically uses the operating mode it's receiving from the adapter. This multiple-mode operation allows computers with network adapters that only recognize one mode to connect without the need to change adapters.

The configuration program for your access point probably includes an option that specifies the operating modes that the access point can use. Unless you want to limit access to your network to a limited set of network adapters, it's best to use the most flexible mode setting, one that recognizes all available operating modes.

Security

Wi-Fi networks can use either of two different encryption schemes to keep people who do not have the proper electronic key code out of the network: WEP (wired equivalent privacy) and WPA (Wi-Fi protected access). As Chapter 12 of this book explains, WEP encryption is not particularly effective against a determined eavesdropper, but it's better than nothing. The more recent WPA method is more secure, but if some of your users have older Wi-Fi adapters that only accept WEP encryption, you might have to use the older system (or insist that your users replace their old Wi-Fi adapters with new ones that can use WPA).

It's generally easier to set up a wireless network with encryption disabled, but it's a very good idea to turn it on when you start moving real data through the network. The encryption keys must be identical in each of your access points' configuration utilities and in all the client devices that you expect to use with that network.

WEP Encryption

Every access point can use a 64-bit WEP encryption key to restrict unauthorized access, and some offer the choice of either a 64-bit key or a more secure 128-bit key. Because the 64-bit key is actually a 40-bit key combined with a 24-bit initialization vector string, some configuration programs call it 40-bit encryption. Similarly, 128-bit encryption is a 104-bit key combined with a 24-bit initialization string, and it is sometimes called 104-bit encryption. Some access points might support proprietary WEP methods that use larger keys; they require all users of the network to have cards that support them. Access points and network adapters that use 40-bit WEP encryption are completely compatible with those that use 64-bit WEP encryption.

Unfortunately, some manufacturers request a string of letters and numbers as a WEP key, and others expect you to provide a series of hexadecimal numbers, either as five groups of two or as a single 10-digit string. Still others will ask you for a passphrase and automatically generate the hex key for you.

WPA Encryption

Most new access points also support WPA encryption; if yours does not, check the manufacturer's website for a firmware update. When you select WPA encryption for your access point, the setup program will offer a choice of either PSK (Pre-Shared Key) or RADIUS (Remote Authentication Dial-In User Service) mode. Unless your network already has a RADIUS server, choose the PSK option.

Within PSK mode, you can select from two encryption methods: TKIP (Temporal Key Integrity Protocol) or AES (Advanced Encryption System). TKIP is the stronger of the two, so it's usually the better choice. Because the network name (SSID) is used to generate the keys in PSK mode, it's important to change your network SSID from the default because a combination of using dictionary words for the PSK passphrase and a common network SSID can provide determined attackers with an easy route into your network.

DHCP

As mentioned in "DHCP and Other Distractions" on page 148, an access point can act as a DHCP server that automatically assigns numeric IP addresses to the wireless clients in the network.

Remember that only one DHCP server can be active at any time. So if the network already has an active DHCP, disable the access point's DHCP function. If your network includes more than one access point, the DHCP server should be active in only one of them—and then only if no other server is already active.

When the access point's DHCP server is active, the configuration utility might display a list of currently active DHCP clients on the same screen that contains the enable/disable options. Or the utility might offer to open another window or display another screen that contains the list of DHCP clients.

Other Settings

In addition to the settings listed above, you might discover several other options in your access point's configuration utility. Some could control other nonwireless functions built into the same device, and others might be settings that allow a user to specify some arbitrary values that would otherwise be changed in the client device.

The access point manual should give you the information you will need to set these options. When the purpose of a setting is not clear, or if it looks like it won't have any effect on your network, the safest approach is to accept the default value. In other words, when in doubt, leave it alone!

How Many Access Points?

Except for an ad hoc network, the simplest wireless networks operate with just one access point and a handful of network nodes. But when you're trying to cover a large space, an irregular space with obstructions, or if you expect to have many wireless users, you will probably have to add at least one additional access point on a different channel.

If the anticipated coverage area of your indoor network extends more than about 150 feet from the access point, consider a network with more than one access point. Outdoors you should be able to get a reliable signal from an access point at least 200 feet away if a clean line of sight is available.

As a practical limit, if more than about half a dozen computers are trying to connect to the same access point at the same time, the data transfer speed from each wireless node will start to drop. But remember that most of your users won't be trying to move data or use the Internet at exactly the same moment, unless they're streaming audio or video or moving large files around, so that "half a dozen" might translate to 20 or 30 users over the course of a day.

If the number of users on your network increases over time, you might discover that performance is becoming sluggish because your access points are operating at or near full capacity. When that happens, it's time to consider adding more access points to your network. You can either place the new access points midway between the existing ones or use different channel numbers and place them right next to the existing access points. If you can, choose channel numbers that are not being used by other nearby networks.

Assuming your network operates in infrastructure mode, it resembles a hub and spokes design in which each computer or other device is communicating with the network through an access point. Therefore, it's not necessary for all the devices on your wireless network to use the same channel number. If you can distribute your network computers among two or three noninterfering channels, it will reduce the number of links on each channel, which will improve performance across the entire network.

There are several ways to connect multiple access points to the network. If it's practical to string Ethernet data cables to each access point's location, either connect all the access points to a router or use a combined router and access point for the first location and run data cables from there to the other locations.

On the other hand, if there are walls or other obstructions between access point locations, or if it's difficult or impossible to run cables for some other reason, you can use a special type of access point called a *range expander* or *range extender* that uses radio signals to connect to the network's primary access point.

NOTE *When you set up an outdoor network, don't forget to consider the effect of foliage between the access point and the client computers—if you install the network during the winter when trees are bare, you might have poor reception during the summer when the same trees are in full leaf. Placing multiple access points is not an exact science. If your network covers a large open space, you can place them at regular intervals. But finding the best way to cover an irregular space might be more difficult.*

Perhaps the best method is to start with a single access point at the center of the building and confirm that it provides decent coverage within 50 or 100 feet or up to the first major obstacle. You can confirm this by walking around with a computer running your Wi-Fi control program or a site survey program. When the signal starts to fade, move back to a place where the signal is good and measure the distance from the access point. Try to place the second access point about the same distance away from your current location, but in the opposite direction. If the second access point doesn't give you the necessary coverage for the rest of your space, you might have to add still more access points. Your goal should be a maximum of about 30 percent overlap in coverage between any pair of access points.

As a rule of thumb, your users should have no trouble using a signal that shows four or five bars in the control program. Three bars is probably okay for most users, but when the signal strength drops down to one or two bars, you should plan to add another access point.

Locating three or more access points can be more difficult. Remember, your goal in adding more access points is to fill in as much space as possible. With two access points in an open space, you would probably place both of them halfway between the side walls, each about a third of the way from the front and back. If you add another unit, you might want to put the third in the middle and move the other two closer to the front and back, or you can arrange them in some kind of triangular pattern. Figure 9-3 shows typical layouts with two access points and three access points.

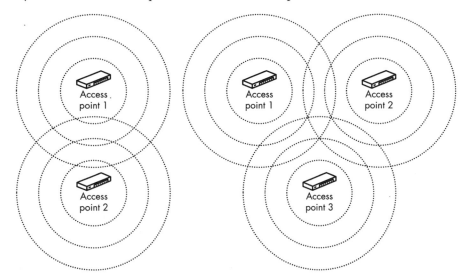

Figure 9-3: For added coverage, use two or more access points.

Each access point in a network should operate on a different channel from the ones used by adjacent access points. If possible, use channel numbers that don't interfere with one another, such as channels 1, 6, and 11. In a very large space, try to keep channel numbers widely separated by staggering the channel numbers over the entire area, like the arrangement in Figure 9-4.

Using Multiple Access Points

When two or more access points on the same network detect a signal from the same client device, the access point with the best signal handles the link. If the client device moves away from the currently active access point and closer to another one, or if the signal quality deteriorates because of interference from other radio signals, the original access point will hand off the link to the access point that is receiving the best signal from the client. This is the same kind of technology that permits cellular telephones to roam without interrupting a conversation.

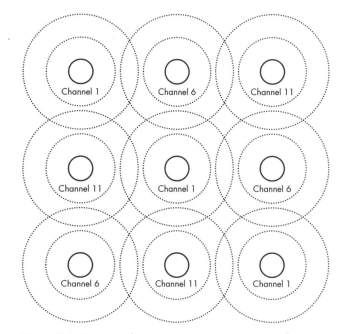

Figure 9-4: Keep overlapping access points separate from one another in a network with multiple base stations.

The early Wi-Fi specifications allowed network adapters and other client devices to move a connection to the network from one access point to another, but they did not explain how to hand off an association. In the absence of a standard, each access point manufacturer came up with its own method, which might not have been compatible with every other manufacturer's system. This is less of a problem with 802.11g and 802.11n networks, but it's still best to use just one type of access point in your network. You can expect a Wi-Fi–compliant network adapter to work with any brand of access point, but it's not always safe to expect two different kinds of access points to work together.

WHICH OPERATING MODE?

The best access points for a new Wi-Fi network can use all available operating modes (802.11b, 802.11a, and 802.11g today, and 802.11n after that specification becomes standard), so they can exchange data with users whose computers have any kind of network adapter. The drawback, however, is that when a user with an older card joins a network that supports a newer, faster standard (such as an 802.11b user joining an 802.11g network), the network must switch all users to the slower standard for compatibility. If you expect all of your users to have newer cards, setting the mode to accept only the faster standards might offer better performance.

Performing a Site Survey

Understanding general networking principles is fine, but you're installing a wireless network in a real location with real walls and real furniture (and most likely, real sources of real interference). Radio waves pass through some materials and bounce off others, so the general estimates of a radio's range and signal strength in an ideal environment are less important than the *actual* performance in the place you want to use it. You should therefore conduct a site survey that tells you how your own radios will operate in your own space.

The first step in a site survey is to identify the area that you want your network to cover. In most cases, that will be the entire area of your office, home, or campus, but there are other possibilities. For example, you might want to provide network access only in common areas, such as a conference room, a reception area, or a library. Or you might want to share a single broad-band network connection among a group of neighbors. Keep in mind that radio signals at Wi-Fi frequencies can pass through many walls, ceilings, and floors, so they will probably reach adjacent spaces even if you don't aim them at those spaces.

For a straightforward home or small office network, your site survey can be very simple. If the whole building is just 50 feet from front to back and 30 feet wide, you can probably place the access point almost anywhere. Just connect the access point to your existing Internet connection, fire up a laptop or other portable computer as a wireless network client, and carry the client device around while a network connection is active. If you can keep the connection alive everywhere in the house or office, you're ready to go.

The spaces covered by a single network don't have to be continuous (or contiguous), although that's the way most networks are constructed. For example, if your business occupies the third, fourth, and ninth floors of a building but none of the floors in between, you can place access points in your own offices, connect them together with Ethernet cables (or connect them to your existing wired LAN), and ignore the other floors. As long as all the access points use the same name (the SSID), your computer will use the same network profile to make the connection. If your LAN extends to more than one building, you can place access points in each building and link them together (if no link is already in place) with a leased line, a virtual private network (VPN) connection through the Internet, or a point-to-point radio link and a bridge router (described in the next chapter).

Make a Site Plan . . .

When you have a rough idea of the space you want your network to cover, it's time to create a more detailed floor plan. If your network will cover more than one floor of a building, or when the network will include space in more than one building, you will want a plan for each floor, a vertical diagram of each building, and another diagram that shows the network's entire coverage area.

Your floor plan should include the location of each wall and partition along with every existing network connection and AC power outlet. If you know about potential sources of interference, such as a 2.4 GHz cordless phone, a Bluetooth network, or a microwave oven, mark their locations on the plan as well. Figure 9-5 shows a floor plan of a small office.

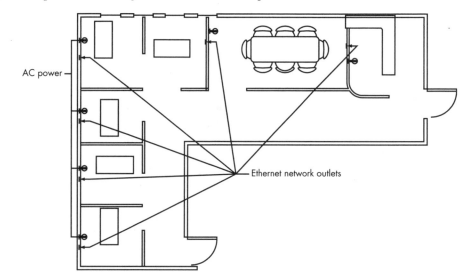

Figure 9-5: An office floor plan

In general, you can get away with a single access point if you can find a spot with a clean line of sight to every location where somebody might want to place a computer or other network client. When that's not possible because of obstructions to the radio signals, you will need additional access points. But don't automatically assume that a clear radio path is the same as a line of sight. The only way to be sure is to fire up an access point and run your own test.

In this case, the best location for a line of sight to everywhere in the office would probably be at the angle of the L-shaped space. If that's not good enough, the next approach to try would be placing one access point at each end. The office in Figure 9-5 contains plenty of network drops and AC outlets, so connecting to the wired network should not be a problem. That's not always the case. In many places, the logical place for an access point might be inside a false ceiling, but if you can't locate an AC outlet up there, you might have to find a different spot or use an access point that supports a power over Ethernet option.

It's less of a problem when the preferred access point location is close to an AC outlet but farther away from a network connection point. You can often solve the problem with a longer data cable, but don't drop a cable from a false ceiling into the middle of a room or over a partition that doesn't reach the ceiling; it looks messy, and somebody will almost certainly yank it out eventually. Your installation will look a lot better if you extend the data cable to a real wall and either drop the cable inside the wall or run it flush to a corner of two walls. Remember to avoid sharply bending or crimping the network cable; be sure to allow for a broad curve. When you want to use a single access point to serve two adjacent floors of a building, the best location would be as close to the shared ceiling and floor as possible. The location is less critical in most houses because the radio signal will pass through wood and plaster more easily than concrete and steel.

The antennas built into most access points and network interfaces are nondirectional or omnidirectional, which means that they radiate equally in all directions. In other words, the useful signal range resembles a sphere or a doughnut with the antenna at the center. Therefore, you will want to place your access point more or less in the middle of the space you want to cover. If you're using an access point with a connector for an external antenna, you can be more flexible. In some environments, a directional antenna at one end of the building might be more effective than an omni in the center.

The built-in antennas on many access points are whips mounted on swivels that allow you to change their positions relative to the box that contains the circuitry. It might not make a lot of difference, but the usual practice is to aim the antennas down when the access point is placed near the ceiling and aim them up when they are close to the floor. In general, you might get slightly better coverage when the antenna is vertical rather than horizontal.

One potential cause of signal loss is *multipath interference.* Multipath loss occurs when the same signal reaches a receiving antenna directly from the transmitter and again a fraction of a second later after bouncing off a reflective surface. On a broadcast television signal, multipath appears on the screen as a ghost or shadow image. In a packet data network, the receiver treats multipath interference as noise, which can slow down the transmission speed. Many access points and network adapters use two separate antennas in a "diversity" receiving arrangement to reduce or eliminate the impact of multipath interference. The receiver compares the strength of the signal from each antenna and automatically selects the better one. Even though the two antennas might be located just an inch or two apart, a diversity system can often provide a cleaner output than a single antenna. If the access point's built-in antenna is inside a package with an odd form, such as a *U*-shaped bar, or if it has two separate antennas, the device is probably using a diversity receiving system. The best way to find out if your hardware uses diversity is to read the specifications.

If your access point does have two captive antennas, you might want to experiment with different relative antenna positions. If your coverage is not adequate when the antennas are aligned north and south, try gradually rotating the access point to align the antennas to the east and west as you watch the signal strength display on a network client computer. If the antennas are on swivels, try moving them around rather than keeping them absolutely parallel.

Outdoors, the rule of thumb is that higher is better, within reasonable limits (for example, don't put your antenna on top of a 100-foot tower). If you possibly can, use an access point with a connector for an external antenna so you can place the box under cover and run a coaxial cable to the antenna. A weatherproof vertical antenna on a roof or a flat-panel antenna mounted high on the side of a building should provide decent line-of-sight coverage up to 300 feet away. When you place an antenna on a roof, try to mount it high enough to make it visible from the ground to prevent attenuation from the building itself, as shown in Figure 9-6. If you can't see the access point's antenna, the signal quality might suffer, but enough of the signal should pass through the structure to provide an acceptable signal.

Figure 9-6: A rooftop antenna might not reach users who are close to the building.

When you mount an omnidirectional antenna outdoors, more gain does not always mean better coverage. As the gain of an omnidirectional antenna increases, the vertical range decreases; the sphere or doughnut shape of the antenna coverage becomes flatter. Mounting a high gain (greater than 8 dB) omnidirectional antenna high up might make it invisible to users above or below it, while a 5 dB or lower antenna might provide perfect coverage. Always make sure to install proper grounding and lightning protection on external installations; a lightning strike on or near your roof can easily travel through the antenna, access point and network cable, and damage your whole buiding's network.

The amount of signal attenuation caused by a structure will be different for different building materials. At 2.4 GHz, radio waves can pass through wood and glass more easily than through concrete or structural steel. As a practical matter, if you're not trying to cover a large college campus or industrial park with your wireless network, you might produce an entirely usable outdoor signal from your indoor access points, especially if they're located near the exterior wall. As you run your site survey, try carrying a portable device away from the building while a connection is active; you might be surprised to discover how far the signal carries.

Remember that we're talking about digital signals. When you achieve the minimum signal quality needed to provide a clean, high-speed data link, a stronger signal won't make any difference unless you have a problem with interference. In other words, a three-bar signal is often all you need to make a connection, and a stronger signal won't improve performance if you're already seeing a five-bar signal. Don't waste your time or money adding an outdoor access point if you can serve your outdoor picnic bench from an existing indoor access point. The signal might be stronger from an outdoor access point, but it won't transfer your data any faster.

Moving vehicles or other large metal objects (such as construction cranes) between the access point and a network client can get in the way of an other-wise clean signal and produce temporary dropouts. If you're trying to provide network coverage to a freight loading yard or some other space that has trucks or other large objects moving around in it, you will want to mount your antenna as high as possible or place a second access point on the other side of the area you want to reach with your network.

Testing, Testing . . .

After all the theoretical planning, you can't avoid real-world testing with actual hardware. A floor plan might give you a good idea of how your network *should* work, but the only way to find out how those radio waves actually move around the area you want to cover with your network is to set up a temporary install-ation and perform some real-world tests.

There are two schools of thought about site surveys: One group believes that they're the best and most efficient way to find the optimal locations for access points in your Wi-Fi network; the other says that adding access points is cheaper than hiring a consultant or buying expensive software, so you might as well just install more of them (access points, not consultants) until your network reaches the whole area you want to cover.

You have several options when you need to perform a site survey:

- Let somebody else do it for you—either a paid consultant or the vendor who expects to sell the network hardware to you

- Use site survey software

- Use the configuration program or the status program supplied with a network interface

The alternative to a formal site survey is old-fashioned trial and error: Install one or more access points and move them around until you achieve the best performance.

Allowing a consultant or sales tech to perform the survey for you has several advantages. First, you can let that person do the work, and you just have to read the report rather than having to run (or crawl) around the whole building with a test unit yourself. More importantly, the people who do this kind of site survey all the time have their own measurement devices that auto-matically store individual readings and produce detailed reports. Unfor-tunately, these measurement units are expensive, and they require some special training, so they're not practical for a one-time user.

If you can't find somebody else to do the job, you'll have to do it yourself. Several hardware vendors, including Cisco, offer site survey software tools for their interface adapters and access points. If you're installing a complex Wi-Fi network, take a look at the Site Survey software offered by Ekahau (*http://www .ekahau.com*) and Covera (*http://www.coverazone.com*). These programs work with many (but not all) network adapters, and they offer long lists of useful features. Free evaluation versions of both programs are available, so you can try them before you buy. Several other free programs also provide site survey information.

If your test hardware doesn't include one of those tools, you can pull enough information out of the standard status and configuration programs that come with every wireless interface to perform a site survey. It's a little easier with the survey tool, but the configuration programs will tell you what you need to know.

Most likely, the first access point location you test will give you completely adequate network coverage, especially in a small office, house, or apartment. But when you're setting up a more complex network, it can be very useful to convince your hardware supplier to let you test network interfaces and access points from more than one manufacturer. Because different manufacturers use different antenna designs and different configuration software, you might discover that one make of network adapters or access points works better than another in your network.

Here's what you should do to complete a site survey:

1. Choose a location for your access point. You might decide to change the location after the initial site survey is complete, but as a start, select a location with a line of sight to as much of your intended coverage area as possible.

2. If you already have a wired LAN in place, connect your sample access point to the LAN and plug in the power supply. If your site does not have an existing LAN, just connect the power unit. Turn on the access point.

3. Configure the access point: Assign an SSID and choose a channel number for each operating mode.

4. If your laptop computer doesn't have a built-in Wi-Fi adapter, plug one into the computer's PC Card socket. For these tests, turn off WEP or WPA encryption.

5. Using your floor plan as a guide, prepare a site survey form, like the one in Table 9-1. Make an entry in the Location column for every room within your coverage area; make two or three entries for different parts of large spaces.

Table 9-1: A Wireless Network Site Survey Form

Location	Signal Strength	Operating Mode
Conference Room, North End		
Conference Room, South End		
Reception Area		
Mike's Office		
Sarah's Office		

6. Take the portable computer to the first location on your survey form.

7. Run the Wi-Fi connection program on your laptop computer. The program should report a signal association between the network node and the access point and show the signal strength (usually as zero to five bars). Check the signal strength for each operating mode (802.11b, 802.11a, 802.11g) that your access point supports.

8. Copy the signal strength for the current location to your survey form.

9. With the connection program running, carry the portable computer to the next location on your list. If necessary, use the Refresh command to obtain new readings. Note the signal strength in your survey form.

10. Repeat the process for each location on your list.

You might also want to wander around the building, noting changes in signal quality as you go. You can expect the signal strength to drop as you move farther away from the access point.

If possible, test using several different brands of wireless card. Different wireless cards perform differently, so it's important to test the signal quality with a range of client cards when you're planning a network for users with mixed hardware.

Don't be surprised if you discover one or more unexpected dead spots, where the signal strength drops below a usable level. This might occur because of some kind of obstruction (like a metal filing cabinet) between the access point and the portable unit or because some source of local interference (like a microwave oven, a Bluetooth device, or a cordless phone) is located nearby. Finding those dead spots is one of the reasons you're doing the site survey. In some cases, moving the test unit just a foot or two away from the original location might be enough to solve the problem. Be sure to note any dead spots on the survey form.

If you find a lot of dead spots as you move around the building, or if any of the dead spots are in critical places, try moving the access point. Keep in mind that some of your Wi-Fi users will probably be using pocket-size PDAs and Wi-Fi–equipped mobile telephones while they walk from one room to another, so you shouldn't forget to test signal quality in hallways and bathrooms.

After you have tested the signal quality in every location on your list, mark the location of the access point on the floor plan and copy the test values for each room or other location. If you're working in a relatively small space, you will probably see consistent numbers for most locations. In a larger area, the limits of the access point's useable signals will probably fit within some kind of irregular curve. Don't be surprised to discover that the signal strength decreases as you move farther away from the access point.

If the signal quality is not acceptable over most of the area you want to cover, try moving the access point to a different location, or if the access point has an external antenna, try moving the antenna. Once again, look for a place with a clean, unobstructed line of sight to as much of the area as possible. Repeat the survey with the access point in the new location.

If you can't find a single location that covers the whole area you want to reach, place one or more additional access points at about two thirds of the distance to the place where the signal begins to fade, and connect each access point to your wired LAN. Use a different channel number for each access point.

SUMMARY: STEPS IN A SITE SURVEY

1. Identify the space you want your network to cover.
2. Prepare a floor plan and a vertical diagram.
3. Choose the ideal locations for access points and antennas.
4. Coordinate with other nearby wireless networks.
5. Install the access points.
6. Test wireless links from many locations.
7. Try moving the access points or antennas.
8. Install additional access points as needed.

Interference Problems

If nobody else is using a Wi-Fi network or any other 2.4 GHz device within about half a mile, you won't have to worry about interference to your network, but that's becoming less likely every day. Other network services, along with cordless phones, microwave ovens, outdoor lighting systems, and radio-controlled toys, all use the same set of frequencies. In addition, several nearby home or office networks are probably using their own Wi-Fi networks. It's often a radio jungle out there.

The type of radio modulation used by wireless Ethernet networks is supposed to overcome interference from all those other services. That's the theory. The engineers who work with the various 2.4 GHz radio services are trying to cooperate so we can all use our networks, phones, microwaves, and toys at the same time. In practice, however, the receivers in your access points and network adapters might listen to the channel that is supposed to contain a nice, clean Wi-Fi signal and perform the digital equivalent of throwing their hands into the air and shouting "Arrrgh!"

Or, more accurately, they do nothing: When that happens, the radio that transmitted the signal waits for an acknowledgment that never comes and then sends the same packet again and again until the receiver acknowledges that it has accepted a clean copy. This means that the channel not only has to be clear enough for the original packet to reach the client but clear enough for the acknowledgment to reach the original sender. The same thing happens with the next packet, and the one after that, and the one after that. This has the same effect as trying to conduct a voice conversation over a noisy phone line or a walkie-talkie, where . . . you . . . have . . . to . . . speak . . . very . . . slowly . . . and . . . listen . . . very . . . carefully. In other words, your nice, speedy network will feel like it's receiving data bits through a pipeline full of molasses.

If there's a lot of radio interference around you, you will probably discover it during your site survey. When you can't establish an 11Mbps link within a clean line of sight to the access point, look for another radio signal nearby. It might be something obvious like the microwave oven in the lunchroom or the cordless phone in the kitchen, but it could just as easily be something harder to find, like another network next door, or a point-to-point radio link that's passing over your roof.

You can try a few things to reduce or eliminate interference: Either remove the source of interference or move your own network to a different channel. Changing channels is often easier, but it's not always effective because your source of interference might be a frequency-hopping radio that jumps around the entire 2.4 GHz band, or a completely different source of interference might be operating on the new frequency.

It's worth a try, however. To try to eliminate interference, follow these steps, in this order:

1. Use the Network Connections tool to identify nearby Wi-Fi networks and the channels that each of them is using.

2. Move to a different Wi-Fi channel as far away from the one where you encountered the problem as possible. For example, if you can't use channel 6, try dropping down to channel 1 or jumping up to channel 11. If the neighboring networks are using more than one channel, look for a channel number that is not in use.

3. Look for a cordless phone, a microwave oven, or some other device that radiates at 2.4 GHz. If possible, replace the offending device with one that operates at a different frequency, such as a 900 MHz cordless phone.

4. If you can change the output power of the radios in your access points and interface adapters, make sure they're set to the high (100 mw) setting. Most adapters use an option in the Network Connection Properties window to control power management.

5. Try moving either your access point's antenna or the antennas on the network interface connected to your computer. Sometimes changing the location by just a few inches can make a big difference in network performance.

6. Ask your neighbors if they are using a wireless network. You can often identify the location of a home network by its name, such as *Smith family*. Because they're likely to experience the same kind of interference from your network that you're getting from theirs, they'll probably agree to cooperate on a "channel assignment plan" in which each network uses a different channel. Remember, if you can keep the networks at least five channel numbers apart, you will keep cross-channel interference to a minimum. If you're trying to coordinate more than three channels, spread the channel numbers across the band as widely and evenly as possible.

Because the only set of three channels that don't interfere are channels 1, 6, and 11, and because one of those three channels is the default setting on many access points, you might discover that they contain more interference from neighboring networks than one of the intermediate channels. You might have better luck with one or two of the intermediate channels instead.

7. Try replacing the omnidirectional antennas on your access point, your network adapters, or both with directional antennas to increase the signal strength and the receivers' sensitivity. You might have to move the access point to a different location or add more access points to cover the same area. If you can convince your neighbors to go to directional antennas, try to align the patterns for a minimum of overlapping coverage.

If none of these techniques solve your interference problem, you can't do much more except to either accept sluggish performance or replace your 2.4 GHz Wi-Fi network with an 802.11a wireless network that operates at 5.2 GHz.

You might encounter one more source of interference, especially in a business or institutional setting, but this one probably won't show up until your network has been in operation for a while. As the wireless network becomes more popular among your users, more and more of them might try to use it at the same time, and the overall network performance will deteriorate. To solve this kind of problem, you can add more access points that operate on different channels.

Advantages of Mixed Networks

Just because you have decided to install and use a Wi-Fi network, you don't have to use a wireless connection for every computer; it's often better to connect some computers through Ethernet cables. All of the major access point manufacturers offer combination units that provide both a Wi-Fi access point and one or more wired Ethernet connection points in a single package.

A wired LAN connection offers several advantages over a Wi-Fi link:

- A cable connection can move data more quickly and with less handshaking overhead.

- When you reduce the number of active Wi-Fi nodes in a network, you also reduce the potential for conflicts among active signals.

- Wired connections are more secure than Wi-Fi connections because it's more difficult for an unauthorized user to intercept the signal.

- When you run the access point's configuration and setup program, it's often easier to establish the initial connection through a cable. Indeed, some routers and access points will only accept configuration commands through a cable connection.

When one or more desktop computers, printers, or servers on your LAN are in the same room as the network router, or if they are accessible through an easy cable run, plan to install a CAT5e or CAT6 Ethernet cable between the router or switch and each computer. Leave the Wi-Fi connections for laptops and other portables and for computers located in rooms that are farther away from the router (such as an upstairs bedroom). If your LAN needs more wired ports than the router/access point provides, look for a multiport Ethernet switch that supports at least 100Base-T (100Mbps) connections, and plug it into one of the Ethernet ports on the router. Consult the router's manual for specific instructions on stacking or chaining switches.

If your network includes one or more fileservers, print servers, and other devices that are shared by the network's users, it's best to use cables rather than wireless links to connect those devices to the network to reduce the amount of wireless traffic. However, this might not be possible for devices such as webcams and other remote sensors that are not close to the router; it's okay to use Wi-Fi to connect such devices to the network.

Access Points Combined with Hubs and Gateway Routers

Many manufacturers offer products that combine the functions of a wireless access point with a network hub, switch, or router. Other combination products include network print servers or broadband (cable or DSL) Internet modems along with access points. A combination unit can be an excellent starting point for a new small network or a good way to add both wired and wireless clients to an existing network. Because a combined device doesn't require separate power supplies, cabinets, and interconnecting cables for each function, the cost is likely to be considerably less than the cost of separate components that perform the same jobs. And the convenience of reducing the number of cables tying everything together can be a huge advantage, especially for a small network that doesn't run everything back to a wiring closet.

To decide whether one of these combination units is the best way to meet your particular requirements, identify those requirements first, and then look at various manufacturers' product catalogs and websites to find a device that comes as close to your needs as possible. Among others, D-Link, Linksys, Netsys, Belkin, and Buffalo all offer a wide variety of access points combined with other functions.

Installing the access point portion of a combination unit is not much different from installing a standalone access point. Each device uses a proprietary configuration utility that offers a place to set the access point's operating channel, the SSID, and other settings, along with other configuration options that apply to the device's added functions. Once again, the manual provided with each product and the maker's website are the only place to find the specific information needed to complete the configuration and setup routines.

In most Wi-Fi networks, the access points are just about invisible in daily operation. They sit on a shelf, or they're on the floor behind a desk, where they move data between client computers and the wired network. After you get the access point up and running, you can just about forget it until you need to change the configuration.

Extending the Network

The original idea behind the Wi-Fi specification was to provide wireless connections to LANs in limited areas such as businesses, homes, and public institutions. Wi-Fi was supposed to be a simple extension of traditional Ethernet to laptops and other computers that could not be conveniently connected through a cable. Other radio services would provide wireless access to the Internet from public spaces.

That was the plan. But Wi-Fi gear is inexpensive, it doesn't require a license, and it's relatively easy to set up and use. So an entire culture of "guerilla networkers" emerged to develop alternative uses for the technology that extend the reach of wireless networks beyond their own offices, classrooms, and homes. Hobbyists and community organizers have installed antennas on rooftops and hillsides where they can reach entire neighborhoods with public or private wireless access to the Internet and create point-to-point data links over distances of several miles. Many colleges and universities have added outdoor wireless access points to their campus-wide networks. And a handful of cities have started to build public Wi-Fi networks that might eventually cover their entire downtown areas.

These wide-area Wi-Fi networks have the potential to create some serious competition to the multibillion dollar 3G (third-generation cellular) wireless networks that were supposed to be the next wave of mobile connectivity. If these noncommercial networks that have been thrown together with duct tape and antennas in coffee cans ever come close to providing widespread reliable and cheap wireless network access at 6Mbps, the 3G cellular folks will have a lot of trouble convincing people to buy their expensive 384Kbps services. Therefore, the commercial cellular and wireless network operators are watching the community network movement very carefully.

It's relatively easy to install and use a Wi-Fi network to move data between buildings or to provide network access to your back yard, parking lot, or other open space. Outdoor antennas are widely available, or if you prefer, you can build your own.

This chapter contains information about the legal and practical issues related to operating and using a wireless network outside your own property and technical information about outdoor access points and antennas. In Chapter 10, you can learn how to use Wi-Fi equipment to construct and use long range, point-to-point network links.

Legal Issues

Wi-Fi networks do not require licenses, but the FCC and other regulatory agencies have established some rules about the radio transmissions that make those networks possible. Most of these rules exist to minimize the likelihood of interference among wireless networks, cordless phones, and other services that share the same radio frequencies, so nobody has an unfair advantage over nearby users.

When you're trying to create a Wi-Fi network with the largest possible footprint, rather than just reaching all the computers in your own building, the strength of the radio signals from your access points and network adapters becomes a lot more important. There's a direct relationship between the strength of your signal and the distance it can travel, so it's essential to understand just exactly what the regulations allow.

The specific rules that apply to unlicensed wireless devices appear in Part 15, Section 15.247 of the FCC's regulations. Here's what they say:

> (b) The maximum peak output power of the intentional radiator shall not exceed the following:
>
> (1) For frequency hopping systems operating in the 2400–2483.5 MHz band [. . .] and all frequency hopping systems in the 5725–5850 MHz band: 1 watt.
>
> (3) For systems using digital modulation in the 902–928 MHz, 2400–2483.5 MHz, and 5725–5850 MHz bands: 1 Watt.
>
> (4) Except as shown in paragraph (c) of this section, if transmitting antennas of directional gain greater than 6 dBi are used the peak output power from the intentional radiator shall be reduced below the stated values in paragraphs (b)(1) or (b)(2) of this section as appropriate, by the amount in dB that the directional gain exceeds 6 dBi.
>
> (i) Systems operating in the 2400–2483.5 MHz band that are used exclusively for fixed, point-to-point operations may employ transmitting antennas with directional gain greater than 6 dBi provided the maximum peak output power of the intentional radiator is reduced by 1 dB for every 3 dB that the directional gain of the antenna exceeds 6 dBi.
>
> Source: *http://www.fcc.gov/Bureaus/Engineering_Technology/ Documents/cfr/1998/47cfr15.pdf*, section 15.247

What does that all mean? First, the rules allow the radio transmitters in access points and network adapters to have a maximum power of 1 watt. And second, the maximum amount of antenna gain is 6 dBi unless you reduce the transmitter power as you increase the gain. Highly directional point-to-point systems are permitted to use more antenna gain than point-to-multipoint systems. The maximum power *to the antenna* can't be more than 1 watt, but you can use a directional antenna to increase the effective radiated power to 4 watts.

The rules in other countries might be somewhat different, so you should check with your own country's regulators, especially about the channels and maximum power allowed, but the United States rules should provide some useful guidelines for calculating your equipment's power output and antenna gain.

When you calculate the output power of a radio, you must also consider the signal loss in the cable between the radio and the antenna. For example, the output of an access point might be 20 dBm (equal to less than half a watt), but a particular cable to the antenna might lose 6 dB at 2.4 GHz.

Therefore, the antenna would only receive 14 dBm from the radio. That's a lot less than a watt, so there's room for some gain in the antenna.

The radios built into most Wi-Fi access points and adapters transmit at less than half of a watt, so they're well within the legal limits unless you connect one to a huge antenna with a tremendous amount of gain. An RF amplifier between the radio and the antenna could boost power beyond the 1 watt limit, but of course, that would violate the FCC's regulations.

Two different types of Wi-Fi signal could benefit from more transmitter power: point-to-point signals, where the added power could increase the distance between the two sites; and point-to-multipoint, where increased power at the access point could expand the footprint within which client devices could successfully join the network. A point-to-point link typically uses high-gain directional antennas at both ends; in a point-to-multipoint system, the antenna at the access point usually covers a broad area, but the client adapters might use directional antennas.

If anything, the FCC's power restrictions on radio transmitters in the 2.4 GHz band are too conservative. It would be nice to be able to push, say, 5 watts into a high-gain antenna to create a clean and reliable data link over a distance of 5 or 10 miles or more, or use a single access point to cover a larger area. But the telephone companies and communications common carriers who sell data services have enough influence with the regulators to keep the low power rules in place, and stronger signals would create a lot more interference. So the one-watt limit is probably here to stay.

As a responsible, law-abiding citizen, you should always take those federal regulations very seriously. And as a responsible, law-abiding author and publisher, we would never encourage you to do anything else. However, it's extremely unlikely that a hypothetical individual or small business using a hypothetical high-gain antenna to boost the signal strength of their hypothetical wireless LAN would ever attract any attention from the FCC or other law enforcement types, unless that hypothetical signal created significant interference to somebody else's network or other radio service, or if it attracted attention from a local telephone company or a major Internet service provider. Operating your Wi-Fi network within the FCC's power restrictions is the right thing to do, but that's too bad, because it would not be difficult to boost the strength of your signal.

As a general rule, the FCC doesn't care to spend its time and resources dealing with interference complaints on unlicensed frequencies like the 2.4 GHz ISM band used by Wi-Fi networks. But the law is the law, so as a matter of principle, nobody with the good sense to buy and read this book would ever consider blatantly boosting the power from their access points and network adapters or using very-high-gain antennas. Of course not.

Remember that the FCC's rules only apply to the United States. The regulators in other countries have set their own limits, which are sometimes even lower than the American numbers. And their enforcement policies might be a lot more severe. So it's important to consult technical and legal experts with experience in your own country before you try to install a high-gain antenna or an RF amplifier in your network.

Outdoor Antennas and Access Points

Several factors contribute to the signal strength (and therefore the maximum distance) of a radio link between an access point and a network client in a Wi-Fi network:

- Antenna gain
- Transmitted power
- Antenna height
- Cable attenuation

Keep in mind that a Wi-Fi link moves data in both directions: from the access point to the network adapter, and from the adapter to the access point. So the antennas and radios in the link must be able to both transmit and receive radio signals. Fortunately, the gain and directional characteristics of an antenna are identical for both transmitting and receiving, so the same antenna that boosts the effective power of an outbound signal can also increase a receiver's sensitivity to a weak incoming signal.

An outdoor antenna must also survive in the physical environment where it is operating. High winds can shift a directional antenna away from the direction it was originally aimed; accumulated ice and snow can block the signal and increase the amount of weight that the physical mounting hardware must support; and sunlight can cause a plastic enclosure to deteriorate. Therefore, many antennas are sealed inside radomes or other enclosures that offer additional protection. The maximum output power of a Wi-Fi transmitter is less than a watt, so just about any antenna durable enough for outdoor use should be hefty enough to handle the signal without any trouble.

Antennas for the 2.4 GHz band exist in many shapes and sizes. An omnidirectional antenna can be a single element just a few inches long, with or without an enclosure. The antennas built into PCMCIA adapters are even shorter. The most common directional antennas are yagis (smaller versions of rooftop TV antennas), patch antennas that resemble smoke detectors, parabolic reflectors that can be up to three feet high, and large panels with extremely wide aperture angles.

Remember that a wireless data network uses digital radio signals, so there is absolutely no advantage to using higher power, or a fancy antenna, or placing your antenna on a rooftop, if you can send and receive adequate signals with smaller, cheaper equipment. If an antenna with a moderate amount of gain produces acceptable signals, your data won't be any better or move any faster when you replace it with something bigger and more expensive. And smaller antennas are a lot less conspicuous, which can reduce the likelihood of complaints from neighbors and local zoning agencies.

Antenna Characteristics

Wireless network devices use the same antennas for both transmitting and receiving radio signals. An antenna handles a lot more energy when it's transmitting than when it's receiving, but the performance characteristics are identical. The same antenna that increases the effective radiated output power of a transmitted signal also boosts the sensitivity of a receiver by the same amount; an antenna connected to a Wi-Fi access point or network adapter will improve the strength of the radio signals moving in both directions across the radio link. The most important characteristics that define the performance of an antenna are *aperture angle* and *gain*.

The aperture angle of a directional antenna is the angle or arc within which the antenna radiates or detects energy at maximum power or sensitivity. If, for example, an antenna's aperture angle is 20 degrees, the window of maximum signal strength extends 10 degrees to each side of the front of the antenna. The signal strength will drop when both antennas in a radio link are not within the aperture angle of the other. Figure 9-7 shows the effect of aiming a pair of directional antennas at each other.

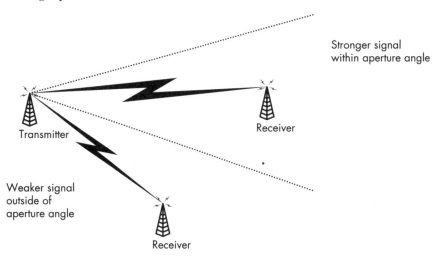

Figure 9-7: Directional antennas can increase signal strength.

The specifications for a nondirectional antenna (also called an omnidirectional antenna) don't include an aperture angle, but if they did, the aperture angle would be 360 degrees. Omnidirectional antennas might have a vertical aperture angle listed; as the gain of an omnidirectional antenna increases, the vertical range decreases. As the name suggests, the antennas in a point-to-point link should be aimed directly at each other, so their aperture angles can be extremely narrow.

An antenna's gain is its effective output power or sensitivity relative to a standard dipole antenna. If you measured the strength of signals from two identical transmitters, or the same signal through two separate receivers, the signal that passes through an antenna with a gain of 3 dBi will be 3 dB stronger than a signal through a reference dipole antenna. The gain of an antenna increases with the size of the antenna and as the signal is focused within a narrow aperture.

It's useful to think about antenna angles and gain as similar to focused lights. A standard light bulb radiates the same amount of light energy in all directions (except back to the base of the bulb). But if you place a reflector behind one side of the light source, or if you focus the light in a particular direction, the apparent brightness of the light will increase within the target area, but it will look dimmer when you move away from the target area. The total amount of light radiated by the bulb is the same, but more of that light is concentrated in certain places.

Radio antennas work the same way, more or less. A nondirectional antenna will radiate equal amounts of energy in all directions, while a directional antenna can concentrate more energy in some directions than in others.

Directional antennas with tight aperture angles are useful for point-to-point links, but that's not the only way to take advantage of a directional antenna in a wireless network. When you have a potential problem with interference from other radio signals, it's often helpful to place a directional antenna with the source of interference off axis from the aperture angle so the receiving antenna is much less sensitive to the source of interference than to the signal you want. When you're trying to provide network coverage to your own property while limiting the amount of spillover to your neighbors, you can place one or more directional antennas at the edge of the area you want to reach and aim the antennas inward.

An antenna with a greater surface area is more effective than a smaller antenna, but the exact size of the antenna is also extremely important. The ideal antenna for any radio frequency is cut to a length exactly equal to the wavelength of that frequency or some multiple or fraction of that wavelength. So it's important to use an antenna specifically designed for operation at 2.4 GHz (2,400 MHz) with your 802.11b network. An antenna of the correct size will receive Wi-Fi signals far more efficiently than an antenna with a random length.

Power

The maximum amount of power produced by a Wi-Fi radio transmitter is determined by the design of the radio; the people operating the network usually can't adjust it, or if they can, it's most often nothing more than a choice between high and low power. However, the output power of one of those radios is often considerably less than the legal maximum, so it's often possible to increase the amount of power that reaches the antenna without breaking the law.

You can't boost the amount of power produced by the transmitter, so the only way to increase the power of the signal from a radio in an access point or a network adapter is to place a device called an RF amplifier (*RF* stands for *radio frequency*) between the radio and the antenna. You can think of an RF amplifier as a black box that takes a low-power radio signal at its input and provides a stronger signal with exactly the same content at the output.

Some RF amplifiers are designed for use indoors next to the access point, router, or network adapter. Others can be mounted outdoors on the tower or mast next to the antenna. Indoor amplifiers are usually easier to install and maintain, and they're a lot easier to connect to an AC power source, but they're less efficient because a long feed cable to the antenna will absorb some of the RF power coming out of the amplifier. An amplifier in a weatherproof enclosure near the antenna will supply more power to the antenna, but it will be more difficult to reach when you have to repair or replace it. If you do use an outdoor amplifier, look for one that obtains DC power through the antenna feed cable.

HyperLink Technologies and other manufacturers offer RF amplifiers for use at 2.4 GHz. Many of these devices amplify both inbound and outbound signals. This is a useful feature because it makes it possible to install an amplifier on just one end of a link and still increase the signal strength in both directions. When you use a bidirectional amplifier, *make sure* that it is designed for use with the 802.11 standard you are actually using. Bidirectional amps must determine when a card is transmitting and change the amplifier mode accordingly, since an amplifier designed for 802.11b might not detect an 802.11g card that is transmitting, and it could even damage the device.

Antenna Height

Radio signals at 2.4 GHz travel along a line-of-sight path, so you can increase the distance that a signal can travel by raising one or both antennas. That's why it's common practice to place radio antennas on rooftops, hilltops, and tall towers. To compensate for the curvature of the earth, the average height of the two antennas must increase as the *signal path* (the distance between antennas) gets longer.

Radio line of sight is actually broader than the visual path between the two antennas. Radio waves travel within a cigar-shaped region called the *Fresnel zone* (pronounced *fru-NEL* zone) that surrounds the direct path between the transmitting and receiving antennas. For the best possible transmission, the Fresnel zone must be free of hills, trees, buildings, and other obstructions.

The maximum distance that a wireless network signal can travel depends on the average height of the two antennas, with allowance for the curvature of the earth and the requirement for unobstructed Fresnel zone clearance. Table 9-2 lists one set of estimated minimum heights required for various distances at 2.4 GHz. Remember that these are estimates, so you might actually move your data over somewhat greater distances.

Table 9-2: The Relationship Between Antenna Height and Maximum Signal Path

Distance	Average Antenna Height
1 mile	13 feet
3 miles	27 feet
5 miles	35 feet
8 miles	48 feet
10 miles	57 feet
15 miles	83 feet
20 miles	115 feet

Note that the height of the two antennas is the average height above average terrain: If one antenna is higher than the average height, the other antenna can be closer to the ground. For example, if one end of a five-mile link is on a hillside or on the roof of an eight-story building, the other end of the link could be close to ground level if there are no obstructions between the two locations. If one antenna is on a mountaintop, the maximum signal path might be several times greater.

When you're trying to provide Wi-Fi network coverage to a large area, it's more efficient to place the access point's antenna as high as possible rather than trying to raise a lot of antennas connected to individual computers. On the other hand, if you're trying to connect just one or two computers to a distant access point, it could be better to place the antennas connected to their network adapters on a rooftop.

For a really long Wi-Fi link, you will want to place both antennas as high as possible, but unless you're trying to provide access to a remote mountaintop or something like that, there's probably a better and more reliable way to create a broadband connection to the Internet or your own LAN.

Cable Attenuation

The cable that carries a radio signal from a radio transmitter to an antenna, or from the antenna to a receiver, is not a perfectly efficient transmission medium; every foot of cable absorbs a small but measurable amount of power. So the amount of power that reaches the antenna drops as the cable length increases.

The effect of cable attenuation on a short cable is usually insignificant, but it can make a huge difference over longer runs. If the antenna is high on a tower or rooftop, or if you're trying to estimate the antenna gain necessary for a long point-to-point link, you must allow for cable loss when you calculate the strength of the signal reaching the antenna. The amount of loss in a particular type of cable depends on the diameter of the cable and the materials used to produce the cable. The specifications for each type of cable will include the amount of attenuation, often expressed in dB per 100 feet at different operating frequencies.

If the cable loss is rated at 6.80 dB at 2,500 MHz, you can estimate that a 20-foot cable at 2.4 GHz (2,400 MHz) will lose about 1.3 dB (20 ft = 100 ft × 0.2; 0.2 × 6.80 dB = ~1.3 dB). If the output power from an access point or network adapter is 20 dBm (100 milliwatts), the antenna will only receive 18.7 dBm (74.1 milliwatts) through that cable. So when you push that signal through an antenna with a gain of 6 dBi, the effective radiated power would be about 24.7 dB (20 − 1.3 + 6 = 24.7), or about 295 milliwatts.

Every foot of feed cable increases the amount of cable loss, so you should place your access points and network adapters as close to the antenna as possible. If the antenna is mounted on a roof or the wall of a building, try to place the radio in a nearby equipment closet or other space where you have access to AC power and your Ethernet cables. It's a lot more efficient to run a longer Ethernet cable to the access point and a shorter antenna feed cable.

When you install an antenna feed cable, it's good practice to allow a little slack at each end to make it easier to connect and disconnect the cable from the antenna and the radio. But don't leave a lot of excess cable coiled up on the floor just because the premade cable is longer than you need. All that cable wastes signal with no compensating benefit.

Each coupler or connector in the cable run is also a point of loss; a typical guideline is 0.3 dB of loss per connector, so a short pigtail connector from a wireless card to a standard antenna connector would include two connectors, then both ends of the long cable run would have two more, and the connector on the antenna itself would be a fifth point of loss. Therefore, in addition to the loss of the cabling itself, you will have an additional 1.5 dB of loss due to connectors. Whenever possible, keep the number of connectors in your antenna cable to a minimum.

Campus Networks

A campus network usually provides wireless access to the Internet, and sometimes to a LAN, for users in two or more buildings, and to the outdoor spaces that surround those buildings. A campus network can exist on a college or university campus, but the same kind of planning and design can also apply to other locations. For example, a campus network might also operate in an office park or an industrial park, in a public space such as a green park or a shopping and entertainment center, or even a farm or a marina. Several cities have installed campuslike networks to provide public Internet access throughout their central business districts. Another form of temporary campuslike network might exist at a special event such as a music festival, a Boy or Girl Scout jamboree, or a gathering of old-car enthusiasts. They're also common at flea markets and swap meets where many people want to use the Internet to consult specialty websites before they decide to buy.

The simplest campus networks occur by accident: The radio signals from the access points that provide network service to the interior of a building don't stop at the building's walls, so a user in the parking lot or the back yard can also establish wireless access to the network. A larger and more complex campus network might have additional access points in locations specifically chosen to reach network clients on the college lawn or the coffee shop across the street.

A campus network might be a complement to a set of wireless links that connect two or more buildings to the same network, but it's not the same thing; a campus network should provide broad coverage to a lot of outdoor space, while a point-to-point link simply extends a single LAN to spaces inside several buildings.

Setting Up a Campus Network

In general, the same rules apply to a campus network that you would use in designing a Wi-Fi network that serves a single building. Choose locations for your access points that will provide signals to as much of the area as possible, and allow for some overlap from one footprint to each adjacent footprint. Each pair of overlapping coverage areas should use a different radio channel.

When you're setting up an outdoor network to provide Wi-Fi access to the Internet, remember to place your Internet modem and first access point close to a source of electric power and within a short cable run to a telephone line or other Internet point of presence. If possible, place the antenna within a clean line of sight to campsites, picnic tables, and backstage areas (as appropriate) where your users will want to use their laptop computers.

In almost every case, the access points that serve an outdoor network should connect to external antennas rather than the captive antennas built into many access points designed for indoor use. Choose the antenna with the best characteristics for your particular needs, and use a waterproof cable to connect it to an access point located out of the weather.

Connecting the Access Points to a LAN and the Internet

If your access points are all located in buildings that already have network service, you can treat the access points with outdoor antennas as a simple extension of the existing network. But if you don't already have a network connection at your access point, you'll have to create one.

To connect your campus network to a LAN or the Internet, you must provide a point of network presence for every access point. The connection can be through an Ethernet cable, a data circuit leased from the telephone company, or a point-to-point radio link.

Every access point requires a source of electric power, but it's not always necessary to run a long extension cord from the nearest AC outlet. Many access point manufacturers offer a power over Ethernet option that carries power for the access points through the same cable that carries the Ethernet data. And don't forget solar power as a possible alternative.

Ethernet cables are easy to connect to an access point, but they're not the best choice for links between buildings except in very specific situations. First, you must have a secure path for the cable to follow; you can't just string the cable through the trees or run it across the lawn. On a college campus, it's sometimes possible to run cables through steam or other utility tunnels, but that's not practical in most other locations. Even if you have a way to route the cable from one building to another, the maximum practical distance for a 10Base-T or 100Base-T twisted pair cable connection is only about 100 meters. If your access point is more than a hundred meters from the network hub, you'll have to add one or more repeaters to the line or replace the twisted pair cable with a fiber optic connection. Either way, the cost is probably greater than using a radio link or connecting each access point to a separate Internet router and assigning the same SSID to each network.

Sometimes the ideal location for an access point is on a building that has existing Internet service, but it's not part of the LAN you want to use for your campus network. In that case, you can set up a VPN link that creates a "tunnel" through the Internet back to your own network. The access point will pass data to and from your own network through the VPN just as if it was connected through a short cable.

The third alternative is often the most practical choice. Use point-to-point wireless links between the network hub and each of your remote access points. Outdoor routers and related hardware and software that are designed specifically for this purpose are available from Cisco, D-Link, and many other suppliers.

Networking Your Neighborhood

Someplace between the relative simplicity of a home-based wireless network and a complex campus network, you might want to think about extending your own home or small-business network: You can share a high-speed Internet connection with one or more nearby neighbors or allow your employees to take their laptop computers to the coffee shop next door. If you or your children like to play multiplayer games with the family next door, or if you want to go online from your Palm handheld or Pocket PC while schmoozing with your neighbors at the annual block party, a neighborhood network might be the way to go.

But before you decide to hang an antenna on your roof, consider exactly what you want to accomplish with your neighborhood network and how you plan to maintain security in the rest of your network. If you're trying to add a particular location to your network (such as a particular neighbor's house, or the cafe that has become your de facto branch office), use a directional antenna that will focus your signal to the specific location you want to reach. On the other hand, if you want to provide an Internet hot spot for everybody within half a block or more, you can place a high-gain nondirectional antenna at the highest point on your own building. If you're using the same LAN for both in-house and neighborhood use, make sure a firewall keeps your own computers separate from the public portion of the network.

If your network adapter has a connector for an external antenna, you might want to either buy or build a directional antenna that you can point toward the community network's nearest access point. It's quite possible that you will discover nearby signals that were not detected by the low-gain omnidirectional antenna built into the adapter.

Many neighborhood network initiatives use an alternate distribution method, called wireless distribution system (WDS) or mesh. In a mesh network, each access point connects to other access points that are in wireless range, and it provides access to clients. Mesh networks trade raw speed for ease of connectivity—when additional access or range is required, simply turn on another access point. But remember that each access point in the mesh that does not also have a dedicated Internet connection can reduce the bandwidth by up to half.

Several free and commercial mesh solutions exist, as well as the standard WDS supported by many routers. Typically all access points in a WDS or mesh network must be the same brand to properly connect.

Keeping Your ISP Happy

It seems like a perfectly logical idea: Share your high-speed cable modem or DSL service with your next-door neighbor, and split the cost. Or let everybody in your apartment building or on your suburban block share a single wireless network.

But consider the potential aggravation factor of dealing with your Internet service provider, who might view your generous sharing of a cable or DSL account as a threat to its (real or potential) revenue stream and a violation of its terms of service. Some major ISPs have specific policies that do not allow customers to share connections through neighborhood networks. Many other ISPs don't care, and a few even encourage the practice.

The ISPs are legitimately concerned that neighborhood networks might generate a lot more demand for network bandwidth than a single user connection. When you design and construct a communications network, you calculate the maximum capacity of your network based on predicted peak demand. If you get it right, your network can handle the demand with enough capacity to spare for emergencies, but if the demand increases beyond your expectations, the whole system overloads and you have to add more capacity.

This kind of planning applies to telephone systems, highways, and even streetcar lines, as well as Internet connections. If you have enough streetcars (or bandwidth) to handle your rush hour traffic, the system runs efficiently and the number of dimes and quarters in the fare box should cover your expenses. But when a big new factory opens at one end of the line, 500 more passengers suddenly want to use your system. Unless you add more capacity, the cars are too crowded and everybody complains.

Experience can give you a pretty accurate idea of how much demand will exist at any given moment—you might not know exactly who is online at 10:15 on a Tuesday morning, but you can predict how many streetcars or how much bandwidth you will need to handle the demand.

In the case of an Internet account, the ISP has built enough bandwidth to handle the peak demand (in an office, it's probably first thing in the morning and at lunchtime; in a residential neighborhood, it's after school). But if that demand doubles, they'll have to buy and install more equipment and find a source of revenue to pay for it. They want to prevent the kind of unexpected additional demands for bandwidth that can break down the whole system, or, more accurately, they want to know about it and plan (and charge) accordingly.

You have three choices: Ask your ISP if it has a policy on shared connections and follow its guidelines (which might mean finding a different ISP); go ahead and install your neighborhood access points and hope the telephone company, cable service, or other ISP doesn't find out about it; or investigate a commercial connection type such as synchronous DSL or even a T1-class line, which will cost more but should have less restrictive terms of use.

Network Security: Everybody Is Your Neighbor

The most basic configuration of a neighborhood network is a single access point with a wide coverage footprint and an unprotected connection to the Internet. Anybody with a network adapter within range of your signal can use your network to exchange data through the Internet. That includes the family next door, but it also includes the guy in the van parked on the street who's using your network to download pornography.

Unless you are intentionally creating a public Internet hot spot for everybody who comes along, you should use some of the security tools built into the Wi-Fi specifications. Chapter 12 covers security in more detail, but here are the most important security tools:

- Turn on WEP or WPA key encryption. This one is crucial. It's true that a dedicated intruder can crack a WEP key in less than an hour, but it does discourage the casual drive-by user and serves as a "do not disturb" sign.
- Use MAC address filtering to restrict access to your network to specific network adapters. Again, it's not difficult to spoof a MAC address with the right software, but it's one more impediment to unauthorized access.
- Turn off the DHCP function that automatically assigns a numeric IP address to each client, and assign a specific address to each authorized user.
- Turn on the firewall function in your access point or router.
- Use an external server or a firewall that forces each user to supply a username and password before it connects them to the Internet.
- Use a VPN.

If you're using the same network to link two or more of your own computers, use a firewall to isolate that part of the network from the public access point. Encourage all of the legitimate users of your network to pay close attention to file sharing so they don't allow outsiders to read or write the data stored on their computers. Also, be sure to change the access point's administrative password. Do not use *admin* or any other widely used default password. An intruder who breaks into your access point can cause massive damage to your network.

10

LONG RANGE
POINT-TO-POINT LINKS

 As low cost Wi-Fi equipment has become widely available, many users have thought about aiming an antenna at a nearby building or a hillside 5 or 10 miles away to create a cheap, high speed, two-way data link. Some experimenters and tinkerers with more time than money have even designed their own antennas out of tin cans, potato chip canisters, and junk from their basement workshops. They have generally discovered that Wi-Fi links can be a reliable way to move data across a lot of ground.

This chapter contains information about designing and using point-to-point wireless network links. A *point-to-point wireless link* can be part of a larger Wi-Fi network, it can act as a simple bridge between two wired LANs, or it can add a single distant site to an existing LAN. Point-to-point service differs from other Wi-Fi networks because it moves data between two specific locations rather than broadcasting a network signal to any network client within range of the radio signal. It's also possible to use Wi-Fi as part of a wireless gateway that provides Internet access to a community or an isolated location where affordable landlines are not available.

Why extend a wireless network? Point-to-point links can serve several purposes:

- It can extend a single network to include users in more than one building. In an office park or on a college campus, a business or academic department that occupies space in more than one building can use wireless to share LAN services across all the organization's locations.

- It can move data across a barrier such as a highway or a river. If there's a clean line of sight, a wireless link can jump across a gap that could make it difficult or impossible to string cables from one building to another.

- It can provide LAN and high-speed Internet access to users and unattended computers in remote locations. A wireless link can extend a broadband connection to places that are not served by broadband DSL or cable modem Internet service, or even by Plain Old Telephone Service.

- It can establish wireless network links as an inexpensive alternative to leased lines. Private data circuits supplied by the telephone company or other common carriers normally involve a one-time installation fee and a recurring monthly payment. The annual cost of a leased line can often be many times greater than the one-time cost of buying and installing a radio link.

In a sense, a point-to-point Wi-Fi network link is a completely different category from a wireless LAN. Both use the same radio technology, and it's quite possible to extend a wireless LAN beyond the limits of a single building, but a point-to-point link could just as easily use some other type of radio modulation at some other frequency, rather than DSSS at 2.4 GHz, and perform the same function. You can find some pointers to alternative methods for connecting remote sites to your network later in this chapter.

Extending the LAN

A point-to-point wireless network link can be either a LAN at one end connected to a single client device at the other end or a bridge between two LANs. In other words, the end points of a link can be either a single computer or other device, or a full network.

A wireless LAN with a remote client, like the one shown in Figure 10-1, works the same way as a network with two or more access points within a single building. The only difference is that one or more access points connected to the LAN use an outdoor antenna aimed at a client computer in a remote location. The remote computer appears to the network exactly like every other computer on the same LAN.

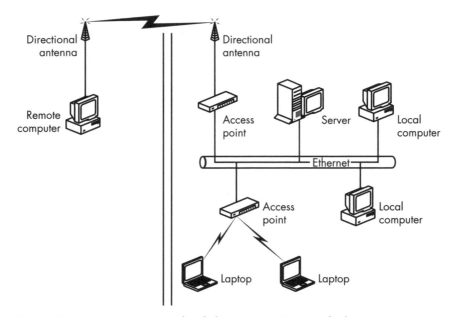

Figure 10-1: A point-to-point wireless link can connect to a single device in a remote location.

A wireless network bridge, like the one shown in Figure 10-2, is a link between two segments of the same LAN. The two segments might be separated by as little as a few hundred feet or as far apart as several miles or more.

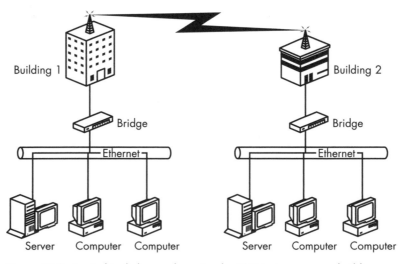

Figure 10-2: A wireless link can also extend a LAN to two or more buildings.

If the distance between the end points is too far for a single radio link, or if there are obstructions to the line-of-sight signal path, a point-to-point link can include one or more repeaters at relay points between the origin and the destination. A relay point can be situated at an isolated location, such as a radio tower or a rooftop, or a place with additional network clients, such as a third building between the two end points.

A point-to-point link can use any access point and network adapter that has connectors for external antennas. However, several manufacturers offer wireless routers that have been specifically designed for outdoor bridging applications, which are often a better choice. Routers made by Plexus, HyperLink Technologies, Cisco, and other manufacturers all combine access points with routers, so they make the network a lot easier to assemble.

Bridge Routers

A bridge router is the opposite of an access point: An access point connects to a wired LAN and converts the network connection to Wi-Fi signals; a *bridge router* connects to the network through a Wi-Fi link and provides one or more wired Ethernet ports. In other words, a bridge router provides a wireless link between two parts of the same LAN. Many of the same manufacturers that make access points and network interfaces also offer bridge routers as part of their product lines. Figure 10-3 shows a Wi-Fi bridge router as part of an extended LAN.

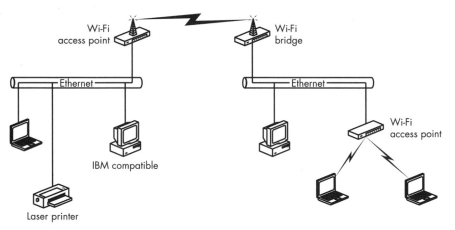

Figure 10-3: A bridge uses Wi-Fi to connect a remote location to a LAN.

You could use a bridge router to share a LAN or single broadband Internet connection among two or more buildings. For example, you can use a bridge router to distribute your neighbor's DSL or cable Internet service to two or more computers in your own house (with your neighbor's permission, of course). Or if your business has offices in two or more nearby buildings, a bridge router could extend the LAN between buildings.

Point-to-Point and Point-to-Multipoint

An indoor access point uses either a nondirectional antenna that radiates equal amounts of energy in all directions from the middle of the intended coverage area, or a directional antenna with a wide aperture angle located at one edge (or a corner) of the coverage area. An access point that provides wireless service to any location within a designated area (such as an office or a house) is a *point-to-multipoint* service; it can exchange data with many network clients at the same time.

A point-to-point link has a different objective: It moves as many of the radiated signals as possible between two fixed locations. Radio signals move across the link in both directions, so each access point, router, or network adapter uses the same antenna for both transmitting and receiving. The goal is to focus the radio signal toward the antenna at the other end of the link, so at least one of the end points uses a directional antenna. If the link covers a long distance, both antennas should be directional for the strongest possible signals.

In a campus or similar area where the network connects several buildings, the network links can be split to distribute network service from a central location to remote sites in more than one direction. In this kind of system, the central access point uses a nondirectional antenna, and each remote uses a directional antenna, as shown in Figure 10-4. In a system where two remote sites are in the same general location relative to the primary base station, the best choice might be a directional antenna with a wider operating angle. A more complex system might include a combination of directional and omnidirectional antennas.

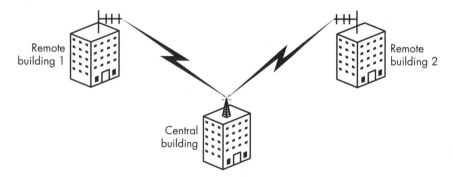

Figure 10-4: An omnidirectional antenna can distribute signals to two or more remote locations at the same time.

Installing a Point-to-Point Link

The first step in conducting a point-to-point site survey is to identify a possible signal path. In theory, it ought to be possible to calculate the required height of both antennas and identify the path between them, but it almost never works out that way. There's almost always a certain amount of tweaking required before you can fire up your radios and start to move data across the network. You can perform a preliminary survey with a good map (such as a topographical map from the US Geological Survey), but at some point you will want to climb up onto the roof (or look out the window) and confirm that there's a line of sight to the place you want to put the other end of the link. If the path extends more than a few hundred yards, bring a pair of binoculars with you.

You can generally place an antenna on your own building without any special permits, but if you want to use the roof of a commercial building, you will probably need permission from the property owner and possibly from the local zoning board or other land-use agency. This probably won't be a problem when you're mounting an inconspicuous antenna, but keep it in mind if you have to use a relatively large dish or something similar. If you're using an existing pole or tower to support the antenna, make sure you're not producing or receiving interference with other antennas nearby.

Climbing a pole or tower with a belt full of tools and securely mounting a bulky antenna in a precise position 30 or more feet in the air is not a casual afternoon project. Don't even consider it without appropriate safety equipment, including hard hats for everybody involved—a dropped wrench or bolt can be lethal. If you don't have experience with this kind of work, there's no shame in hiring somebody to do the job for you. The people who sell point-to-point antennas can tell you where to find a qualified antenna rigger in your area.

Choose a Signal Path

The first step in installing a link is to decide exactly where it will go. If you're just extending the network across a parking lot or a highway, the path will be obvious; choose a location that avoids the big tree in front of the building. But if the distance between antennas is more than about half a mile, you will probably want to lay out the path on a map first.

Topographical maps, either on paper or online, will give you the best level of detail. See *http://www.topozone.com* for maps of the entire United States; *http://toporama.cits.rncan.gc.ca* is the source for maps of Canada. If the exact locations for both end points are not immediately obvious on a map, a GPS device can provide precise geographic coordinates.

Reaching the Boondocks: Long-Range Links

The distance covered by most point-to-point wireless network links can probably be measured in yards rather than miles (or if you prefer, in meters rather than kilometers), so installing the link is relatively easy. The other end of the link is in plain sight, so the antennas are easy to aim at each other. Signal strength is usually not a problem on a short hop, especially with directional antennas.

A longer link is possible, but it's more difficult to set up because the signal will be weaker, and it's a lot more important to point the antennas accurately. Figure 10-5 (and some common sense) shows why a receiver becomes harder to find as you move farther away from the transmitter.

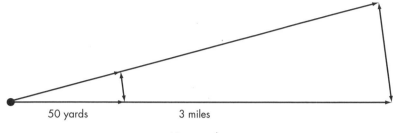

50 yards   3 miles

Not to scale

Figure 10-5: A small angle change in the direction of an antenna can have a huge effect on the connection if a receiver is several miles away.

It's also more difficult to locate a particular building or other end point with the unaided eye when it's one of many buildings on a hillside or in a valley several miles away, so a telescope or a pair of binoculars is an essential part of your installation tool bag. Starting at the location where the network connection is already in place, look for the target site from the roof or an upper-story window. If you can find it, you can probably install a network link from here to there.

However, at least one of the antennas in a long-range link must be high enough to overcome the obstructions caused by Fresnel zone interference and the curvature of the earth. This isn't a serious problem for a one- or two-mile link—the roof of a two-story building is probably high enough to give you the clearance you need unless there are a lot of trees in the way—but if you're trying to push a signal five miles or more, the height of the antenna is a significant issue. This is the reason you often see radio towers on top of hills and tall buildings.

Aligning the Antennas

For best performance, a directional antenna must be aimed directly toward the antenna at the other end of the link. If the antennas at both end points are directional, they must both be pointed correctly. In most cases, the best place to locate an antenna is on the roof or a tower, or bolted to an outside wall, but sometimes it's possible to place it indoors next to a window if there's a clean line of sight to the other end of the link.

It's entirely possible to align a pair of antennas by watching the signal strength display in your Wi-Fi configuration software, but when you're working with long-range links and weak signals, a piece of test equipment called a spectrum analyzer will provide much more precise information. A *spectrum analyzer* is a special-purpose radio receiver that displays a portion of the radio spectrum as a visual image. Because the display shows any radio signal it detects as a spike in the graphic display, the spike will grow larger as the signal strength increases. Therefore, you can use the display to find the best possible positions for your antennas.

Unfortunately, most general-purpose spectrum analyzers that can display a 2.4 GHz signal are quite expensive devices—a new one will probably cost several thousand dollars or more. However, MetaGeek (*http://www.metageek .net*) makes a simple and relatively inexpensive USB spectrum analyzer called Wi-Spy, which is designed specifically for evaluating signals within the 2.4 GHz band. Figure 10-6 shows the display from a laptop connected to a Wi-Spy analyzer. If you can't find a spectrum analyzer easily, don't worry about it; the signal strength display in the Wi-Fi software will work well enough.

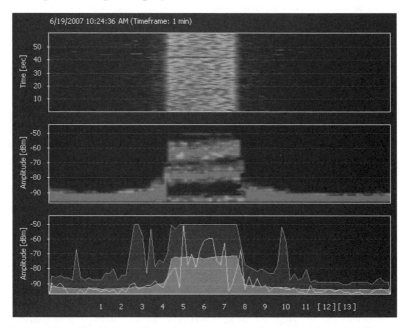

Figure 10-6: The MetaGeek Wi-Spy spectrum analyzer provides a graphic display of Wi-Fi radio signals.

Installing and aligning the antennas for a point-to-point link is not a one-person job. At a bare minimum, you will need one person at each end to adjust the antenna's positions to find the strongest signal; if an antenna is not right next to the computer or spectrum analyzer, you will want one person watching the screen while another moves the antenna. If you can place a team at each end of the link with telephones or two-way radios, it will save a lot of time and aggravation.

To aim the antennas properly, follow these steps:

1. Choose the exact location where you want to install each antenna and securely mount the masts or poles that will hold it.

2. Use the mounting hardware supplied with each antenna to attach it to the mast, pole, or other supporting structure. Point the antenna toward the other end point of the link, but don't tighten the mounting screws yet; you will want to adjust the antenna's position more precisely.

3. Run the feed cables from the antenna to your wireless router, access point, or network adapter. If you have access to a spectrum analyzer that can operate at 2.4 GHz, connect it to the feed cable coming from the antenna.

4. Connect the routers or access points to their respective networks and turn on the radios at both ends. If you are using a spectrum analyzer, tune it to the frequency of the radio channel that your access point or router is using. If you don't have a spectrum analyzer, start the configuration utility on your network device. If only one end of the network link has a directional antenna, that's the one to adjust.

5. Slowly move the antenna connected to the router or the spectrum analyzer. You should see a peak in the signal strength display when this antenna is aimed directly at the other end of the link. Move the antenna left and right first, and then adjust the vertical angle. When the signal strength display or the spectrum analyzer shows the strongest signal, tighten the antenna mounting hardware to maintain that position.

6. If the other antenna is also directional, repeat the signal peaking process. If you have a second team at the remote site, they can make the adjustments on their antenna while they communicate via radio or telephone with the people at the point of origin.

7. If it's not already connected to the network device, connect the feed line from the antenna to your router, access point, or network adapter.

At this point, you should be able to exchange data between the two end points in both directions. If you can't get enough signal through the link to produce a usable network connection, make sure both the network adapter and the access point are set to operate at full power. If that's not enough to provide a useful signal, you might have to boost the signal with an RF amplifier or replace one or both antennas with other antennas that have more gain.

Obstructions and Relays

Each antenna in a point-to-point link must have an unobstructed line of sight to the antenna at the other end of the link. If there's a building or a mountain between the origin and the destination, you'll have to find a way to get your signal over or around it. If the signal path goes through a wooded area, try to run your site survey during the spring or summer because a signal that passes through bare branches without any trouble can often be shut down by leaves and other foliage.

You can't bend a radio signal around an obstruction, so the only way to get past it is to use a repeater at a location that has a line of sight to both end points. A repeater can be a single router with space for two radios, such as the Proxim Outdoor Router, two separate routers connected through an Ethernet network cable, or a pair of access points connected through a network hub. To reduce the effects of interference between the two antennas, each segment of a multihop network link should use a different radio channel.

As a side benefit, the same router that relays the network to a second radio can also provide network service to the building where the relay is located, or it can split the network and relay signals to two or more remote end points. So, for example, the central control point of a Wi-Fi network might be located on a valley floor with a link to a relay point on a nearby hilltop or rooftop. From the hilltop repeater, the same network can be extended to two or more locations in as many different directions.

Alternatives to Wi-Fi for Point-to-Point

Long-range Wi-Fi links are not the only way to connect remote clients to a LAN. Other methods for extending a network are often easier or more reliable.

The main reasons to use Wi-Fi equipment in a point-to-point wireless link are that the equipment is widely available and relatively inexpensive, it doesn't require a special license, and the link can be part of an existing wireless LAN. But it's also possible to use other radios that use different (licensed or unlicensed) radio frequencies or different types of radio signals.

The IEEE 802.11 specification (without any other suffix letter) covers radios that use both direct-sequence spread spectrum (DSSS) and frequency-hopping spread spectrum (FHSS) modulation. In a radio environment where interference from other wireless LANs is a problem, a different technology can often cut through the noise to produce a stronger and cleaner stream of data.

Each type of radio offers a different combination of data transmission speed and signal range. For example, BreezeCom's PRO.11 family of wireless network products use FHSS radios that can move data at up to 3Mbps over a distance of up to 30 miles. A BreezeCom Workgroup Bridge connects directly to a 10Base-T Ethernet LAN.

If the 11Mbps data speed of an 802.11b is not fast enough to meet your requirements, other devices can provide faster connections, but they generally have shorter ranges than a Wi-Fi link. 802.11a equipment has a maximum data speed of around 54Mbps at 5 GHz. C-SPEC's OverLAN HS 100 has a top speed of about 100Mbps, but the signal range is significantly shorter than a Wi-Fi link.

For links with a degraded line of sight, modified Atheros radios from Ubiquity Networks use the 802.11g OFDM encoding at 900 MHz, which can handle interference from foliage and buildings much more effectively.

This is a book about wireless networks, but sometimes it's useful to remember that the point of the exercise is to establish a network connection or access to the Internet and not a wireless link. If a broadband connection to the Internet already exists at the remote location, go ahead and use it. Just because a point-to-point wireless link is possible, it's not always necessary.

For example, a virtual private network can provide all the advantages of a point-to-point wireless link without the hassles of setting up a pair of antennas. As far as the people using the network are concerned, a single network with a VPN tunnel connecting two or more buildings looks just like a network with a radio link. Another approach that can often be effective is to run cables from one building to the next through utility tunnels.

Antennas for Network Adapters

If you're using a point-to-point link to reach a single distant network client, you will need a network adapter that accepts an external antenna. You might find a PC Card adapter with an antenna connector, but Buffalo and other manufacturers offer USB Wi-Fi network adapters that can use an external antenna.

Because some adapters use proprietary antenna connectors, they require a special cable called a *pigtail* with a standard antenna cable connector at one end and a plug that matches the adapter's connector at the other. A proprietary pigtail can cost more than the network adapter, but comparable pigtails are also available at less than a third of the adapter maker's prices from several other sources, including Fleeman Anderson & Bird (*http://www.fab-corp.com*) and HyperLink Technologies (*http://www.hyperlinktech.com*). The small cables used for pigtails can often be the most poorly shielded component in your network; always keep pigtails as short as possible to maximize the signal strength.

Build Your Own Antenna?

Many community network enthusiasts have designed and built their own antennas out of odd hardware, plastic spacers, copper wire, and empty cans. Depending on the contents of your junk box and your pantry, the materials for a homemade high-gain directional antenna might cost as little as three or four dollars, not counting the price of a can of coffee, beef stew, or potato chips. If you have to go out and buy all the parts and hand tools necessary for the project, you might spend $20 or more.

However, when you add the value of the time necessary to assemble the antenna and tweak it for optimal performance, it's not at all clear that rolling your own would be less expensive than buying an inexpensive commercial antenna. It's not unusual to spend three to six hours or more assembling one of these "cheap" home brew antennas. A few minutes of online searching (look for "2.4 GHz antenna") should find several sources for store-bought directional antennas under $25 that will work at least as well as the ones you can build. Keep in mind that your access point or network client adapter doesn't need an antenna that can handle high power, so you can get by with a relatively lightweight unit.

The most common type of directional antenna for point-to-point communication is called a *yagi*, or more properly, a Yagi-Uda antenna system. It was named for the two Japanese engineers, Professor Hidetsugu Yagi and Professor Shintaro Uda of Tohuku University, who designed and constructed the first ones around 1926. A typical yagi antenna, like the one shown in Figure 10-7, has a single active element whose length is exactly half the wavelength of the radio frequency at which the antenna will operate (at 2.4 GHz, that's about 2.35 inches). Quarter-wavelength elements will also work. Additional elements, called reflectors and directors, are located parallel to the active element at very specific intervals determined by the size of the active element. Reflectors are located behind the active element, while the directors are in front of it. Most of the rooftop television aerials that were common before the days of cable and satellites were yagis.

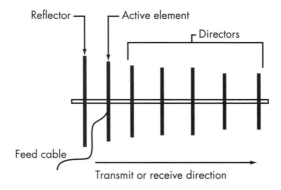

Figure 10-7: A yagi antenna has one active element, one reflector, and several directors.

A yagi always has just one reflector, which is about 5 percent longer than the active element, and several directors, which are about 5 percent shorter than the active element (each additional director should be slightly shorter than the one behind it). As you add more elements to a yagi, the amount of gain increases. If you want to consider building a yagi of your own, take a look at Rob Flickenger's antenna built inside a Pringles potato chip can at *http://www.oreillynet.com/cs/weblog/view/wlg/448.*

Many designs for home brew 2.4 GHz yagi antennas use one-inch washers as reflectors, directors, and active elements. This will work, but it's not ideal for two reasons: First, at 2.437 GHz (the center frequency of Wi-Fi channel 6) a quarter-wavelength active element should be about 1.16 inches long, so those washers are about 16 percent smaller than they ought to be for ideal performance; and second, the reflector and directors are the same size as the active element, which reduces the gain (or sensitivity) of the antenna. But considering that the whole thing was built out of about $7 worth of parts, it's close enough. If a pair of these antennas gets your signal from here to there and back again at high speed, it really doesn't matter that the reflectors and directors aren't exactly the right size.

Darren Fulton's more traditional 13-element design at *http://www.users .bigpond.com/Darren.fulton/yagi/13_element_yagi_antenna_for_2.htm,* shown in Figure 10-8, uses antenna elements cut to length from heavy-gauge brass or copper wire and a reflector made of sheet aluminum.

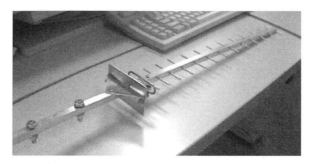

Figure 10-8: Darren Fulton's home brew yagi antenna has a total of 13 elements.

A yagi isn't the only type of directional antenna that lends itself to build-it-yourself designs. Waveguide antennas, with a radiating element inside a reflective metal cylinder or cone, use another extremely effective design. The antenna's performance depends on the size of the enclosure, the length of the radiating element, and its exact position. Greg Rehm's instructions for assembling a tin can waveguide antenna are online at *http://www .turnpoint.net/wireless/cantennahowto.html*.

If you want to boost your signal gain in all directions, you should use an omnidirectional antenna. The instructions at *http://jgomsi.com/obelix/wireless/ guerrilla2/* are a good place to start.

Based on the tests and measurements posted on the Internet for these and other home brew antennas, it appears that they're both effective and cheap, especially if you don't include the value of your time when you calculate the cost. It's all a matter of attitude: If you thought "that sounds like a fun project" when you read about building a home brew antenna, go for it. But if spending an afternoon with a soldering iron in your hand sounds like a form of cruel and unusual punishment, remember that an inexpensive commercial antenna will do the same job just as well, with a lot less effort.

11

CONNECTING TO AN EXISTING WI-FI NETWORK

For many people, connecting to the Internet when they're away from home or the office is more important than operating or using their own network. Wi-Fi signals in schools, libraries, airports, coffee shops, and conference centers, aboard trains and buses, and even in city parks and highway rest areas go a long way toward making your laptop computer or other portable a go-anywhere Internet appliance. In many urban areas, it seems as if there are Wi-Fi networks almost everywhere. When you open your computer's wireless network setup program in a city center or a residential neighborhood, it often detects half a dozen or more Wi-Fi signals. Depending on your location, many of these signals are likely to be business office LANs or home networks, but many others are public networks that welcome connections from outside users (that's you). Some of these services charge by the hour (or by the month) for Internet access, but many others are free.

This chapter explains how to find Wi-Fi access points that will allow you to connect and how to choose the best access point when your computer detects more than one nearby network.

Public Wi-Fi Is Not Secure

Any time you use a public Wi-Fi hot spot, there is a very real possibility that somebody else is reading everything that moves to and from your computer, including your login names and passwords, email, instant messages, and personal information on web pages. Wi-Fi network monitor programs that can capture and display Wi-Fi data packets as they move through the air are easy to find and use. Other programs can use that captured data to crack your WEP or WPA keys. Figure 11-1 shows a network monitoring program in action.

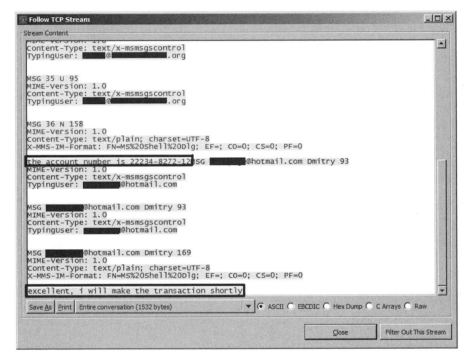

Figure 11-1: Wireshark, a freely available packet sniffer, allows unsavory latte drinkers to listen in on your online coffee house conversations. The figure shows a sensitive chat session in MSN Messenger—but whenever you're on a public network, remember that all your unencrypted email, chats, and web browsing are subject to similar public scrutiny. Behave accordingly!

Just because a Wi-Fi hot spot is operated by your hotel or a well-known chain of coffee shops or bookstores doesn't meant that your data is secure. Somebody in a car parked nearby (or the hotel room next door) could be watching your keystrokes as you type them—or even modifying them as they go.

Therefore, it's essential to remember that public Wi-Fi connections are not secure. Don't use a Wi-Fi hot spot in a hotel, coffee shop, conference center, or any other location to send or receive information that you would not want to share with everybody else in the room (or in the hotel room next door).

On the other hand, there isn't a Wi-Fi data thief behind the potted plant in every hotel lobby and airport waiting area. If you exercise some common sense—don't conduct online banking or send your credit card number (or any other confidential information) from a public hot spot—you should be able to strike a balance between security and convenience.

Whenever possible, encrypt your traffic with a VPN or other mechanism (see Chapter 15 for ways to do this). This will not only protect your data from prying eyes, but it will help prevent someone from injecting malicious data into your system.

Remember that not all websites use SSL (denoted by *https* in the URL and the padlock icon at the top or bottom of the window in most browsers, as shown in Figure 11-2) to encrypt the entire session. Often only the login is encrypted to protect the username and password, but the following pages are not protected to save CPU resources from encrypting data from thousands or millions of users.

Figure 11-2: All browsers use variations on the padlock icon to signify a secure (HTTPS) connection.

Finding a Wi-Fi Hot Spot

The easiest and most obvious way to find a Wi-Fi network is to turn on your computer and run its Wi-Fi control program. The network adapter will scan for nearby signals and display a list like the one in Figure 11-3, which shows the unsecured signals available in the lobby of a hotel next to Seattle's Lake Union. When you're in an unfamiliar neighborhood (or even just a few blocks away from your usual haunts), you might not know which networks would welcome your connection and which ones are private. Just because the owner of a network hasn't bothered to turn on encryption doesn't mean it's an open invitation for you to use that network.

AD HOC NETWORKS

You can also see a bogus public network in Figure 11-3 that claims to offer "Free Public WiFi." Notice, however, that the icon next to the Free Public Wifi network displays a computer-to-computer link—an *ad hoc* network. This could really be a direct link to a computer operated by a thief trying to steal your passwords and other private data that he can later use to read your email or drain your bank account. More likely, it's a victim of the ad hoc network bug described later in this chapter. If your computer identifies a nearby network as a free Wi-Fi site, you should not trust it. Don't bother connecting to open ad hoc networks without the "Free Wifi" name—they won't let you get online anyway. The only time you should trust an ad hoc network is when you're deliberately exchanging data with another computer in the same room.

In Figure 11-3, the two *ibahn* signals are the hotel's Wi-Fi hot spots; *cascadelink* and *kenmoreair* are access points in the waiting room for the Kenmore Air seaplane base across the street.

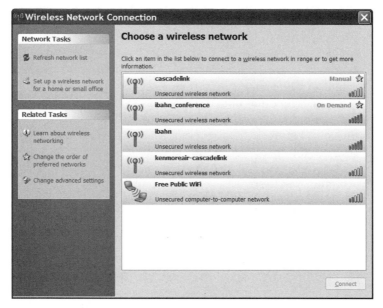

Figure 11-3: The Windows Network Connection window provides a list of nearby networks.

The best approach is often to do some research *before* you try to connect—either consult an online directory of hot spots (such as *http://www.wifinder.com, http://www.netstumbler.com/hotspots,* or *http://www.wififreespot.com*) before you leave home, or look for some kind of "Wi-Fi Here" sign near the door or cash register at a coffee shop, the information desk at the library, or some other obvious location. If you can find an instruction sheet or information card that provides details about a public network you want to use, be sure to connect to that network's SSID rather than some other unknown signal that your system detects nearby.

If you subscribe to a specific public Wi-Fi service, such as Boingo or T-Mobile, you can download and install a program that can identify that company's sites and automatically set up a connection. Figure 11-4 shows the T-Mobile Connection Manager.

When you choose the Wi-Fi option at the right side of the window and choose Networks, the Connection Manager program scans for nearby signals and displays a list in the window shown in Figure 11-5. This image was taken at the same location as the one in Figure 11-1.

NOTE   *If you have trouble connecting to your email server or IM system on a paid Wi-Fi network, try running a web browser such as Internet Explorer or Firefox first. Many subscription services use the browser to display a login/password screen.*

Figure 11-4: The T-Mobile Connection Manager provides access to Wi-Fi and other broadband wireless networks.

In spite of your best intentions to check out the directories and guides before you leave home, you will probably find yourself in a new location where you want to find and use a Wi-Fi network to connect your computer to the Internet. The control programs supplied with your Wi-Fi adapter, your computer's operating system, and your computer all make it easy to identify and choose the best nearby network signal; sniffer programs such as NetStumbler (also called Network Stumbler) provide even more information about each network that you can use to make a more informed choice.

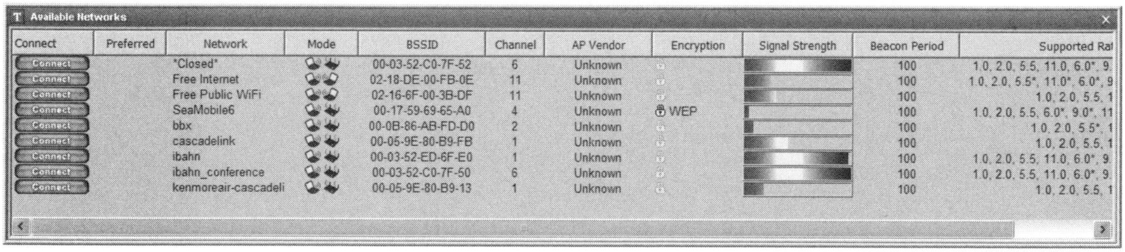

T Available Networks											X
Connect	Preferred	Network	Mode	BSSID	Channel	AP Vendor	Encryption	Signal Strength	Beacon Period		Supported Rat
Connect		*Closed*		00-03-52-C0-7F-52	6	Unknown			100		1.0, 2.0, 5.5, 11.0, 6.0*, 9
Connect		Free Internet		02-18-DE-00-FB-0E	11	Unknown			100		1.0, 2.0, 5.5*, 11.0*, 6.0*, 9
Connect		Free Public WiFi		02-16-6F-00-3B-DF	11	Unknown			100		1.0, 2.0, 5.5, 1
Connect		SeaMobile6		00-17-59-69-65-A0	4	Unknown	WEP		100		1.0, 2.0, 5.5, 6.0*, 9.0*, 11
Connect		bbx		00-0B-86-AB-FD-D0	2	Unknown			100		1.0, 2.0, 5.5*, 1
Connect		cascadelink		00-05-9E-80-B9-FB	1	Unknown			100		1.0, 2.0, 5.5, 1
Connect		ibahn		00-03-52-ED-6F-E0	1	Unknown			100		1.0, 2.0, 5.5, 11.0, 6.0*, 9
Connect		ibahn_conference		00-03-52-C0-7F-50	6	Unknown			100		1.0, 2.0, 5.5, 11.0, 6.0*, 9
Connect		kenmoreair-cascadeli		00-05-9E-80-B9-13	1	Unknown			100		1.0, 2.0, 5.5, 1

Figure 11-5: The T-Mobile Connection Manager detects nearby Wi-Fi networks.

To find a Wi-Fi network, simply turn on your computer and run your favorite Wi-Fi network setup program. Some public networks are open to anybody who wants to use them, but many others require an account (paid or otherwise) with the network's operator. When you connect to an account-holders-only network, you will see a login screen each time you try to use your web browser or other Internet application program with the network.

Keeping Your Data Secure

Any time you connect to the Internet through a public hot spot, be sure your computer's firewall is active to keep other people from connecting to *your* computer while you're collecting email, swapping instant messages, or blogging about the current speaker at the conference you're attending.

Both Windows (XP and Vista) and Mac OS X include built-in firewalls, as do all the standard Linux distributions. For more about firewalls and other network security issues related to wireless networks, see Chapter 12.

It's equally important to remember that nonelectronic methods of stealing data can be just as effective as monitoring your wireless signals through another computer. When you send and receive email or instant messages, and when you type an unsecured account name and password in a public place such as a coffee shop, a library, or a conference, you're running two kinds of risks: a data monitor program (also known as a *snooping* program) on a nearby computer can capture your password as you send it, and a shoulder surfer can watch your screen and keyboard and note your login information as you type it into the computer.

The best way to protect your data from over-the-air monitoring is to use a virtual private network (VPN) between your portable computer and the LAN at your office or home. Chapter 15 offers detailed information about installing and using a VPN. If that's not possible, wait for a secure connection before you conduct financial transactions or send private email. The only way to keep your critical data absolutely secure is to never send it through a Wi-Fi network. That might sound like an extreme statement, and it probably is, but it's nonetheless true.

NOTE *Don't assume that your Wi-Fi connection is secure just because you're alone in a hotel room or an office. That Wi-Fi signal can easily pass through walls and floors to a data snoop in another room or in a car parked on a nearby street.*

Keeping other people's eyes away from your screen requires a different kind of protection. If possible, find a table in a coffee shop or other public location where you can sit with your back to a wall so nobody can look over your shoulder without your knowledge. If that's not practical, when you're in a lecture hall or the audience of a public event, or when you're aboard an airplane or a train, consider using a privacy filter (made by 3M and others) over your computer's screen that makes it impossible to see the image unless you're directly in front of it. Once again, the most effective way to protect your data from unwanted attention is to wait until you can use the computer privately.

NetStumbler and Other Sniffer Tools

A *sniffer tool* is a program that uses a wireless network adapter to scan for active networks and displays the characteristics of each network. NetStumbler is a very slick Windows utility that will find network characteristics and display a list, like the one in Figure 11-6, that shows everything you need to know about a detected network signal, including the MAC address, SSID, channel number, and the signal strength and quality. If you have a global positioning system (GPS) device connected to your computer, NetStumbler can also identify the exact latitude and longitude of the location where it detected the strongest signal from each access point, and it can estimate the distance between your current location and the access point. Among other things, NetStumbler displays numeric values for the signal strength and noise level of each network, rather than just a set of bars. This can be particularly helpful when you're looking for the best possible location for an access point or aiming a directional antenna to find the strongest possible signal.

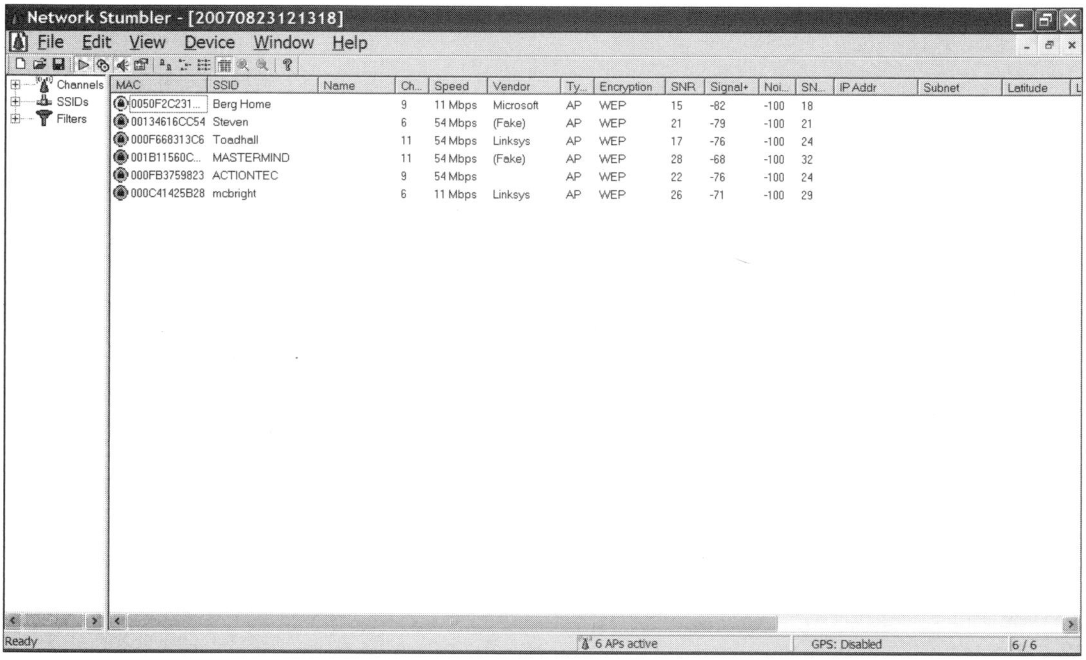

Figure 11-6: NetStumbler finds and displays extensive details about every wireless Ethernet signal that it can find.

For most of us, NetStumbler and other sniffers can pull more Wi-Fi information out of the air than we'll ever need, but if you're trying to map all the signals and compare the signal quality of your own complex Wi-Fi network, or if you're curious about the technical details of nearby networks, sniffers can be useful tools. NetStumbler is *beggarware,* which means that it's available at no cost, but users who consider it to be useful are invited to send an unspecified donation to the developer. You can download NetStumbler from *http://www.netstumbler.com/downloads.*

Several other more complex Wi-Fi sniffer tools are also available, but most of them require a computer running Linux or Unix. The TuxMobil website (*http://tuxmobil.org/linux_wireless_sniffer.html*) is a good source for links to information about Wi-Fi sniffers and scanners. One of the most popular is Kismet (available from *http://www.kismetwireless.net*), which includes tools for sniffing wireless packets, identifying networks, and detecting intrusion into your own computer. Kismet was created by Mike Kershaw, the technical reviewer of this book. You can find descriptions of more of these programs at the usual software sources for your own Unix or Linux distribution or from SourceForge.net (*http://www.sourceforge.net*).

Public Hot Spots

If you don't know which public wireless service has the network service contract at the airport where you're waiting to change planes, or at the convention center where you're attending meetings, you'll have to let your computer search for a signal. If you don't already have an account with a particular wireless service provider, most of them allow new users to set up new accounts on the spot.

Airports and Conference Centers

Providing public wireless network service to airport terminals is a new and growing industry that appears to be simple from the consumer's point of view—just install enough access points to cover all the concourses and the airlines' lounges, connect them to a broadband Internet trunk, and wait for customers to start paying for network access. It sounds like a license to print money. Of course, it's not that simple. Nothing that involves a government-owned airport authority and a facility that supports dozens of different radio services for everything from air traffic control to rental car returns and shuttle buses is ever easy. Things get even more complicated when the airport signs a franchise agreement with one wireless service and every airline contracts with a different company to provide wireless service to all of their VIP clubs.

It seems as if the management of every airport has come up with a slightly different set of answers to these questions. Therefore, you can't assume that the account you set up to connect in the Admirals' Club in Chicago will also work at the waiting area near gate A-14 in Seattle. The only way you can find out is to fire up the computer and see what signals it detects. If the Wi-Fi utility tells you that it has found a signal, remember to look at the menu or window that shows the names of all the networks within range. If you have an account with one of those networks, go ahead and log in. If not, choose the network with the best signal quality and set up a new account. To avoid falling into a theft-of-data trap, be sure to avoid connecting to any signals that your computer identifies as ad hoc networks.

If you travel through the same airports a lot, or if you belong to one or more of the airlines' VIP clubs, you will want to set up a prepaid account with the company that provides service to those locations. When you find yourself in an airport (or any other location) that uses a different service, you can sign up for a pay-as-you-go account on the spot.

Wi-Fi service in conference centers is similar. You might need a paid subscription to one of the public Wi-Fi services, but more and more conference organizers provide free Wi-Fi connections. To connect, turn on your laptop or other wireless device and look for a strong signal. If necessary, ask a conference official for the SSID of the hot spot supplied by the hotel or conference center.

Hotels

Wi-Fi is available in most upscale hotels, major brand-name motels, and luxury vacation resorts. Wireless access to the Internet has become almost as common as a television in each room and free morning coffee. Some properties include Wi-Fi service as a standard amenity at no extra charge, while many others require guests to pay extra for Internet use.

To avoid an unpleasant surprise on your bill, it's always a good idea to ask about Wi-Fi charges when you check into a hotel. Some places might automatically add an inflated charge for network access unless you specifically refuse it, even if you connect to their network for just a few minutes. Like wildly expensive long-distance telephone calls, some innkeepers treat Internet access as one more potential opportunity to gouge their guests.

If you're staying at a hotel or motel that charges an unreasonable amount for Wi-Fi (more than about $10 per day), tell the desk clerk that you will not be using the service, so they should not charge you for it. Take your laptop computer to a nearby coffee shop, café, public library, or some other nearby hot spot where you can connect at a lower cost, or even better, for free. Or if you travel a lot, consider using a broadband wireless data service like the ones described in Chapter 13 to completely bypass the hotel's Wi-Fi network.

Many networks in hotels and other businesses will ask you to provide a login and password before they allow you to connect to the Internet, even if they don't charge for the service, to restrict access to their own customers. You should receive an instruction sheet when you check in or find one on a table or desk in your room that explains exactly how to connect.

Aboard Planes, Trains, Buses, and Other Moving Targets

Mass transit systems and long-distance passenger railroads around the world also offer Wi-Fi service to their passengers; you can even find Wi-Fi networks aboard the ferry boats that sail across Puget Sound in Washington and Sydney Harbour in Australia. Wi-Fi on commercial airliners is less common, but a few international carriers do offer Wi-Fi service on long-haul flights. You can expect to find a lot more airborne wireless access in the next few years.

Connecting to a mobile hot spot is no different from connecting to any other Wi-Fi network, but it's particularly important that you select the onboard service rather than one that might be coming from outside the vehicle; otherwise you will move out of signal range almost immediately. Turn on your computer, run the Wi-Fi control program, and choose the network you want to use. The mobile network that travels along with you on the bus, boat, or train should be obvious from its name.

Wi-Fi services that offer connections from moving trains, buses, or whatever generally cost more than other public Wi-Fi services because the Internet connection is more complicated and because you're a captive audience— either pay the fee or go without a connection.

Municipal Wi-Fi Networks

Public Wi-Fi services with multiple access points that cover an entire neighborhood or even a whole city seem like the logical extension of individual hot spots. It seems like a very good deal for city governments, who often think they can collect franchise fees or payments to place Wi-Fi antennas on utility poles and possibly obtain free wireless Internet service for government agencies while they provide high-speed Internet access to their communities. The idea of use-it-anywhere Wi-Fi, both for laptops and other portables, and as an alternative to cable and DSL connections, seems like a logical new type of public utility, just like electricity and the public water supply. Therefore, many towns and cities around the world are looking at either building their own wide-area Wi-Fi networks or contracting with a private service provider.

Public Wi-Fi hasn't worked out as well as many vendors and local governments had hoped and expected, especially in major urban centers. The trade magazines and websites that keep track of such things are full of reports that one city after another has either delayed the start-up of their municipal Wi-Fi networks or had the private networking company that was building the system for them fail to deliver the service on schedule or even cancel their contracts. The initial gold rush mentality that seems to drive entrepreneurs toward any new technology has been replaced by a wait-and-see position: Until somebody figures out how to actually make money on a citywide system, the vendors are hesitant to move forward.

It turns out that community Wi-Fi networks have several possible problems. Signals from outdoor antennas don't always provide reliable signals inside houses and commercial buildings without additional hardware; many people who already subscribe to wired DSL or cable Internet services don't want to pay for another subscription that duplicates what they already have; and some of the new broadband wireless data services, such as the ones we'll describe in Chapter 13, don't require nearly as many individual access points, so they're far less costly to build and maintain. Without a base of new subscribers, the network suppliers don't want to spend money on the network infrastructure.

In spite of these initial difficulties, a few towns and cities are already offering municipal Wi-Fi services, and others will follow. If you live or work in a place where a public Wi-Fi network is on the air, it can be a convenient alternative to the ones you've been using in coffee shops, bookstores, and other locations as a supplement to your own home and office networks.

After 2009, when many broadcast television stations in the United States move to different channels (2011 in Canada), even more wireless data options will probably appear. Eventually, some kind of wide-area wireless Internet service will probably become available in many cities and towns around the world. Whether that service uses Wi-Fi, WiMAX, or some other technology remains to be seen.

Like most other paid Wi-Fi networks, most municipal networks display a login and password entry window after you connect. In a few cases, the network provides some small amount of access time at no cost so you can send and receive email or conduct a brief instant messaging session before the payment meter begins to run.

"Free Public WiFi"

There's an odd Wi-Fi nuisance that claims to be a network called *Free Public WiFi* or *Free Internet Access* or some similar name, which is caused by a bug in many Wi-Fi control programs (including the one in Windows). Everybody loves something free, so it's very tempting to click on that network and try to connect, especially when the alternative service charges by the hour or by the day. Connecting to one of these networks probably won't damage your computer or destroy any data, but they're false signals that you should know about and avoid. These signals are particularly common at airports, hotels, and other locations where a lot of people are using their laptops at the same time within a relatively small area.

If a Wi-Fi control program has one or more ad hoc networks in its list of preferred networks, it sends out a beacon signal whenever it searches for a connection, and every other nearby Wi-Fi adapter receives and displays the name of that network (for example, *Free Wi-Fi Service*). When the owner of one of *those* computers tries to connect to the "free" network, the control program adds the name to its preferred list, and it sends out yet another beacon signal. And so it goes, quietly creating more useless new beacon signals all the time. In a busy airport waiting area, you might see half a dozen or more separate *Free Wi-Fi* ad hoc network listings in your Wi-Fi control program.

The original *Free Wi-Fi* signal was probably a network cracker who wanted to steal passwords and other data from unsuspecting travelers. However, the bug in the Wi-Fi control programs that causes it to reproduce itself has created a wireless worm that is more of a nuisance than a serious security threat.

Figure 11-7 shows a Windows Wireless Network Connection program that has detected three separate bogus ad hoc networks. In this case, these signals are probably coming from laptop computers in hotel rooms directly above the lobby where the image was captured.

If you look closely at the Wi-Fi control program, you will notice that each of these signals is coming from an ad hoc (computer-to-computer) link rather than a Wi-Fi access point, so there's a different kind of icon associated with that network's listing. If your Wi-Fi control program shows the properties of each signal, you will discover that the addresses of the *Free Public WiFi*, *Free Internet*, and *hpsetup* networks all begin with *02-XX*, which is not a legitimate MAC address number.

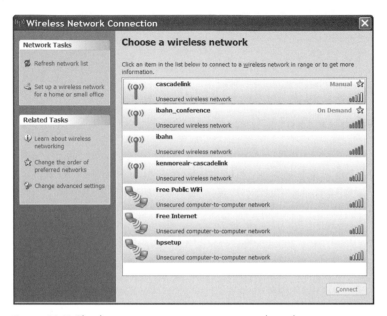

Figure 11-7: The three computer-to-computer networks in this screen are not what they appear to be.

In spite of the tempting names, you should *not* try to connect to any of these networks. In most cases, you probably won't connect to anything, but your computer will add *Free Public WiFi* (or whatever name the beacon is using) to your own list of approved networks, and it will start sending out yet another ad hoc signal with the same name. Worse yet, if your computer does create an ad hoc network with another computer nearby, the person using that other computer might be able to open and read your files.

NOTE   *If you do connect successfully to the Internet through one of these bogus hot spots and read your email, use instant messaging, or do anything else that requires a login and password, there's an excellent chance that somebody will grab your data as it moves through the network. Be sure to change all your account names and passwords—yes, all of them—as soon as possible.*

If your computer connects to one of these sites automatically, disconnect or turn off your Wi-Fi adapter immediately. To make sure your computer doesn't continue to send out a *Free Wi-Fi* beacon, follow these steps:

1.   Open the Network Connection control program you normally use.

2.   If *Free Public WiFi* or any other ad hoc network that you don't normally use appears in the list, select it (but don't click the Connect button) and open the Advanced Settings (in Windows), Profiles window (in Intel PROSet), or the section that controls preset connection profiles. In Windows, open the Wireless Networks tab, as shown in Figure 11-8.

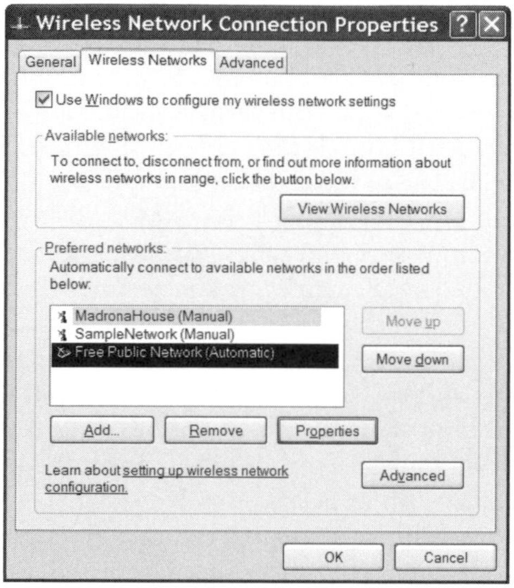

Figure 11-8: Use the Wireless Network Connection Properties window to remove a bogus ad hoc network profile.

3. Select the profile you want to delete from the list of profiles or Preferred Networks, and click the **Remove** button.

4. Click **OK** to save your action and close the window.

In the Intel PROSet program, you can permanently exclude the name of a bogus ad hoc network by selecting any network name in the main control window and clicking Properties. When the Properties window opens, click Manage Exclusions to open the Exclude List Management window, shown in Figure 11-9, where you can add the name of the false signal.

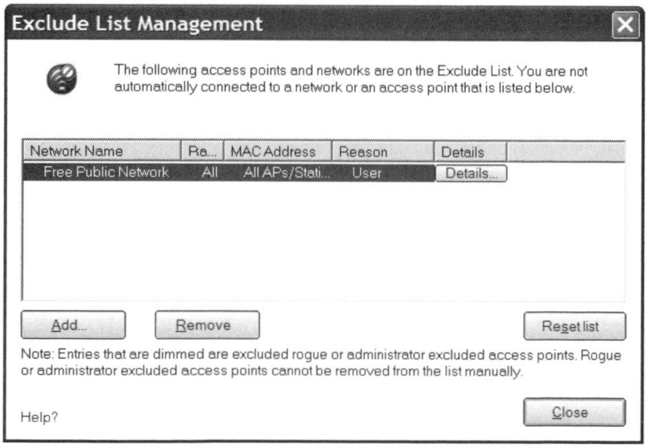

Figure 11-9: Intel's PROSet Wi-Fi software provides an Exclude List.

Unprotected Private Access Points

There's one more source of accessible Wi-Fi signals that we haven't discussed until now: the ones that leak from wireless home and office networks that your neighbors haven't bothered to protect. It can be awfully tempting to grab a connection to one of those networks, but it's both illegal and unethical, even if it is amazingly easy. In many downtown office districts, high-tech industrial parks, and residential neighborhoods, a casual visitor can often find and log in to half a dozen or more wireless networks within a few blocks.

If you can detect a network signal, you might be able to connect through that network to the Internet, but this is legally considered "theft of service"; network managers and law enforcement people frown on it, to say the least.

Of course, nobody with the good sense to read this book would ever consider using somebody else's network or eavesdropping on somebody else's wireless traffic without permission. If you want to try, you're on your own. A few minutes online with a good web search engine can supply a list of factory default SSIDs and WEP codes for many popular network access points and software for cracking WEP encryption. Many users, especially in home networks and small businesses, don't turn on encryption because it's "too complicated" or "too much trouble" or because nobody told them that it's important (consider yourself advised: It's important). Many more never bother to change their default IDs and passwords.

This kind of wireless network hacking is sometimes described as *wardriving*, as an extension of the older hackers' practice of wardialing—using a modem to dial random telephone numbers in search of computers with unprotected dial-in ports.

Some unprotected wireless networks actually welcome public access, so there's a legitimate reason for wardriving (or warwalking with a Wi-Fi enabled PDA or smartphone). Even if you don't actually try to set up a connection to a network, it can be instructive (and yes, entertaining) to wander around to see what's out there, but when you click that Connect button on your neighbor's network without permission, you're breaking the law.

In general, wardriving, or guerilla networking, or whatever you want to call it, is one of those activities, like monitoring your neighbors' cordless telephone conversations, that are sort of fun but not within the limits of polite conduct. Yeah, you can argue that anybody who's dumb enough to operate an unprotected wireless network deserves to have other people use it, or that the bandwidth is right out there for the taking, but that's not likely to convince the owner of the network (or the nice policeman who comes knocking on your car door while you're online) that your intentions are entirely honorable and that you're not doing anybody any harm.

If you treat wardriving as a nonintrusive hobby, like those people who take their radio scanners to a railroad freight yard and listen to conversations between train dispatchers and individual locomotive engineers, or bird-watchers who keep a book that lists every species they've ever seen, then it's probably quite harmless. But when you cross the line and actually establish an unauthorized connection, you should understand exactly what you're doing—stealing bandwidth.

It's not common, but police have actually arrested people for stealing a Wi-Fi connection. In 2006, the owner of a Vancouver, Washington coffee shop complained about a man who had used her Wi-Fi hot spot from his parked truck several times a week for three months without ever buying anything. The cops charged him with theft of services. A year later, the BBC reported that another man in the English town of Redditch, Worcestershire was cautioned for "dishonestly obtaining communications services with intent to avoid payment." And yet another person was fined £500 in London for "hijacking a wireless broadband connection."

And even if the Network Police don't come and arrest you for theft of service (which is possible but highly unlikely), you're also risking your own data; some unprotected networks are operated by people who hope you will use them because they're logging all your keystrokes and other data, including your email password, credit card numbers, and other personal information.

Of course, when you're on the other side of this fence, it's in your interest to prevent unauthorized users from connecting through your access point. At the very least, you should understand that Wi-Fi networks are not absolutely secure, and every access point and network adapter radiates signals that can be detected by outsiders. You can take steps to restrict access to your network, but you can't keep the existence of the network a secret from a serious snoop. As manager of your own wireless network, this should raise a whole lot of questions in your mind. Questions like: Is my network secure? Can somebody on the street connect to my network without my knowledge? How do I keep those #*@&$! out of my network? For the answers to these and other questions about wireless network security, go immediately to the next chapter of this book.

12

WIRELESS NETWORK SECURITY

 Wireless networks are not secure. Let me repeat that: Wireless networks are not secure. They are safe enough for many users most of the time, but it's just not possible to make a network that uses radio to exchange data absolutely private.

Wireless networks are a trade-off between security and convenience. The obvious benefits of a wireless network connection—fast and easy access to the network from a portable computer or an isolated location—come at a cost. For most users, the convenience of wireless operation outweighs the potential security threats. But just as you lock the doors of your car when you park it on the street, you should take similar steps to protect your network and your data.

The simple truth is that a wireless network uses radio signals with a well-defined set of characteristics, so somebody who wants to dedicate enough time and effort to monitoring those signals can probably find a way to intercept and read the data contained in them. If you send confidential information through a wireless link, an eavesdropper can copy it. Credit card numbers, account passwords, and other personal information are all vulnerable.

An entire catalog of tools for cracking Wi-Fi encryption methods is easy to find on the Internet. 3G broadband and WiMAX networks might be more secure than Wi-Fi ones (primarily because capturing data from them is more difficult), and WPA encryption is better than WEP encryption, but no wireless security is perfect. Encryption and other security methods can make data a little more difficult to steal, but they don't provide complete protection against a really dedicated snoop. As any policeman will tell you, locks are great for keeping out honest people, but serious thieves know how to get past them.

NOTE   *Wireless network encryption (such as WPA or WEP) takes place at the data layer of the OSI model (discussed in Chapter 1). The encryption is performed on all data that is sent across the network. Other encryption methods are also available: VPNs (virtual private networks) operate above the TCP layer and can provide additional encryption, and SSL (which secures HTTPS website traffic) is specific to the application.*

To make things even more dangerous, many network managers and home wireless users leave the doors and windows to their networks wide open to intruders by failing to use encryption and the other security features that are built into every Wi-Fi access point and network node. "Drive-by logins" to unprotected private networks are possible in many urban and suburban business districts and in a surprising number of residential neighborhoods. When Wi-Fi was still a new technology, the *San Francisco Chronicle* reported that a network security expert with a directional antenna mounted on the roof of a van in downtown San Francisco could log in to an average of half a dozen wireless networks *per block*. That number would be much greater today. A year later, a group of Microsoft employees who ran an "unofficial" test found more than 200 unprotected access points in a suburban neighborhood outside Seattle. Today, most people have gotten the message about using encryption on their home and office networks, but too many of them are still using the older WEP encryption system rather than the much more secure WPA method. The technical support people at one major telephone company, Qwest, were still advising their DSL customers to use WEP encryption as late as mid-2007.

If you're located in a city center or a suburb, you can probably see this for yourself. When you use your Wi-Fi control program to scan the networks in your neighborhood, you will probably see a list of nearby networks in addition to your own access point. The control program will also tell you what kind of encryption (if any) each network is using. In the example shown in Figure 12-1, one network (RedGoldandGreen) is wide open, and four others are encrypted; two of the encrypted networks use WPA, and the two that are listed as "security-enabled" without an encryption type use WEP.

Do the math: your access point has a range of 150 feet or more in all directions, so the signal probably extends beyond your own property lines (or the walls of your apartment or office). A network device in the building

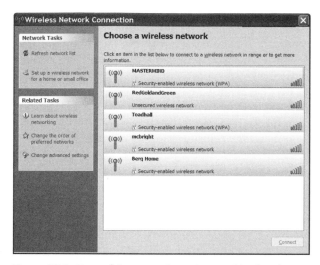

Figure 12-1: Four of the networks in this neighborhood require an encryption key before they will connect.

next door or across the street can probably detect your network. And so can a laptop or PDA inside a car parked on the street. If you don't take some precautions to prevent it, the operator of that device can log in to your LAN, steal files from your servers, and tie up your Internet connection with streaming videos or multiplayer games.

It's important to understand that we're talking about two different kinds of security threats to a wireless network. The first is the danger of an outsider connecting to your network without your knowledge or permission; the second is the possibility that a dedicated eavesdropper can steal or modify data as you send and receive it. Each represents a different potential problem, and each requires a different approach to prevention and protection. While it's certainly true that none of the encryption tools currently available can provide complete protection, they can make life more difficult for most casual intruders. And as long as they're out there, you might as well use them.

An unsecured wireless network presents many opportunities to an attacker. Not only are the network crackers able to monitor any data that moves through the network, but they might also be able to modify it. If, for example, there is a vulnerability in your web browser, an attacker can replace images as you view them with an image that exploits that vulnerability and installs a trojan on your computer, allowing the attacker to steal data stored on the computer that *you never sent over the wireless network*. This type of attack might be relatively rare (casual snoopers are unlikely to take the time on the chance you have something interesting), but it still presents a serious risk. Also, many popular websites encrypt the login page with SSL encryption via HTTPS, but they don't encrypt subsequent pages to reduce the drain on processing power—your password might be secure, but any email you read via the webmail interface might not be, and attackers might be able to steal the cookie (a unique piece of data included with web information) that identifies your login and access your mailbox directly.

Protecting Your Network and Your Data

As the operator of a Wi-Fi network, what can you do to discourage intruders? There are a few techniques that can make things difficult for them. First, you can accept the fact that wireless networks are not completely secure and use the built-in network security features to slow down would-be intruders; second, you can supplement your wireless router's built-in tools with a hardware or software firewall (or both) to isolate the wireless network; and third, you can deploy additional encryption such as a VPN to secure traffic to the network.

The security features of the early Wi-Fi protocols (WEP encryption) were not adequate to protect data. The WEP protocol was flawed in several ways. The basic encryption method (the RC4 algorithm) was known to have weaknesses in certain applications, it required all users to know the key, and provided no secure mechanisms for distributing new keys. Most of these shortcomings were acknowledged and dismissed as being outside the scope of the goal of providing the same protection that a user on a standard wired network would receive, but, in fact, the result was that wireless equivalent privacy was little better than no protection at all. Recent attacks (such as those performed by the aircrack-ptw tool) have further undermined WEP because they've often been able to disclose an encryption key in a matter of minutes by analyzing a limited amount of traffic. With these developments, WEP should be treated more as a "do not disturb" sign than as a real means of protection.

The WPA and WPA2 standards attempt to fix the shortcomings of WEP, but they only work when all of the users of a network have modern cards and drivers. Most, if not all, cards made in the last few years will support WPA or WPA2.

For most of us, the more serious danger is not that people will eavesdrop on our messages, but that they will create their own connection to our network and either read files stored on computers on the LAN or steal the broadband connection to the Internet without our knowledge. However, business networks must take extra precautions to protect their (and their customers') data. Several high-profile compromises of customer credit card data in major retail chains have been traced to inadequate network protection.

It's essential to maintain control of your network. Here are some specific steps to take:

- Don't use your access point's default SSID. Those defaults are well known to network crackers.

- Change the SSID to something that doesn't identify your business or your location. If an intruder detects something called BigCorpNet and they look around to see BigCorp headquarters across the street, they'll home right in on that network. Same thing for a home network; don't use your family name or the street address or anything else that makes it easy to figure out where the signal is coming from.

- Don't use an SSID that makes your network sound like it contains some kind of fascinating content—use a boring name like, oh, *network5*, or even a string of gibberish, such as *W24rnQ*. If a would-be cracker sees a list of nearby networks, yours should look like it's the least interesting of the lot.

- Change your access point's IP address and password. The factory default passwords for most access point configuration tools are easy to find (and they're often the same from one manufacturer to another—hint: don't use *admin*), so they're not even good enough to keep out your own users, let alone unknown intruders who want to use your network for their own benefit. If an outsider gets into the access point's software, they could lock you out of your own network by changing the password and the encryption key.

- If possible, place your indoor access point in the middle of the building rather than close to a window. This will reduce the distance that your network signals will extend beyond your own walls.

- Use WPA encryption rather than WEP. WPA encryption is a lot more difficult to break, especially if you use a complex encryption key.

- Change your encryption keys often. It takes time to sniff encryption keys out of a data stream; every time the keys change, the miscreants trying to steal your data are forced to start again from scratch. Once or twice every month is not too often to change keys in a home network. An office LAN should change keys at least once a week.

- Don't store your encryption keys in plaintext on the network where they are used. This seems obvious, but in a widespread network, it might be tempting to distribute them on a private web page or in a text file. Don't do it.

- Don't use email to distribute encryption keys. Even if you're not sending emails in plaintext, an intruder who has stolen account names and passwords will receive the messages with your new codes before your legitimate users get them.

- Add another layer of encryption, such as Kerberos, on top of the encryption built into the wireless network. See *http://web.mit.edu/kerberos/www* and *http://www.isi.edu/~brian/security/kerberos.html* for downloads and more information about Kerberos.

- If it's practical on your network, turn on the access control feature in your access point. Access control restricts network connections to network clients with specified MAC addresses. The access point will refuse to associate with any adapter whose address is not on the list. This might not be practical if you want to allow visitors to use your network, but it's a useful tool in a home or small business network where you know all of your potential users. MAC address filtering will not prevent a determined attacker from copying the address of an authenticated user, but it could provide an additional layer of protection.

- Test your network's security by trying to find and use your network from outside your own building. Take a laptop computer running a sniffer program, such as NetStumbler or your network adapter's control program, and start walking away from the building. If you can detect your network from a block away, so can an intruder.

- Turn on the security features, but treat the network as if it was wide open to public access. Make sure everybody using the network understands that they're using a nonsecure system.

- Limit file shares to the files that you really want to share; don't share entire drives. Use password protection on every share.

- Use the same firewall and other security tools that you would use on a wired network. At best, the wireless portion of your LAN is no more secure than the wired part, so you should take all the same precautions.

- Consider using a VPN for added security.

Protecting Your Computer

Network security goes both ways—the network manager doesn't want unauthorized users messing with the network, and individual users don't want anybody to get to their personal files. When you're logged in to a public network, you should take some precautions to prevent anybody else on the network from reading your files.

In Windows Vista and Windows XP, there isn't a central place to turn off file shares, so you must turn off each share separately. Follow these steps to turn off sharing:

1. Open the **My Computer** window.

2. The icons for some or all of your shared drives and folders might appear with a hand "serving" the icon. To turn off sharing, right-click the icon and choose **Sharing and Security** from the menu.

3. Turn off the **Share this folder on the network** option.

4. Click the **OK** button to close the dialog box. When the My Computer window appears, the sharing hand will no longer be under the name of the folder or drive letter.

5. Repeat the process for every shared folder or file. Don't forget the Shared Documents folder.

When you get back to your own office or home network, you'll have to reverse the procedure to start sharing your files again.

What about the danger of somebody grabbing your data as it passes through the radio link? It can be done, even if you're using encryption. You have to assume that any data transmitted through a wireless network is not secure. A determined eavesdropper with the right equipment and software can copy your data packets as they move through the air. It's possible, but it's not likely unless you are a target of government surveillance or industrial espionage.

The only way to be absolutely sure that nobody is monitoring your wireless network is to stop using it. But it's even easier to monitor the cordless phone in your kitchen. In general, you can assume that a connection through a public network is no more or less secure than a link to your own network. If somebody is serious about stealing your network packets, they will probably find a way to do it.

Wi-Fi Security Tools

The security tools in the Wi-Fi specifications aren't perfect, but they're better than nothing. Even if you choose not to use them, it's essential to understand what they are and how they work, if only to turn them off.

Network Name (SSID)

As you learned in Chapter 3, every wireless network has a name. In a network with just one access point, the name is the basic service set ID (BSSID). When the network has more than one access point, the name becomes the extended service set ID (ESSID), but your computer's control program displays both types in the same list. The generic designation for all network names is the SSID, which is the term you will see most often in wireless access point and client configuration utility programs.

When you configure the access points for a network, you must specify the SSID for that network. Every access point and network client in a network must use the same SSID.

When a network client detects two or more access points with the same SSID, it assumes that they are all part of the same network (even if the access points are operating on different radio channels), and it associates with the access point that provides the strongest or cleanest signal. If that signal deteriorates due to interference or fading, the client will try to shift to another access point on what it thinks is the same network. This transfer is called a *hand off*.

If two different networks with overlapping signals have the same name, a client will assume that they're both parts of a single network, and it might try to perform a hand off from one network to the other. From the user's point of view, this misdirected hand off will look as if the network has completely dropped its connection. Therefore, every wireless network that could possibly overlap with another network must have a unique SSID.

The exceptions to the unique SSID rule are public and community networks that only provide access to the Internet but not to other computers or other devices on a LAN. Those networks often have a common SSID, so subscribers can detect and connect to them from more than one location. In other words, if you have an Internet access account at your local coffee shop, you might find and use exactly the same SSID when you visit another shop owned by the same company.

A network's SSID provides a very limited form of access control because it's necessary to specify the SSID when you set up a wireless connection. The SSID option in an access point is always a text field that will accept any name you care to assign, but many network configuration programs (including the wireless network tools in Windows XP and those supplied with several major brands of network adapters) automatically detect and display the SSIDs of every active network within their signal range.

It's not always necessary to know the SSID of a network before you try to connect; the configuration utility (or a network monitor or sniffer program like NetStumbler) will show you the names of every nearby network in a list or a menu (the exceptions are networks in which the Broadcast SSID feature has been turned off). For example, Figure 12-2 shows the result of a NetStumbler scan at Seattle-Tacoma Airport, where Wayport served the passenger terminal and MobileStar provided coverage in the American Airlines VIP club.

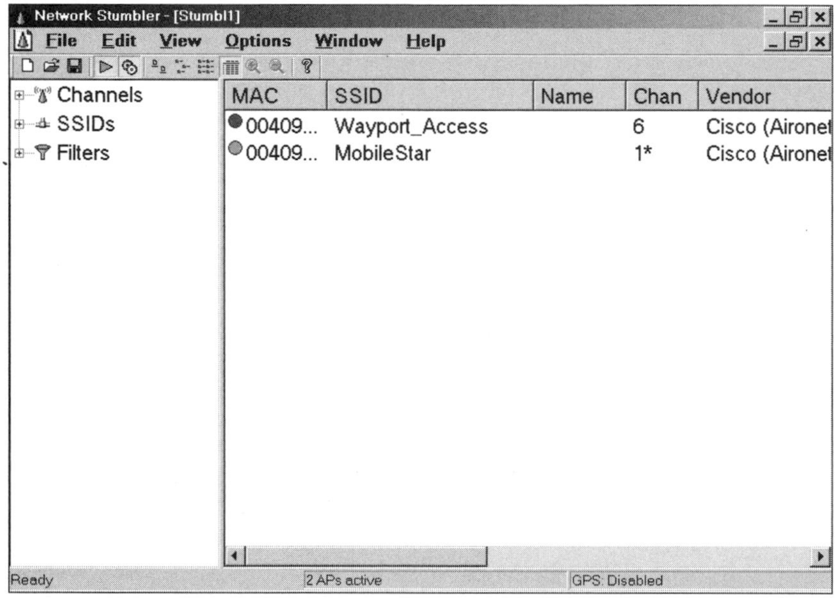

Figure 12-2: NetStumbler and many configuration utilities display the SSIDs of every nearby wireless network.

WARNING   *Every access point comes with a default SSID setting. These defaults are well known and documented within the community of network snoops (see, for example, the lists of access points and defaults compiled by members of SeattleWireless.net at* http://seattlewireless.net/arlan/ssid_defaults-1.0.5.txt). *Obviously, the defaults should never be used in any active network. Make sure you change the access point's administrative login and password while you're at it.*

Normally, most Wi-Fi access points send out beacon signals that broadcast the network's SSID. When a network adapter performs a radio scan, it detects those beacon signals and displays a list of nearby SSIDs in its control program.

However, it's possible to disable the SSID broadcast so the network doesn't show up on most control program scans. To connect a computer to a network whose name is not visible, you must instruct your control program to search for the relevant SSID.

Nonbroadcast SSIDs are not completely invisible. A sniffer program (such as NetStumbler) can still detect it and display the SSID, and every time a user connects to the network, the network adapter sends the SSID in a packet that can easily be sniffed. Disabling the SSID broadcast might, in some cases, make it easier for an intruder to later attack the laptop of one of your users (this is a more serious issue for businesses or corporate network administrators than for people running home networks). Because the laptop cannot know if the hidden network is available, it must constantly probe for it, announcing its presence and giving an attacker much of the information needed to spoof the hidden network. Because a hidden network must be in a laptop's Preferred Networks list, it will automatically connect to the spoofed network.

WEP Encryption

WEP encryption is an option in every Wi-Fi system, so it's important to know how it works, even if you choose not to use it. As the name suggests, the original intent of the wired equivalent privacy (WEP) protocol was to provide a level of security on wireless networks that was comparable to that of a wired network. That was the goal, but a network that depends on WEP encryption is almost as vulnerable to intrusion as a network with no protection at all. It will keep out the casual snoops (and your freeloading neighbors, if they're not particularly adept at cracking encryption), but it's not particularly effective against a dedicated intruder. The more recent WPA encryption is *always* the better choice.

WEP encryption is intended to serve three functions: it prevents unauthorized access to the network, it performs an integrity check on each packet, and it protects the data from eavesdroppers. WEP uses a secret encryption key to encode data packets before a network client or an access point transmits them, and it uses the same key to decode the packets after they have been received. The original standard used shared authentication, in which the access point sends a challenge packet that a client must encrypt with the proper WEP key and send back. However, this technique opens a significant vulnerability by allowing a snooper to watch both parts of the exchange and figure out the key. The "open" authentication method, which should be used by any network using WEP (not that any network should use it), simply discards packets that cannot be decrypted by the network's WEP key.

Therefore, the WEP settings must be exactly the same on every access point and client adapter in the network. This sounds simple enough, but it gets confusing because manufacturers use different methods to identify the size and format of a WEP key. The functions don't change from one brand to another, but identical settings don't always have identical descriptions.

How Many Bits in Your Encryption Key?

A WEP key can have either 64 bits or 128 bits. Although 128-bit keys are more difficult to crack (but they are still pretty insecure), they also increase the amount of time needed to transmit each packet. However, confusion arises because a 40-bit WEP key is the same as a 64-bit WEP key, and a 104-bit key is the same as a 128-bit key. The standard 64-bit WEP key is a string that includes an internally generated 24-bit initialization vector and a 40-bit secret key assigned by the network manager. Some manufacturers' specifications and configuration programs call this *64-bit encryption*, but others describe it as *40-bit encryption*. Either way, the encryption scheme is the same, so an adapter that uses 40-bit encryption is fully compatible with an access point or another adapter that uses 64-bit encryption.

Many network adapters and access points also include a *strong encryption* option that uses a 128-bit key. Devices that support strong encryption are downward compatible with 64-bit encryption, but it's not automatic, so all of the devices on a mixed network of 128-bit and 64-bit devices will operate at 64 bits. If your access point and all of your adapters accept 128-bit encryption, use a 128-bit key. But if you want your network to be compatible with adapters and access points that only recognize 64-bit encryption, configure the entire network to use 64-bit keys.

In practice, the choice of 64- or 128-bit WEP encryption doesn't make much difference. Tools are easily available that can crack both types, although cracking a 128-bit key might take a bit longer.

Is Your Key ASCII or Hex?

The length of the key is not the only confusing thing about setting WEP encryption. Some programs request the key as a string of ASCII characters, but many others want the key in hexadecimal (hex) numbers. Still others can generate the key from an optional passphrase.

Each ASCII character has 8 bits, so a 40-bit (or 64-bit) WEP key contains 5 characters, and a 104-bit (or 128-bit) key has 13 characters. In hex, each character uses 4 bits, so a 40-bit key has 10 hex characters, and a 128-bit key has 26 characters. In Figure 12-3, the Wireless Setting screen for a D-Link access point, the 40-bit Shared Key Security field uses hex characters, so it has space for 10 characters. The D-Link program runs all 10 characters together in a single string, but some others split them into 5 sets of 2 digits or 2 sets of 5. The key looks the same to the computer either way, but it's easier to copy the string when it's broken apart.

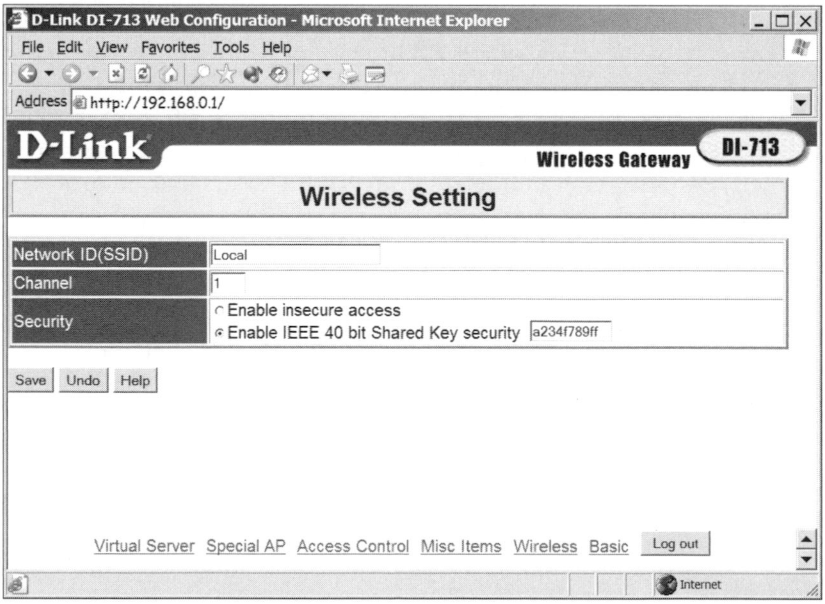

Figure 12-3: The configuration utility for a D-Link access point accepts WEP keys in hex format.

A passphrase is a string of text that the adapters and access points automatically convert to a string of hex characters. Because humans can generally remember actual words or phrases more easily than hex gibberish, a passphrase can be easier to distribute than a hex string. However, a passphrase is only useful when all the adapters and access points in a network come from the same manufacturer.

What Are the Options?

Like just about everything else in a Wi-Fi configuration utility, the names of the encryption options are not consistent from one program to the next. Some use a straightforward set of options such as "enable WEP (or WPA) encryption," but others use technical language taken from the formal 802.11 specification.

Some access points also offer an optional shared key authentication option that uses encryption when a network client has the key, but uses unencrypted data with other network nodes.

Mixing Hex and ASCII Keys

Setting up a mixed network becomes more complicated when some network nodes use hex only and others require ASCII keys. If that's the situation in your network, you will want to follow these rules for setting the encryption keys:

- Convert all your ASCII keys to hex. If a configuration program demands an ASCII key, enter the characters *0x* (zero followed by lowercase letter *x*), followed by the hex string. If you're using Apple's AirPort software, you'll have to enter a dollar sign ($) at the beginning of a hex key.

- Make sure all your encryption keys have exactly the right number of characters.

- If all else fails, read the security sections of the manuals for your network adapters and access points. It's possible that one or more of the devices in your network has some obscure proprietary feature that you don't know about.

Is WEP Secure Enough To Use?

Several academic computer scientists have published reports about WEP encryption that argue against trusting it to protect confidential data. They all point to serious flaws in the cryptographic theory and practice that were used to define the WEP encryption algorithms. These experts are unanimous in their recommendations: If you use an 802.11 wireless network, you cannot rely on WEP for security; you should employ WPA to protect your networks.

A group at the University of California, Berkeley has identified numerous flaws in the WEP algorithm that make it vulnerable to at least four different kinds of attacks:

- Passive attacks that use statistical analysis to decrypt data
- Active attacks that construct encrypted packets to mislead the access point into accepting false commands

- Attacks that analyze encrypted packets to construct a dictionary that can be used to automatically decrypt data in real time
- Attacks that alter packet headers to divert data to a destination controlled by the attacker

The Berkeley report, which you can read online at *http://www.isaac .cs.berkeley.edu/isaac/wep-faq.html*, concludes with an unequivocal statement: "Wired Equivalent Privacy (WEP) isn't. The protocol's problems are a result of misunderstanding of some cryptographic primitives and therefore combining them in insecure ways."

Researchers at Rice University and AT&T Labs published a description of their attack against WEP encrypted networks (*http://www.securitytechnet .com/resource/hot-topic/wlan/wep_attack.pdf*) that led them to a similar opinion: "802.11 WEP is totally insecure." They were able to order and receive the necessary hardware, set up a network for testing, design their attack tool, and successfully capture a 128-bit WEP key in less than a week.

Both the Berkeley and the AT&T Labs reports are written by and for technical experts who have a background in cryptography. Their conclusions are clear, but their methods assume that an intruder has some serious technical knowledge. However, it doesn't take a network expert to crack WEP encryption; tools for less sophisticated code breakers are also easy to find. Both AirSnort (from the Shmoo Group, *http://airsnort.shmoo.com*) and WEPCrack (*http://sourceforge.net/projects/wepcrack*) are Linux programs that monitor wireless network signals and exploit the weaknesses in the WEP algorithm to extract the encryption key. There are dozens of others. Just a few minutes with Google or any other Internet search tool is all it takes to find WEP cracking tools and detailed instructions for using them.

Recently announced attacks against WEP, implemented in tools such as aircrack-ptw, can break WEP keys in a matter of minutes using a very limited amount of data—sometimes as little as 10 megabytes of data gathered from a single network user and a few seconds of processing on a modern laptop.

Bottom line: Go ahead and encrypt your network data, but use WPA rather than WEP if you possibly can. Encrypted data is more secure than plaintext transmission, and it takes time to crack a WEP key, so WEP does add another (extremely weak) layer of security, especially if you change keys frequently. WEP encryption might not do much to protect you against serious attackers, but it will probably keep out the casual network eavesdropper who stumbles onto your network from across the street and the drive-by network snoop. It's a lot easier to break into an unencrypted network (and there are still plenty of them out there), so a cracker who detects your encrypted signal will probably move on to a target with less protection.

WPA Encryption

WPA encryption was developed as a partial solution to the security problems that make WEP encryption less than totally secure. WPA is much safer than WEP, but cracking WPA is still possible.

WPA is more secure because it uses a method called *Temporal Key Integrity Protocol (TKIP)* to automatically change the encryption key after a specified period of time or after the system exchanges a specific number of packets. Because WPA changes the key frequently, it's a lot more difficult for a cracker to gather enough information to decipher its encryption code.

In large networks, WPA uses an authentication server to verify the identity of each network user. The server uses Remote Authentication Dial-in User Service (RADIUS) and the Extensible Authentication Protocol (EAP) to exchange encryption keys with the computers and other devices that are connected to the wireless network.

In home networks and smaller business networks that don't have a server, a method called *pre-shared key (PSK) mode* uses a passphrase stored in the access point in place of the authentication server. To connect to the network, users must enter the same passphrase on their computers or other network devices (or set their devices to automatically enter the passphrase). When you set up WPA encryption, you must specify whether the network uses a server or PSK mode.

Any access point and network adapter that supports 802.11g or 802.11n should also recognize WPA encryption. If you're using an older 802.11b or 802.11a access point, it might still be possible to add WPA encryption by installing the latest versions of firmware and drivers. Look in the support or downloads section of the manufacturer's website for free upgrade instructions and software.

PSK Passphrases

A WPA-PSK passphrase can be a string of either 8 to 63 ASCII characters or 64 hexadecimal digits. The passphrase that you enter into a network device must be exactly the same as the one stored in the access point. Obviously, typing 64 digits correctly is not something that you want to do frequently, so the ASCII alternative is the better choice for most users. For optimal security, the ASCII passphrase you assign to your network should be a random mixture of at least 20 characters including letters (capitals and lower case), numbers, and punctuation marks.

A PSK network uses the passphrase to set up the initial connection between a client (such as a computer or PDA) and the access point. After the connection is in place, the TKIP assigns new encryption keys to every packet or group of packets.

The PSK combines with your network SSID to calculate the final key value. It is important to choose a unique SSID and a strong passphrase. Attackers can build large tables of SSID and PSK pairs for common network names and dictionary words, performing weeks of calculation once with the payoff of nearly instantly determining the key of any network that matches that pair of values. Choosing strong passphrases and unique SSIDs can mitigate this type of attack.

Using WPA Encryption

When you set up a new network, the security section of the access point's configuration software will ask if you want to use encryption, and if so, whether you want WEP or WPA encryption. Unless you're planning to run an open-access network, you should choose WPA.

In many cases, the access point will offer two or more types of WPA encryption. If your network includes a RADIUS server, choose EAP. If the network has no encryption server, use the WPA-TKIP option.

For a network user, providing a WPA key is just as easy as providing a WEP key. Most network adapters made in the last few years automatically recognize the type of encryption embedded in each Wi-Fi signal that they detect, so the control program might ask for an encryption key without specifying whether it's a WEP key or a WPA key.

WPA Security

It was probably inevitable that somebody would take the added security features in WPA encryption as a challenge and develop a WPA cracking tool. Several such tools are out there, so WPA does not provide the impenetrable protection that some of its proponents might want you to believe. In particular, programs called coWPAtty and Aircrack-ng both use *dictionary attacks* on WPA-TKIP networks to try thousands or millions of possible keys until it finds the correct ones. Because each additional letter, number, or other character in a key increases the key's complexity, a long key takes much longer to crack than a short one. This kind of cracking technique takes time because the programs can only try about 50 different encryption keys per second, but eventually, they will find the right passphrase and connect to the target network.

Fortunately, neither of these programs or any of the others aimed at cracking WPA encryption are easy to use, and they can take a lot of time to crack a network, so successful attacks on WPA are not particularly common. It might not be possible or practical to completely protect yourself against attacks, but a long passphrase that includes random numbers and punctuation marks in odd places is usually a better choice than a string of words or numbers alone. In other words, something like *hdt%mzx33wolf$fgilxxq&#smedbxor* is a better passphrase than *nostarchpressbooks*.

Access Control (MAC Authentication)

Most access points include an option that permits the network manager to restrict access to a specific list of client adapters. If a network device with a MAC address that does not appear on the list of authorized users tries to connect, the access point will not accept the request to associate with the network. This can keep intruders from connecting to a wireless LAN, but it forces the network administrator to keep a complete list of users' adapters and their MAC addresses. Every time a new user wants to join the network, and every time an established user swaps adapters or gets a new laptop, PDA, or other device with a built-in adapter, the network manager must add one more MAC address to the list. This is probably manageable in a home or small office network, but it could be a major undertaking for a larger corporate or campus-wide system, if it's practical at all.

MAC authentication does not provide unbreakable protection against unauthorized users because a determined cracker could monitor radio signals from approved users, intercept their adapters' MAC addresses, and load an approved address onto a different adapter. But combined with encryption and other security tools, authentication adds one more impediment in the path of a network cracker.

Every access point configuration utility uses a different format for its access lists. The manual and online documentation supplied with your access point should provide detailed instructions for creating and maintaining an access control list.

The Wi-Fi standards do not specify a maximum size for an access point's access control list, so the numbers are all over the map. Some access points limit the list to a few dozen entries, but others, such as the Proxim Harmony AP Controller, will support as many as 10,000 separate addresses. Still others accept an unlimited number. If you plan to use a list of addresses to control access to your network, make sure your access point will work with a large enough list to support all of your users, with enough expansion space for future growth. As a rule of thumb, the access point should accept at least twice as many MAC addresses as the number of users on your network today.

Some access points also include a MAC address exclusion feature that allows the network manager to block one or more MAC addresses from access to the network.

Virtual Private Networks

Virtual private networks can add one more layer of useful security by isolating the connection between network nodes from other network traffic. A VPN is an encrypted transmission channel that connects two network endpoints through a "data tunnel." Many network security experts recommend a VPN as an effective way to protect a wireless network from eavesdroppers and unauthorized users. You can find more detailed information about setting up and using a VPN in Chapter 15.

Authentication: The 802.1x Standard

Because of the security gaps in the WEP encryption specification, many wireless network equipment manufacturers and software developers have adopted yet another IEEE standard, 802.1x, to add another layer of security to their networks. The 802.1x standard defines a structure that can support several additional forms of authentication, including certificates, smart cards, and one-time passwords, all of which offer more protection than the access control built into 802.11. In 802.11 networks, a technique called the Robust Security Network builds upon the 802.1x framework to restrict network access to authorized devices.

Most end users need to know two things about 802.1x: First, it's built into some (but not all) Wi-Fi hardware and software, including the wireless configuration utility supplied with Windows XP and many recent access point products, so it can provide one more potential layer of security; and second, it has serious flaws that a dedicated network cracker can exploit to break into a wireless network. The ugly technical details are in an analysis prepared by two researchers at the University of Maryland, available online at *http://www.cs.umd.edu/~waa/1x.pdf.*

Firewalls

If you accept the idea that encryption and 802.1x do not provide adequate protection for a wireless LAN, the next logical step is to find another way to keep intruders out of your network. You also need a firewall.

A firewall is a proxy server that filters all the data that passes through it on the way to or from a network, based on a set of rules established by the network manager. For example, a firewall might reject data from an unknown source or files that match a particular source (such as a virus). Or it might pass all data moving from the LAN *to* the Internet, but only allow certain types of data *from* the Internet. The most common use of a firewall in a LAN is at the gateway to the Internet, as shown in Figure 12-4. The firewall monitors all inbound and outbound data between the computers on the local network on one side and the Internet on the other. This kind of firewall is intended to protect the computers on the LAN from unauthorized access from the Internet.

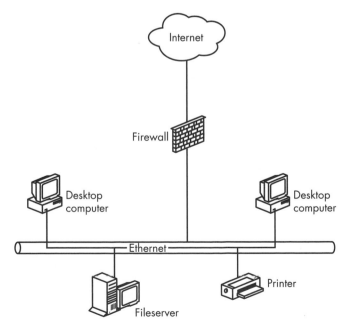

Figure 12-4: A network firewall isolates a LAN from the Internet.

In a wireless network, a firewall can also be placed at the gateway between the wireless access points and the wired network. This firewall isolates the wireless portion of the network from the wired LAN, so intruders who have connected their computers to the network without permission can't use the wireless connection to reach the Internet or the wired part of the LAN. Figure 12-5 shows the location of a firewall in a wireless network.

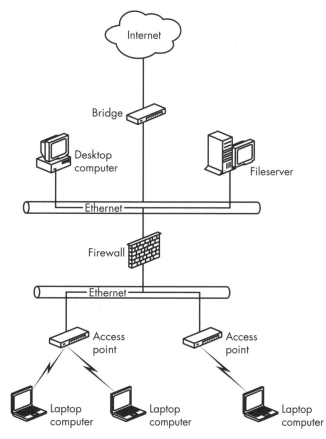

Figure 12-5: A firewall in a wireless LAN can act as a protected gateway to the wired portion of the same network.

Keep Wireless Intruders at Bay

Most people who try to tap into a wireless network don't care about the other computers on the local network; they're looking for free high-speed access to the Internet. If they can't use your network to download files or connect to their favorite web pages, they'll probably move on to find some other unprotected wireless hot spot. That doesn't mean you should store confidential data in file shares on unprotected computers, but if you can limit or restrict access to the Internet, it will make your wireless network a lot less attractive to intruders.

A firewall in a wireless network can perform several functions: It acts as a gateway router between the wireless network and a wired LAN or a direct connection to the Internet, blocking all traffic moving from the wireless side to the wired network that doesn't come from an authenticated user, but it does not interfere with commands, messages, and file transfers from trusted users. Therefore, a legitimate user can connect to network nodes on the wired part of a mixed LAN or onto the Internet, but an intruder would be cut off at the firewall.

Because authorized users and intruders are both on the unprotected side of the firewall, it does not isolate wireless nodes from one another. An intruder can still gain access to another computer on the same wireless network and read shared files, so it's a good idea to turn off file sharing in any computer connected to a wireless network.

A firewall for a wireless network should use some kind of authentication to allow legitimate users through the gateway, but it should reject everybody else. If the access control based on MAC addresses is built into Wi-Fi networks, and the added authentication in 802.1x is not adequate, then an outboard firewall should require each user to enter a login and password before they can connect to the Internet.

If your wireless network includes computers running more than one operating system, your firewall must use a login tool that works on any platform. The easiest way to accomplish this is with a web-based authentication server, such as the one included in the Apache webserver (*http://httpd.apache.org*).

The Apache webserver is available as a Unix application that can run on an old, slow computer with an early Pentium, or even a 486 CPU, so it's often possible to recycle an old junker that is no longer in daily service and use it as a firewall. Both the Apache application and a Unix operating system are available as open source software, so it ought to be possible to build an Apache firewall at extremely low cost.

If you prefer to use Windows rather than Unix, or if you don't want to assemble your own firewall, you have several options. You can use the Windows version of Apache, or you can use a commercial utility such as the ones listed at *http://www.thegild.com/firewall.*

Isolate Your Network from the Internet

Attacks on a wireless LAN don't all come through the air. A wireless network also requires the same kind of firewall protection against attacks from the Internet as every other network. Many access points include configurable firewall features, but if yours does not, the network should include one or more of these firewalls:

- A firewall program on each computer
- A separate router or a dedicated computer acting as a network firewall

Client firewall programs provide another line of defense against attacks through the Internet from outside your own network. Some of these attacks come from miscreants who are looking for a way to read your files and other resources that you don't want the entire world to see. Others might want to use your computer as a relay point for spam or attempts to break into some other computer halfway around the world in order to make the real source more difficult to identify. Still others spread viruses or use Really Unpleasant programs that take over control of a PC and display threatening messages. An unprotected system with a lot of unused storage space can be an attractive target for hackers who want to distribute pirated software, music, or video files (you don't think they store that stuff on their own computers, do you?).

The number of such idiots and creeps out on the Internet is surprisingly large; if you install a firewall that notifies you when an outside computer tries to connect to your network, you will probably see several break-in attempts every day.

Access Points with Firewalls

The easiest firewall to use with a wireless network is one that's built into an access point, such as the D-Link DI-524 Wireless Router (shown in Figure 12-6) and similar products from other manufacturers. This model combines the functions of a wireless access point with a broadband router and an Ethernet switch, so it supports both wired and wireless network clients.

Photo courtesy of D-Link

Figure 12-6: The D-Link DI-524 Wireless Broadband Router
contains configurable firewall firmware.

As you know, a network router provides translation services between the numeric IP address that identifies the LAN to the Internet and the internal IP addresses that identify individual computers within the local network. The firewall normally blocks all incoming requests for data to network hosts, but this creates problems when you want to use one or more of the computers on the local network as fileservers. So the firewall includes a virtual server that redirects certain types of requests to the appropriate computer inside the firewall.

Each request for connection to a server includes a specific port number that identifies the type of server. For example, webservers operate on port 80, and FTP servers use port 21, so those port numbers are part of the request for access. To accept requests for access to a server, you must instruct the firewall's Network Address Translation (NAT) function to forward those requests to a specific computer within the LAN. In Figure 12-7, the virtual server is configured to use the computer with the local IP address 192.168.0.177 as a webserver and 192.168.0.164 as an FTP fileserver. Table 12-1 lists the most common service port numbers.

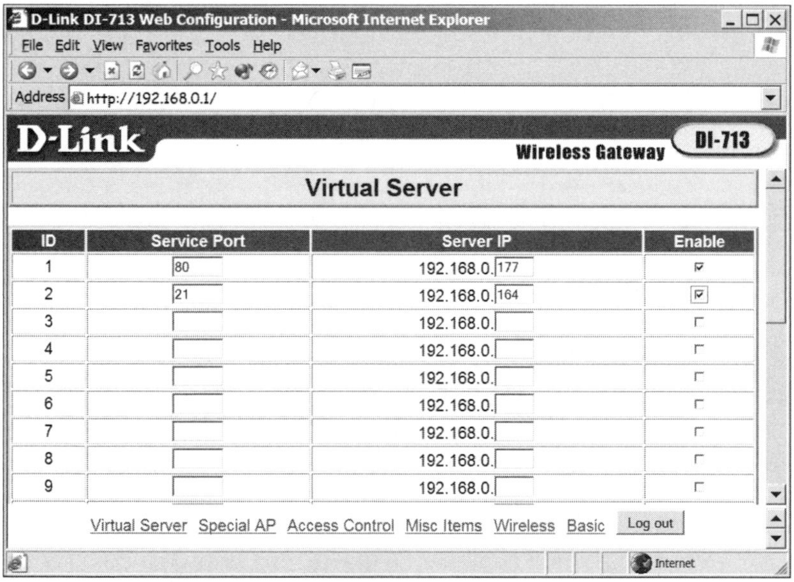

Figure 12-7: The D-Link access point directs requests for access to fileservers to specific computers within the network.

Hundreds of other port numbers have been assigned, but you will never see most of them in actual use. The official list of port assignments is online at *http://www.iana.org/assignments/port-numbers*.

NAT translation assumes that the IP addresses of each virtual server don't change from one request to the next. A webserver on 192.168.0.23 today won't migrate to 192.168.0.47 next week. That's generally not a problem on a wired network, but in a wireless setting where network clients join and depart the network all the time, the DHCP server automatically assigns the next available address to each new client. If one of those clients is also the home of one of the network's service ports, the NAT probably won't find it. This is not a common problem because most networks don't use portable computers as servers, but it can happen. The solution is either to turn off the DHCP server and assign a permanent IP address to each client or move the service port to a computer than has a wired connection to the network and assign a fixed IP address with a number at the high end of the DHCP range (for example, if the range of addresses assigned by the DHCP is from 192.168.1.100 to 192.168.1.200, set the server's address as 192.168.1.199).

Table 12-1: Common TCP/IP Service Port Numbers

Port Number	Internet Service
20	FTP-Data (FTP Default Data)
21	FTP (File Transfer)
23	Telnet
25	SMTP (Outgoing Mail)
37	Time
53	DNS (Domain Name System)
70	Gopher
79	Finger
80	HTTP (Webserver)
88	Kerberos
110	POP 3 (Incoming Mail)
119	NNTP (Network News)
1863	Microsoft MSN Messenger
5190	AOL Instant Messenger
7070	Real Audio and Video

Firewall Software

A wireless gateway firewall at the interface between the access point and the wired part of your LAN will keep intruders from using your network to reach the Internet, and a firewall at the Internet connection will turn away attempts to connect to your network *from* the Internet, but there's still one more form of protection necessary in a wireless network. If somebody gains access to your wireless LAN without permission, you want to keep him out of the other legitimate computers on the same network, so you need to install a client firewall program on each network node.

Client firewalls perform the same functions at a computer's network interface that a LAN or enterprise firewall performs for the entire network; it detects attempts to connect to TCP service ports and rejects them unless they match one or more of the firewall program's configuration settings.

Several good firewall products are available as shareware, and others are free to noncommercial users. It's easy to try them on your own system and choose the one you like best. There's also a firewall built into Windows XP and Windows Vista that is adequate for most home and small-business networks.

Here are some Windows programs:

ZoneAlarm   *http://www.zonealarm.com*

LANguard   *http://www.languard.com*

Unix and Linux users also have plenty of firewall options. Most of them were written for use on stand-alone firewall computers that are commonly used as network gateways, but they could be equally appropriate as protection for individual network clients.

In Linux, the iptables firewall is part of the kernel. It is well documented at *http://www.netfilter.org/projects/iptables/index.html*. Portsentry is a port scan detection tool that is integrated into several widely used Linux distributions. It's available for download from *http://linux.cudeso.be/linuxdoc/portsentry.php*.

IP Filter is a software package that provides firewall services to FreeBSD and NetBSD systems. The official IP Filter website is *http://coombs.anu.edu.au/~avalon*, and there's an excellent HOWTO document at *http://www.obfuscation.org/ipf/ipf-howto.txt*. The program can deny or permit any packet from passing through the firewall, and it can filter by net mask or host address, establish service port restrictions, and provide NAT translation services.

OpenBSD, FreeBSD, and NetBSD can all use the PF, or Packet Filter, facility to perform firewalling functions. More information is available at *http://www.openbsd.org/faq/pf*.

NetBSD/i386 Firewall is another free Unix firewall. It will operate on any PC with a 486 or later CPU and uses as little as 8MB of memory. The NetBSD/i386 Firewall Project home page is *http://www.dubbele.com*.

Turn Off DHCP

The DHCP server in an access point or router automatically assigns a numeric IP address to each computer that is connected to the network. Therefore, it will also assign an IP address to an unauthorized computer that makes it through your encryption and other security tools.

On the other hand, if your network uses fixed IP addresses for each computer, and the access point or router is set to only recognize those particular addresses, the access point or router will reject a connection attempt unless the computer or other device is set to the correct address.

The most common ranges of IP addresses for a LAN are:

- 192.168.0.0 to 192.168.0.255
- 192.168.1.0 to 192.168.1.255

If you use a less common range of fixed IP addresses, it will be more difficult for an outsider to guess a correct address. Several other ranges are also reserved for LANs, including:

- 10.0.0.0 to 10.255.255.255
- 172.16.0.0 to 176.31.255.255
- 192.168.0.0 to 192.168.255.255
- 169.254.0.0 to 169.254.25.255

If, for example, you have 10 computers on your home network, you could set the range of acceptable IP addresses to 172.16.234.20 through 172.16.234.40 and assign a static IP address within that range to each computer.

Of course, this is not as practical for a public network where many users come and go, but it's useful in a home network in which you control all the network nodes.

Don't confuse using static IP addresses with MAC authentication. Both methods restrict access to a specific set of computers, but they use different parts of the connection process to accomplish that goal. While both offer an additional layer of security, they are imperfect. Neither method should be your only means of securing your network.

Turn Off the Power

An intruder can't break into your wireless network if the access point and all of your computers are turned off. If you and your family, or the people in your office are not using your Wi-Fi network, there's usually no reason to let anybody else use it, especially without your permission or knowledge. When you leave home for a few days, or even a few hours, or when you are done with your computers for the night, you can shut down your wireless network by disconnecting the power connector on the access point or using a power strip to turn off power to all of your computers and peripheral devices, including the network access point. When you want to use the computer and the network again, reconnect the power connector or turn on the power strip. Remember to wait until the lights on your DSL or cable modem and wireless access point stop flashing before you try to use the network.

This technique has the added benefit of reducing the amount of electric power the access point and other devices consume. Neither the access point nor any of your other equipment uses more than a watt or two when they're idle, but if you reduce that number to zero, you might see a small reduction in your monthly electric bill.

Physical Security

Up until now, we've been talking about keeping electronic intruders out of your wireless network. It's easy enough to gain access to a network using off-the-shelf equipment that hasn't already been configured for that network; it's even easier when the intruder has stolen a laptop from an authorized user. Losing a laptop computer to a thief is bad enough. Letting the thief use a stolen computer to log in to a network is even worse. As a network operator, you should remind your users that their portables are attractive targets for thieves, and offer some guidelines for protecting them. As a user yourself, you should follow the same precautions.

The first rule is simple: Don't forget that you're carrying a computer. It seems obvious, but London taxi drivers found about 2,900 laptops (and 62,000 mobile phones!) left in their cabs during a six-month period. Uncounted others have been abandoned in airplanes, hotel rooms, commuter trains, and conference centers. It doesn't take a thief to separate a computer from its owner if the owner just walks away.

Don't advertise the fact that you're carrying a computer. Those nylon bags that say *IBM* or *COMPAQ* on the side in great big letters might be handy, but they're not as safe as an ordinary briefcase or a conservative carrier bag.

Next, keep your laptop in your hands or on your shoulder whenever it's not locked in a closet or storage locker. Look away for a minute, and a skilled thief can make it disappear. Airport terminals, railway stations, and hotel lobbies are common places for quick snatch-and-grabs. If you have to use the computer in a public space, use a lock with a steel cable to secure it to an immovable object.

Don't leave an unsecured laptop computer in an office overnight.

Watch out for airport scanners. Make sure you're able to retrieve the computer as soon as it comes off the conveyor belt. Two people working together can do a fine job of delaying you and grabbing the computer before you can get to it. If somebody tries to steal your computer from a security check, make some noise and get help from the security guards.

Make sure your computers and loose components like PC Cards have property labels both inside and out. Engrave your name or company name and telephone number on network interface cards and other removable parts. A company called Security Tracking of Office Property (*http://www.stoptheft .com*) offers registered security plate labels with a cyanoacrylate adhesive that requires something like 800 pounds of pressure to remove and an indelible chemical tattoo marked "Stolen Property" that appears if somebody removes the label.

If you can convince your users to use alarm devices on their computers, that might improve the chances of recovering them. Caveo Anti-Theft PC Cards (*http://www.caveo.com/products/anti-theft.htm*) are motion detectors that analyze a computer's motion and both sound a loud alarm and prevent access to the computer's operating system when the computer has been carried beyond a preset distance. Similar alarm products are available from other manufacturers.

Tracking software is another approach to laptop security. Subscription services such as LoJack for Laptops (*http://www.lojackforlaptops.com*), Computrace (*http://www.absolute.com*), CyberAngel (*http://thecyberangel.com*), and XTool Laptop Tracker (*http://www.stealthsignal.com*) use the computer's communications software to send a "Here I am" signal back to the service. When a subscriber reports that a computer has been stolen, the service uses the locator signal to assist law enforcement authorities in finding it.

Finally, keep a list of models and serial numbers separately from the devices themselves. You'll need that information for your police report and your insurance claim.

When you discover that one of the computers that uses your wireless network has been lost or stolen, it's essential to protect the rest of the network. If possible, change the network's passwords and encryption keys as soon as you can. If your network uses a list of MAC addresses to control access, remove the stolen device's MAC address from the list of authorized connections. Some tools (such as ArpWatch for Linux) provide a mechanism for watching for specific MAC addresses and raising an alert when it detects one of those addresses.

Sharing Your Network with the World

If you use your wireless network to provide public access to the Internet to your neighborhood or campus, or if you want to allow customers and other visitors to connect to your wireless net, you won't want to use encryption or other security tools to limit access to known users, but you should still give some thought to security. Just because you want to give people a direct connection to the Internet, that doesn't mean you want to let them poke around in the other computers connected to your network, so it's necessary to isolate the wireless access points from the rest of the network.

If all of the local nodes on your LAN are connected through wires, the best approach is to place a firewall between the wireless access point and the wired LAN that only allows the access point (and the computers connected to it through wireless links) to communicate with the Internet but not with any local nodes on the wired LAN, as shown in Figure 12-8.

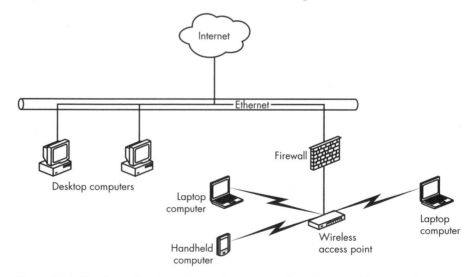

Figure 12-8: The firewall isolates the wireless segment from the rest of the network.

If one or more of your in-house computers uses wireless connections, you must protect them from access by outsiders who are using the public portion of your network. There are several ways to do that: Figure 12-9 shows a wireless network with a software firewall in each in-house computer; Figure 12-10 shows a system that uses two separate wireless networks with different SSIDs that are both connected to the same Internet hookup. In general, the basic rule is to use one or more firewalls to isolate the public portion of your network from the computers that you don't want open to everybody in the world.

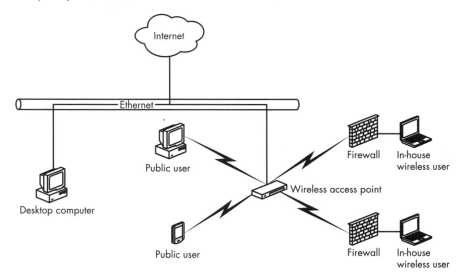

Figure 12-9: Every in-house computer includes a software firewall.

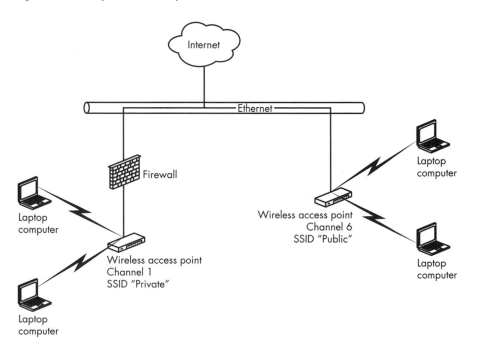

Figure 12-10: The public wireless access point has a different SSID from the access point for in-house users.

Some Final Thoughts About Wi-Fi Security

It seems as if a pattern is emerging, doesn't it? Engineers from interested hardware and software companies gather under the flag of an IEEE task force to develop yet another new set of network security tools to make their products safe from hackers, crackers, eavesdroppers, and other miscreants—and a few months later, an independent researcher at some university or government agency discovers that the new tools have their own serious problems that expose the "protected" data to break-ins and leaks, and yet another cracking program shows up on the Internet, "just to demonstrate the concept." In the meantime, the poor end users of the world are running as fast as they can to keep up, but their wireless networks still aren't completely secure.

If you look at wireless security as a cat-and-mouse game, it's pretty clear that the mice (or is it the cats?) need some sophisticated knowledge and equipment to work around the existing encryption and authentication tools. On the other hand, some of the most advanced tools are freely available to anyone with an Internet connection.

What to do? Is a secure wireless network an unreachable goal? Don't give up hope. WPA encryption is secure enough to keep most intruders out of the vast majority of Wi-Fi networks, and the additional security features included in the new 802.11n specification will provide even more protection. If that's not good enough, you can add a VPN to provide yet another layer of security for your data.

Think of wireless security like the front door to your house: If you leave the door wide open, anybody can walk in and steal your stuff. But when you lock the door and latch all the windows, it will be *much* more difficult for a burglar to enter. An expert can pick the lock, but that takes a lot of time and trouble, and most thieves will look for an unprotected house instead.

13

ALTERNATIVES TO WI-FI: WIRELESS BROADBAND DATA

 Wi-Fi is not the only way to connect a computer to the Internet. Several other methods are also out there, and each of them offers a unique combination of advantages and drawbacks. Wired LANs and connections through power lines are often faster and more convenient than Wi-Fi for fixed installations such as home and office networks; other radio services might be better for connecting your smartphone, laptop, or PDA.

Every connection method is a trade-off among data transfer speed, ease of access, cost, and other features. For many users, the added convenience of a single connection that's available without the need to search for an access point is worth the added cost and the sacrifice in data transfer speed.

This chapter describes the currently available wireless services and offers advice about choosing the best one for your particular needs.

What's Wrong with Wi-Fi?

Thousands of Wi-Fi networks blanket most urban and suburban areas in North America and Europe. Almost every new laptop computer includes a Wi-Fi adapter, and separate plug-in adapters are cheap and easy to install. Access points are inexpensive and convenient. Wi-Fi network connections are generally fast and reliable. So what's not to like?

In spite of its many attractive features, Wi-Fi is not the ideal wireless service for all occasions. Wi-Fi networks have these drawbacks:

- Every time you move to a new location, you must set up a new Wi-Fi connection, often through a different network that requires a different account.

- Public Wi-Fi networks are not available everywhere. Just because your computer detects a handful of signals from Wi-Fi access points doesn't mean that you can connect to them; many are likely to be encrypted private networks.

- Wi-Fi networks have a limited signal range. Unless you're using some kind of high-gain antenna, a network with a single access point typically reaches no more than 300 feet (100 meters) outdoors or a lot less if there are walls between your computer and the base station.

- Wide area campus-wide or larger networks require multiple access points, which can be expensive and complicated to install and maintain.

- Every Wi-Fi network requires a separate login, password, and encryption key.

- Wi-Fi networks are less secure than most wired LANs; even if the network uses encryption and address filtering, a determined snoop can capture and read Wi-Fi data.

- Using a Wi-Fi network adapter can expose your computer to access from other users who could read your files and steal your identity. This is not common, but it's possible.

None of these problems should discourage you from ever using Wi-Fi; it's often faster and cheaper than any other wireless service, and sometimes it's the only available option. But just because there's a Wi-Fi adapter built into your laptop computer, it's not always the best way to connect it to the Internet.

Broadband Data Services

Each type of wide-area broadband wireless service uses a different set of radio frequencies and a different type of modulation, but from a user's point of view, they're all very similar. A built-in network adapter or a plug-in PC Card or USB adapter exchanges data with a network of base stations that covers an entire metropolitan area, highway corridor, or other large geographic region. Unlike Wi-Fi, there's no need to search for an access point before you connect your computer to the Internet; within the service area, you can assume that there's always a usable signal wherever you are. The characteristics that set each service apart from its competitors include the specific coverage footprint, the cost of a monthly subscription, the proprietary control software, and the data transfer speed.

Wide-area broadband services offer these advantages over Wi-Fi:

- Each service offers coverage over an entire region; roaming from one location to another is no problem.

- It's not necessary to maintain separate subscriptions for more than one hot spot or service provider.

- A single connection profile is all you need to connect anywhere; there's no need for a different profile for each access point or service provider.

- The service providers operate and maintain the access points.

- These services operate on licensed frequencies, so interference with other sources of radio signals is not a serious issue.

- Each service provider supplies the network adapter hardware already configured to its frequencies and modulation types; it's not necessary (or possible) to shop for hardware separately.

In practice, if you're within the footprint of a broadband wireless service provider's signal, you can turn on your wireless adapter and expect to connect to the Internet. However, many wide-area broadband networks are often significantly slower than Wi-Fi, and the cost of a monthly subscription is still relatively expensive (although both of these conditions might change in the next few years). Until the broadband providers build out their service areas and expand their roaming agreements with other carriers, no single service offers anything close to universal coverage.

As a general rule, the speed of a wireless Internet service decreases as the coverage area of a single access point expands, so a Wi-Fi link is almost always much faster than a cellular data service. However, there are some exceptions: When WiMAX networks become available, they might be just as fast as Wi-Fi links. Older mobile phone modems are even slower, but they use obsolete technology (such as GPRS), so they're not part of this discussion.

The difference in speed between Wi-Fi and broadband wireless can be dramatic, so some broadband control programs can choose a Wi-Fi signal when it's within range and switch to the slower broadband service when that's the only signal available. When Apple introduced the iPhone, many users complained that AT&T's broadband EDGE connections were much slower than a Wi-Fi signal.

In the future, we can expect to see modems built into new laptop computers that will automatically find and use the fastest available wireless connection to the Internet from any location; if there's a speedy Wi-Fi hot spot nearby, the computer will grab and use that signal, but if it can't find a usable Wi-Fi network, it will connect through your cellular network's slower broadband service instead. Today, some broadband control programs (like the T-Mobile Connection Manager shown in Figure 13-1) allow you to manually select either type of connection from the same window.

Figure 13-1: The T-Mobile Connection Manager controls both Wi-Fi and broadband network connections.

In the T-Mobile program, the panel at the right side of the window shows the relative signal strength of the Wi-Fi and EDGE/GPRS signals that it has detected. *EDGE/GPRS (Enhanced Data rate for GSM Evolution/General Packet Radio Service)* are the technologies that T-Mobile uses for its broadband wireless service. If the faster EDGE service is available, the program automatically uses it; otherwise, it drops down to a slower GPRS data link. When you choose the type of service you want to use, you can either click the Connect button in the center of the window or click the name of the service type to see a list of available signals. In the next generation of wireless control programs, this will all be automatic; the program will choose the best signal and automatically connect your computer to that network.

Comparing Technologies

Today's broadband wireless data services use several different transmission specifications: some of them, including EDGE (Enhanced Data GSM Evolution) and EV-DO (Evolution-Data Optimized), are part of the latest generation of cellular telephone networks. Others use dedicated data-only wireless technologies, such as WiMAX (Worldwide Interoperability for Microwave Access).

In North America, the cellular service providers offer either EDGE or EV-DO. If your cellular carrier uses CDMA (code division multiple access) technology, its broadband wireless data service uses EV-DO; if the cellular service uses GSM (Global System for Mobile Communications), its data service uses EDGE. Both EDGE and EV-DO are sometimes called *3G (third-generation cellular)* services, but EDGE is technically not a true third-generation technology.

Both systems provide data networks that can reach a large area, but the various cellular service providers are still in the process of expanding their coverage footprints. Before you commit to a particular service, it's absolutely essential to test it in the specific locations where you want to use it most often.

There can be a substantial difference in speed between EDGE and EV-DO; EDGE is limited to average speeds of 400 to 700Kbps. The maximum speed of the original (Revision 0) EV-DO networks was only about 300 to 700Kbps, which is similar to EDGE, but the newer EV-DO Revision A (often called *Rev. A*) networks can operate at maximum download speeds up to about 2.4Mbps under ideal conditions (but the average speed is generally around 1.0 to 1.5Mbps, or maybe a little faster). Therefore, you should make sure that your modem and your local service provider are both capable of using Rev. A signals.

Rev. A is not the end of EV-DO development. The hardware manufacturer Qualcomm has announced that it is ready to start making Revision B chip sets (the essential integrated circuits inside modems, adapters, and base stations), which will allow data to move through two or three radio carriers (similar to channels) at the same time. Allowing for handshaking and other network overhead, Rev. B should offer data transfer speed at about 4.5Mbps. By the time the broadband service providers complete their product development and marketing, it will probably be another few years before commercial Rev. B service becomes available.

Either network type (EDGE or EV-DO) offers a substantial improvement over a dial-up link or a GPRS connection, but an EDGE network link is pretty pokey when compared to a Wi-Fi or EV-DO (Rev. A) network.

Both EDGE and EV-DO provide download speeds (from the Internet to your computer) several times faster than their upload speeds (from your computer to the Internet). Unless you're playing multiplayer games, sending huge music or video files, or transmitting some other kind of very large files, this probably won't make much difference to your real-world performance.

The price of wireless data service through either an EDGE or EV-DO network in the United States or Canada is about the same (typically about $60 per month in mid-2007), but you can often find promotions and special deals that might reduce that cost. At a minimum, look for an offer that includes a free network adapter. When WiMAX and other competitive services become available, you can expect the prices of both EDGE and EV-DO access to drop.

NOTE   *If you choose a low-cost measured broadband service (rather than an unlimited "all you can eat" account), remember that the price is based on the total number of bits that pass through the network to and from your computer. Every time your computer checks for new email or instant messages, the bit count increases by a small amount, even if you don't send or receive new messages. All those no-new-messages exchanges can add up over the course of a month.*

Many broadband wireless carriers offer a choice of network adapters as either PC Cards or USB devices. Both contain similar radios, so the performance is likely to be the same with either type. If your computer has a PCMCIA socket, a PC Card is often more convenient than a USB unit, but when you're using your computer in a location with a weak signal, you might be able to find a stronger signal by moving the USB device. If you're indoors, you can sometimes improve performance by placing the USB box close to a window or using a third-party signal booster. Figure 13-2 shows three typical broadband network adapters.

Photo courtesy of Verizon Wireless.

Figure 13-2: Broadband network adapters are available as USB, ExpressCard, and PC Card.

Unlike Wi-Fi adapters, which are sold separately from the wireless services that use them, almost all broadband wireless devices are either supplied to new customers directly from the network service providers or built into new laptops and other portables (often as an extra-cost option). It might be possible to buy a network adapter directly from the hardware manufacturer, but it's a bad idea for several reasons: It will almost certainly cost more than the one supplied with your network contract, a generic adapter won't include the specific firmware that each service provider requires, and the service provider's technical support center won't want to talk to you.

NOTE   *When a broadband adapter is built into a new laptop, that adapter is usually limited to a single service provider that has a marketing deal with the laptop's manufacturer or distributor. Most laptop suppliers offer access to only one or two broadband service providers, so it's important to choose the service provider you want to use. If your laptop is not available with an adapter from your preferred service provider, order the computer without a built-in broadband adapter and use a separate PC Card supplied by the carrier you want to use.*

Choosing a Service Provider

As a general rule, the companies that offer cellular mobile telephone service in your town or city also offer broadband wireless data.

AT&T is the major national EDGE service provider in the United States. Its adapters are available as low-cost options in many brands of new laptop computers, including Dell, Lenovo, HP, and Sony, and it's also the captive broadband service provider for Apple's iPhones (although a quick Internet search should point you to instructions for unlocking an iPhone). The T-Mobile broadband network also uses EDGE. Unless you're living in an area that is not served by a faster EV-DO service, the slower EDGE network service is probably not the best choice because an EV-DO connection will be noticeably faster.

The major national providers of EV-DO service in the United States are Verizon, Sprint, and Alltel. Several other cellular services and telephone companies also offer access to EV-DO wireless data networks, but most of them are resellers of service from one of the big three. For example, Qwest Wireless offers its own branded EV-DO service, but it uses the Sprint network. In Alaska, the major EV-DO provider is ACS wireless. In Canada, both TELUS and Bell Mobility (part of Bell Canada) offer EV-DO service in major population centers nationwide, and some smaller carriers provide their own service in certain provinces.

All the service providers that use the same technology get their wireless network adapters and base station hardware from the same two or three manufacturers, so their performance and reliability are just about the same. The most important differences from one provider to another are often the locations of their radio towers and the quality of the companies' technical support and billing staffs.

The best approach is to compare offers from two or three providers. Total cost per month, cost of a network adapter, and coverage in all the places you expect to visit should all be part of your selection process. If you travel outside your own country, look for a package that includes international roaming. It might also be instructive to call each company's technical support telephone line to see how long you have to wait for a live technician and whether the technician is fluent in English (or your own native language). If possible, ask for a brief trial period for any new service. Most companies will let you return an adapter and cancel your account within a few days if you can't get an acceptable connection.

Many cellular phone companies offer package deals that combine broadband wireless and mobile telephone service, sometimes with other services such as long distance and satellite television as a package deal; call your account representative or visit their retail store for specific details.

Coverage

The first and most important issue to consider when you're shopping for a broadband wireless data service is whether the service provider's signal reaches all the locations where you're likely to use it. If the coverage area (sometimes called the *footprint*) doesn't include your small-town customers' places of business or the highway corridors where you travel, it doesn't matter how good the service might be in downtown Chicago or Denver.

All the service providers are constantly adding new locations to their coverage areas, so you can't always trust the printed coverage map that you might receive from a salesperson. The most reliable coverage maps are the ones on each carrier's website:

Sprint   *http://www.sprint.com*
T-Mobile   *http://www.t-mobile.com/coverage*

Verizon	*http://www.verizonwireless.com*
AT&T	*http://www.wireless.att.com/coverageviewer*
Alltel	*http://content.alltel.com/business/enhanced/ mobilelink_coverage.jsp?state=nat*

If you can convince a service provider to let you try its service in the locations where you're most likely to use it, that's the best possible test. Look for either a try before you buy deal or a satisfaction guaranteed offer that allows you to return the network adapter and cancel your subscription within a week or two for a full refund.

Data Speed

Assuming that more than one service provider can offer service in the place where you want to use it, the service that offers the highest data transfer speed is the best choice. Therefore, an EV-DO (Rev. A) service is preferable to either EV-DO (Rev. 0) or EDGE, and any kind of broadband service is better than an older GPRS service.

Many service providers are gradually improving their higher-speed coverage, so a salesperson might tell you that your neighborhood might not have high-speed service right now, but it's coming soon. Even if this claim is true, if a competing service can supply broadband today, that service should be your first choice (at least for now; you might want to reconsider when your initial contract expires).

Selecting the broadband data service that can provide the fastest connection is particularly important if you use the connection to receive high-bandwidth network content, such as streaming audio and video and image-rich web pages. On the other hand, if you only use your wireless Internet service for email, instant messages, and viewing websites that are limited to text, data transfer speed might not be as important as cost and good reception.

Cost

Broadband wireless service is expensive compared to either wired DSL or cable modem service, and it's extravagant when you compare it with free Wi-Fi access in a library or coffee shop. Therefore, it's worth the time and trouble to compare offers from all of the service providers in your area.

Assuming that the local wireless services are all using the same technology (EV-DO Rev. A if possible) and the coverage footprint of each service includes all the places you expect to take your computer, look for the least expensive offer, both in terms of startup cost and monthly fees.

Many telephone companies offer discounted package deals if you buy more than one service from them. If you order some combination of wired home or business telephone service, long distance, cellular mobile voice, and wireless data from the same company, the service provider might offer you a substantial discount.

Some service providers might offer a lower price or a free network adapter if you commit to a long-term contract, often for two years or more. Read the terms and conditions of the agreement before you sign up for more than a single year—it's quite possible that today's bargain might be more expensive than next year's competitive deals. As wireless technology continues to improve, you might regret locking yourself into a relatively slow network service.

Choosing a Network Adapter

Some broadband service providers call them *modems* rather than network adapters, but just about everybody uses similar PC Cards and USB adapters. Each company loads its own licensed radio frequencies and firmware, but the basic modems are all just about the same.

Each of the major service providers offers a free or very low-cost modem to new subscribers along with one or more extra-cost alternatives. Before you choose an adapter, read the specifications carefully to make sure that the modem supports either EDGE or EV-DO (Rev. A) technology, depending on the service provider. EV-DO (Rev. 0) and GPRS are older, slower systems.

Unless you need the added flexibility of a USB adapter or your computer requires an ExpressCard, choose the service provider's free or least expensive PC Card modem. Remember that the PC Card will operate inside your computer, so you shouldn't care about its physical appearance—a shiny expensive modem probably doesn't work any better than the cheap one that costs $50 or $100 less.

Service and Support

All of the wireless broadband service providers except Clearwire are also cellular mobile telephone companies, so you can expect them to treat their wireless data customers the same way they treat their cell phone users. Unfortunately, that's not good news—the only industries that score lower in customer satisfaction than cellular companies are airlines, news media, and cable television companies (see the American Customer Satisfaction Index at *http://www.theacsi.org*).

However, there's a substantial range between the highest- and lowest-rated service providers, so it's often helpful to ask your friends and colleagues about their experiences and look for reports and evaluations on the Internet and in consumer publications. After you read two or three of these comparisons, you will begin to see a pattern: All the carriers have critics, but some appear to provide consistently better service than others.

It can also be instructive to look at the "I hate *name of carrier*" or "*company* sucks" websites and forums, but don't rely on them for objective reports. The people who post reports to those sites about their terrible experiences are the ones who have had bad experiences; they are probably not a random cross section of the company's customers. However, when the same complaint appears repeatedly, it might be a sign that the company has a real problem. And it's also useful to see how the company itself responds to those complaints.

Broadband Wireless Services Around the World

Like the cellular mobile telephone services that came before them, EDGE and EV-DO broadband wireless data services are available in most of the industrialized world. When you travel, it might be possible to find roaming agreements between your service provider and one or more local companies, but the cost can be very high. Before you leave home, ask your account representative about international service and roaming charges, or consult this website: *http://www.gsmworld.com/roaming.*

As an alternative to expensive international roaming, it's often cheaper to establish a separate account with a local company after you arrive. Look for a store or kiosk in the airport when you arrive, or try one of the links from these web pages:

http://www.novatelwireless.com/regions

http://www.gsmworld.com/roaming

http://en.wikipedia.org/wiki/List_of_Evolution-Data_Optimized_service-providers

http://www.3gtoday.com/wps/portal (click **Operators** for a list)

Connecting to a Wireless Broadband Network

Each broadband service provides proprietary control software along with its network adapters, but they all basically do the same things. For example, Figure 13-3 shows the Verizon Broadband and Sprint Mobile Broadband control programs. There's a picture of the T-Mobile control program in Figure 13-1. The control programs from other carriers offer similar combinations of features.

All of these programs offer the choice of setting up the connection manually by clicking the Connect or Go buttons or automatically establishing a live connection every time you run the program. After you establish a connection, you can use your web browser, email or instant messaging program, and any other Internet application, just as if you were using any other type of Internet connection.

When you're not using the Internet, it's usually a good idea to turn off the wireless adapter or remove it from your computer's PC Card slot, especially if you're using your computer on batteries. When the adapter is off and the Internet link is closed, you're not sending or receiving radio signals, and there's no opportunity (however slight) for a wireless intruder to capture your signals and steal your data or read your files.

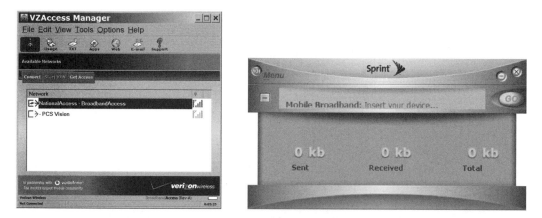

Figure 13-3: Both Verizon and Sprint provide control software with their wireless network adapters.

Using More Than One Computer

Every broadband wireless account is tied to a single modem or network adapter. If you have more than one portable computer, you can either move the modem from one machine to another or obtain more than one account, with a separate modem for each. However, you can use any removable adapter with any computer as long as the control software is installed on the computer; you don't have to tie the adapter to a single computer.

If your family or business owns and uses more than one computer, you have several choices:

- You can buy a broadband account and adapter for each computer.

- You can buy just one account and move the adapter to the computer you're currently using. This might be a good approach if you want to share your broadband account between a desktop computer at home or in the office and a laptop that you use on the road.

- You can buy two or more accounts, with an adapter for each account. Every time you or a family member (or colleague) needs broadband service, you can take an adapter from the pool and return it when you're finished.

If you or your business expects to use more than one broadband account (with an adapter for each), look for a package deal. It might not be listed in the brochure, but every service provider probably has a variety of family plans and special offers for large and small businesses that include free adapters, lower monthly fees, and maybe even a free month or more. Keep asking "Is that your best deal?" until you're convinced that you have a really good offer. Remember that you're a potentially important customer who represents ongoing revenue for the service provider and commissions for the salesperson.

Broadband Security

No wireless network is completely secure, but broadband technology comes closer than Wi-Fi because the service does not share its operating frequency with other radio services, and the service provider controls the hardware at both ends of the network connection. Both EDGE and EV-DO systems use the same methods as mobile telephones to assign a unique electronic serial number (ESN) to each modem and restrict access to the network (and the Internet) to the ESNs that correspond to active accounts. In addition, a broadband connection to the Internet does not move through a LAN, so there's little or no risk that intruders could use a broadband modem as a gateway to the data stored on your computer.

In theory, it would be possible to use a microwave scanner to monitor broadband radio signals or to create a transceiver that spoofs a broadband base station, but we're talking about expensive equipment and sophisticated decoding software. It can probably be done, but it requires a lot more effort than cracking a Wi-Fi signal.

Encryption is not an option, but if you're using a broadband account to connect to a fileserver, email server, or a corporate network, you can use the same kind of VPN that you would use through a Wi-Fi link. Chapter 15 explains how to set up and use a VPN.

Clearwire, Sprint, and Other Pre-WiMAX Services

WiMAX is yet another broadband technology that will combine the speed of a Wi-Fi network and the convenience of EDGE and EV-DO in a single network service. When they become available, WiMAX networks are expected to move data at a maximum speed of about 70Mbps. Even after you allow for a generous amount of overhead, that's obviously a lot faster than anything the current generation of broadband cellular services can offer.

However, full WiMAX service won't be widely available until mid-2008 at the earliest, and it will probably take the service providers several years after that to install base stations and offer comprehensive coverage across the country. By that time, it's possible that today's EDGE and EV-DO networks will be replaced by faster EV-DO (Rev. B) and other high-speed broadband methods. In the meantime, the two major US WiMAX players, Clearwire and Sprint Broadband, are using a slower pre-WiMAX technology that tops out at about 1.5Mbps (many users report even slower connections, depending on their location relative to the nearest radio tower). Between the two companies, pre-WiMAX is available in a growing number of locations. Pre-WiMAX services were initially offered as a wireless alternative to DSL and cable Internet services in offices, homes, and other fixed locations, but Clearwire also offers plug-in PC Cards and, eventually, built-in adapters for both Clearwire and Sprint's Xohm service will be available as an option in new laptop computers. When these become widely available, they're likely to become contenders in the wireless networking marketplace.

Pre-WiMAX systems are as easy to use as wired DSL or cable modem connections to the Internet. After you enter your account information into the modem, it stores those details in its firmware, so it's plug and play: Whenever you turn on the computer and the modem, you have a live broadband Internet link.

If Clearwire's fixed-location pre-WiMAX modems are any indication (the PC Cards were not yet available when this book was written), the network adapters on PC Cards and the laptops that use the same technology will provide clean and reliable Internet connections when they are within range of a base station. However, some users have reported reception problems when the tower is too far away or if there's thick foliage between the tower and their modems.

Clearwire recommends placing the modem (with its built-in internal antenna) next to a window for best performance, and Sprint uses a separate transceiver antenna mounted on the roof or an outside wall. Fixing poor signal quality is usually possible in a fixed-wireless system such as a home or office network, but it's less practical when you're using the same technology with a laptop computer in multiple locations. It remains to be seen whether pre-WiMAX will be practical as a use-it-anywhere wireless Internet access method. When true WiMAX becomes available, the existing pre-WiMAX service providers will supply free or low-cost replacement hardware and software to all their subscribers.

We can expect "real" WiMAX service to be much more reliable because it uses a completely different type of radio modulation and (probably) a different set of frequencies. WiMAX signals will be easier to receive and less susceptible to interference than the current generation of pre-WiMAX services. In the long run, WiMAX might offer a near-ideal combination of high speed and wide coverage without the need to find a new signal and a new account in every new location. If WiMAX fulfills its technical potential, if the business model produces enough money to build widespread networks, and if the WiMAX providers don't take lessons in poor customer service from the cable television and cellular telephone companies, it might become the clear choice for wireless Internet access. In the meantime, pre-WiMAX is worth a look, but don't set your expectations too high.

Broadband Wireless in Automobiles and Other Vehicles

As broadband access to the Internet becomes practical, it's inevitable that many people will begin using online services and resources in their cars, trucks, and other vehicles. Today, many commuter railroads, bus lines, and ferry boats offer onboard Wi-Fi, and similar service is coming to commercial airliners, but that's mostly a matter of passengers using their laptops and other portables from their seats. Mobile Internet services for private vehicles open up a whole new world of possibilities.

Among other things, a live in-car Internet connection could provide instant messaging, email, and some kind of limited access to the World Wide Web, along with live traffic reports and updates to the maps and databases in

GPS receivers and onboard navigation displays. As a supplement or replacement for a car radio, an Internet receiver could also allow drivers and passengers to listen to streaming radio stations and other audio services from around the world; when there's nothing on local radio worth your attention, you can switch to the Internet and choose from a much wider variety of music or talk, even if it's on a station thousands of miles away.

Any mobile Internet connection requires these elements:

- A signal from a wireless Internet service provider
- An antenna to send and receive the wireless signals
- A wireless network interface in a computer, a PDA, or a special Internet appliance

In a vehicle, each of these elements has special requirements that don't usually apply to a stationary connection. The signal must be accessible over a wide enough area that it doesn't disappear as you move from place to place at relatively high speeds (meaning anything faster than walking); the antenna must have a way to bypass the shield created by the metal shell of the vehicle; and the computer or other device must be compact and easy to use, especially if the driver must operate it while the vehicle is in motion.

Today the easiest way to establish an Internet link in a car is to use a laptop, PDA, or other portable with a broadband wireless adapter, possibly with a USB interface to the radio/CD player in the dashboard. If the car is parked within range of a public Wi-Fi signal, you could use Wi-Fi in place of the broadband adapter. Of course, the driver should not try to use a computer unless the car is parked.

Obviously, the control and connection software and the web browser program in a portable computer don't change just because the device is sitting on the passenger seat of an automobile. It still works exactly the same way as it does when your laptop is on a table in a coffee shop or on your lap in an airport's waiting area. The biggest difference is that you and the computer might be moving at relatively high speed, so the network will probably transfer your connection from one base station or radio tower to another.

The broadband wireless and WiMAX networks are designed to handle this kind of hand off, so you might not notice any change as you move around. However, if you move into a location where the network has a lot of active users, you might notice that your connection speed has dropped.

Of course, if you're driving out to the boondocks where there aren't any nearby towers, you could lose the connection completely. This probably won't happen if you stay on the main highways because the network service providers have decent coverage along those roads, but you're on your own when you decide to take the scenic route. If it's absolutely essential to maintain a connection, consult your service provider's website for their current coverage maps before you leave home.

You can also use a broadband wireless service to connect from a recreational vehicle or aboard a boat, as long as you're within range of your service provider's signal. The easiest way to handle this kind of connection is to use a laptop computer and a power adapter that takes power directly from the boat or car's electrical system. For best performance, you will want to mount an external antenna on the roof of your vehicle or the mast of your boat.

TracNet

One possible alternative to a portable computer is the KVH TracNet 100 Mobile Internet Receiver (*http://www.kvh.com/Products/product.asp?id=123*), which is shown in Figure 13-4. It's a special-purpose network router with a PC Card socket for an EV-DO adapter, a choice of external antennas for cars, boats, or recreational vehicles, output audio and video connections to the car's built-in entertainment system, and a Wi-Fi hot spot to connect it to your laptop or PDA. The whole thing runs on 12-volt DC power, so it can operate on the car's electrical system.

Photo courtesy of KVH Industries, Inc.

Figure 13-4: The KVH TracNet 100 offers mobile access to the Internet through in-car video monitors.

The TracNet system comes with a Kyocera EV-DO adapter configured for the Verizon Wireless network; however, if you have an account with a different provider, it ought to work equally well if you swap the Verizon adapter with one from any other EV-DO service provider that uses the same model of adapter card (see *http://www.kyocera-wireless.com/wireless/where-to-buy.htm* for a list of service providers). If you already have a broadband wireless account with Verizon, you can move the adapter card between your laptop and the TracNet router.

A TracNet system is not cheap; the router, antenna, keyboard, and remote control cost about $2,000, plus separate monthly subscriptions to both MSN TV and Verizon Wireless BroadbandAccess Service, so it's not for everybody. But as a demonstration of mobile Internet access, it's a legitimate start, and it's available right now. In the future, we can expect to see less complex systems at lower cost, both as options in new cars and as aftermarket accessories.

External Antennas

Whether you use a built-in wireless system or a portable unit in your car, you will probably need an external antenna mounted on the vehicle's roof or rear deck or attached to a rear window with some kind of adhesive, because the vehicle's metal body is often an effective shield that blocks radio signals. Broadband wireless data services use the same radio frequencies as cellular mobile telephones, so the same antennas work on both, as long as you can find a cable to connect the phone or adapter to the antenna.

The exact type and location of the antenna connector is different on different wireless adapters, so it's essential to use an antenna cable with the correct mating connector at the end. The first place to look for a car antenna with the right kind of cable connector is a local electronics dealer that specializes in installing cellular mobile telephones in cars. Even if they don't have exactly the right antenna in stock, they'll probably know where to find one for you. If you can't find the antenna and cable locally, try an online dealer such as wpsantennas.com (*http://www.wpsantennas.com*) or Wilson Electronics (*http://wilsonelectronics.com*). Both of those companies have online lists of common wireless adapters and mobile phones, with cross references to matching antenna cables.

Safety Issues

Operating a computer while you are driving can be an even greater distraction than using a mobile telephone. It's just not possible to safely use a keyboard or a keypad, or look at a computer's display screen, and concentrate on the road in front of you at the same time. Don't even consider it. Either let your passenger operate the computer, or pull the car over to the side of the road before you try to do it yourself.

This really ought to go without saying, but the number of people who use mobile phones while driving suggests otherwise. Please don't endanger yourself, your passengers, and nearby pedestrians or other drivers by doing anything that distracts you from maintaining control of that large, expensive, heavy car or truck. It's just not worth the risk.

It's also important to remember that a laptop computer or a PDA sitting on the seat of a parked car is likely to attract the wrong kind of attention from a thief who could break into the vehicle and steal it. Remember to place your computer and other valuable objects under cover or out of sight whenever you're away from the car.

14

SMARTPHONES AND PDAs

Wi-Fi and other broadband wireless networks are not limited to full-size computers running full-size operating systems. Palms, BlackBerries, Pocket PCs, iPhones, and other handheld personal digital assistants (PDAs) can all use wireless links to synchronize data with other computers, send and receive email, and download data from the Internet. This new category of hybrid devices automatically switches between relatively slow EDGE or EV-DO networks with wide coverage areas to much faster Wi-Fi networks whenever it's possible to do so.

Every model has a different set of features and functions, from relatively simple phones that offer limited access to text-based information such as weather forecasts or sports scores, to very sophisticated devices that use an operating system such as Windows Mobile or Palm OS to handle email and web browsing. Many phones double as digital cameras that allow users to send and receive pictures, multimedia players that can store and play music and video, and GPS receivers that offer driving directions.

Voice and data services have come closer to converging with each advance from first-generation cellular mobile telephone service (analog voice only) through second- and third-generation (2G and 3G) digital services. Depending on the wireless method the service provider uses, many of the latest mobile telephones can send and receive a limited amount of data (such as text messages and pictures) along with the now-traditional voice connections. These are the same wireless methods that support many PDAs and the broadband wireless adapters described in Chapter 13.

NOTE   *It's also possible to use almost any mobile telephone to connect a portable computer or a PDA to the Internet through a dial-up modem and a special cable, but the connection will be slow and cumbersome because dial-up access is normally limited to a maximum of 56Kbps. Other devices and service plans might offer a significantly faster data connection as well.*

For the purposes of this chapter, a *PDA* is a handheld computer that uses either a specialized Personal Information Manager (PIM) operating system or a version of Linux that has been customized for use with mobile devices. A *smartphone* is a PDA that can be used as a mobile telephone through one of the cellular mobile telephone networks, along with its other PIM functions.

Connecting to the Internet Through PDAs and Other Handheld Devices

PDAs with wireless network adapters can be particularly useful while you're away from your own home or office, when you want to send and receive email or text messages, or when you want to consult an online information source. The combination of a telephone, a camera, a text and voice recorder, a music player, an Internet appliance, and a small general-purpose computer in a convenient pocket-size package is a huge advance in the way people use technology. Fifty years ago, having all that technology in your pocket was inconceivable; even 5 or 10 years ago it would have required half a dozen separate devices (and of course, 50 years from now it will all seem impossibly primitive).

The same Wi-Fi network services that support laptops and desktop computers can also work with handheld devices. One or more access points operate as hubs for the wireless network and double as bridges to the wired portion of a LAN and to the Internet. A single network can include both handheld units and larger computers, so it's entirely practical to use a wireless link to synchronize a PDA with another computer.

NOTE   *A web search for compact flash or SD Wi-Fi adapters will produce thousands of links, but most of them are several years out of date. Just because a product has been discontinued doesn't mean that the web pages that describe it go away.*

Choosing a Smartphone

The best place to find a new smartphone with broadband wireless access is the service provider whose network you want to use. You can either choose the model you want and look for a service provider that supports it, or you can select a service provider and limit your choices to its list of models. Most mobile telephone companies and wireless service providers have retail stores and websites where you can compare the specific models that are compatible with their networks.

Because most PDAs and smartphones have small display screens, their designers have squeezed a lot of program icons and other information into a tiny space. This can make it considerably more difficult to operate a handheld device than a full-size computer with a big screen, a mouse, and a keyboard. Of course, there's usually a learning curve that will make any device easier to use over time, but it's still important to try more than one of them before you buy. "Easy to use" is a subjective call that will not be the same for everyone. Some people will be happier with the iPhone's touch screen, while others will prefer a BlackBerry's keyboard or a simple keypad on a Windows Mobile or Symbian device. Your best bet is to visit one or more retail stores and compare several phones with different operating systems, different feature sets, and different physical layouts.

Every smartphone comes with a basic set of programs, and many others are also available. When you're trying to decide which phone to buy, consider the programs you're likely to use, and be sure to choose a device that either includes those programs with the phone or supports one or more aftermarket programs that fill your requirements.

It's also important to compare the specific wireless services that each device supports. Does it use a fast EV-DO or EDGE connection, or is it limited to the slower GPRS system? Does it automatically search for a nearby Wi-Fi signal before it connects to a broadband network? Does the service provider offer useful signal coverage in all the places you expect to use the device? Of course, some smartphones are bigger than others. If you plan to carry yours in a pocket rather than a purse or briefcase, a smaller unit might be the better choice.

Like mobile telephones, each wireless data device has a unique electronic serial number (ESN) that links that adapter to a specific account. When you buy a smartphone or a PDA with broadband wireless access, you must either set up a new account for your new PDA or transfer an existing account from another device.

NOTE   *If you transfer your phone or PDA from one service provider to another, the new service provider might have to open up your PDA and install a new circuit board with a different ESN.*

Smartphone Operating Systems

A smartphone is a small mobile computer with an operating system that controls its features and performance, including the screen layout and the way it sends and receives data and telephone calls. The most widely used smartphone operating systems are Symbian, Windows Mobile, BlackBerry OS, Palm OS, and Apple's OS X for iPhones. Linux-based phones also exist, but they're not common in North America. Each operating system includes a slightly different feature set, and each has its own strengths and weaknesses, but they all do essentially the same things: They provide the internal software that allows a PDA or smartphone to accept, store, and display text, audio, images, and other data and to communicate through one or more communication channels.

Late in 2007, Google announced that it planned to introduce its own open platform operating system for smartphones, called Android, and it invited third-party software developers to create new applications for it. It will be at least a year or two before Android-based smartphones (Googlephones?) reach any real-world consumers, but when they do, Google will probably offer serious competition to Microsoft, Symbian, and the others.

The Palm, BlackBerry, and iPhone operating systems are all designed for specific hardware platforms, while Symbian, Windows Mobile, and Linux are more flexible; the hardware manufacturers that use them can choose the specific set of features and functions that they want to offer in each device in their product lines.

Some smartphones also include a *tethered modem* feature that connects a laptop or other portable computer to the Internet through a cable, using the smartphone's broadband wireless account. This feature is not available on every model or through every service provider, but it can be a convenient alternative to a separate wireless network adapter card and broadband data account. Tethered modem software is supplied with many BlackBerry models, and June Fabrics Technology (*http://www.junefabrics.com*) offers a similar program called PdaNet for Palm OS and Windows Mobile. Depending on your service provider, tethering might require an extra cost per month, and often it will not be as fast as a dedicated broadband modem (for example, EV-DO Rev. A is typically only available as a dedicated device).

Windows Mobile

Microsoft's Windows Mobile operating system includes built-in support for Wi-Fi networks, along with mobile versions of the Microsoft Internet Explorer web browser, Windows Media Player, and various office applications. Windows Mobile has many design features that are based on the familiar Windows user interface; from the onscreen Start button to the layout of many programs, the look and feel is easy for Windows users to learn and use. Figure 14-1 shows a PDA using Windows Mobile.

Windows Mobile offers all the same basic features as Palm, Symbian, and the others, but it also provides support for Microsoft's Mobile Office programs, including customized versions of Word, Excel, and PowerPoint, and a mobile version of Internet Explorer (shown in Figure 14-1). If your business uses Microsoft Exchange Server, you can easily use a Windows Mobile smartphone to send and receive email. Many additional specialized programs are also available through *http://www.microsoft.com/windowsmobile/catalog*.

Most new Windows Mobile devices include built-in Wi-Fi adapters, and many also support one or more broadband wireless systems, depending on the service provider. You can find a list of currently available Windows Mobile devices on Microsoft's Windows Mobile website, *http://www.microsoft.com/windowsmobile/devices/default.mspx*.

Image courtesy of Microsoft

Figure 14-1: Microsoft offers a wide variety of programs for the Windows Mobile operating system.

BlackBerry

BlackBerry is a family of smartphones made by Research In Motion that are integrated with data communication software and services. In addition to voice telephone service, BlackBerries also offer email, instant text messaging, and access to the Internet through Wi-Fi and broadband wireless data networks. Depending on the BlackBerry model and the service provider, some devices use only the slower GPRS broadband technology, while others support faster EV-DO or EDGE networks. If you plan to use your BlackBerry for Internet access, it's best to look for a model that supports fast data transfer.

Email is the application that made BlackBerry the most popular smartphone in the United States. The screen and keyboard are designed to make reading and writing messages fast and easy. If you're a frequent emailer, a BlackBerry could be your best choice.

Figure 14-2 shows a typical BlackBerry. Notice that the screen shows the signal strength of an EDGE connection in the upper right corner.

BlackBerries are sold and supported by cellular telephone companies and broadband wireless service providers around the world. Like other makes of mobile devices, it's best to buy a BlackBerry through a local company (either directly or through a retailer or other representative) to be certain that it has been optimized for local networks.

Palm

Palm makes two families of smartphones: one group that uses the Microsoft Windows Mobile operating system and another that uses the Palm OS that was originally designed for its handheld Palm PDAs. Smartphones that use Palm OS have a screen layout that many users consider sensible and easy to use. The core Palm OS includes the usual smartphone functions, but it also supports more programs from third-party developers than any other operating system.

Palm OS smartphones are available that support either EV-DO or EDGE networks, depending on the service provider that sells each model. For a comparison of Palm smartphones, including the US service providers that support each one, see Palm's website at *http://www.palm.com/us/products/resources/comparison-smartphone.html*. To find a Palm smartphone in other parts of the world, go to *http://www.palm.com/intl*.

Figure 14-3 shows a Palm Treo smartphone connected to Google Maps.

Image courtesy of Research In Motion Limited (RIM)

Photo courtesy of Palm, Inc.

Figure 14-2: BlackBerry smartphones combine telephone and data communication functions.

Figure 14-3: The Palm Treo 680 smartphone uses the Palm OS operating system.

Apple iPhone

Apple's iPhone is a mobile telephone, an iPod multimedia player, a camera, and a broadband wireless Internet client, all in a handheld device that uses touch-sensitive onscreen icons in place of the traditional push-button keypad or keyboard. Figure 14-4 shows several iPhone screen displays.

Photo courtesy of Apple

Figure 14-4: The iPhone combines multiple functions into a compact package.

Taken as a package, iPhone offers an impressive set of features and functions. The wide-screen (3.5 inch) touch screen display looks good, it feels good in your hand, and the various commands and displays are easy to use and understand. However, wireless Internet access is probably iPhone's weakest feature. It's limited to a single service provider in each country, and it uses relatively slow EDGE connections when it's not within range of a usable Wi-Fi access point. It's not possible to unlock an iPhone from the designated service provider without canceling the warranty and possibly damaging the phone

If you decide that an iPhone offers the best combination of features, or if you're delighted by that nifty touch screen, you can buy one from AT&T (or the captive service provider in your country) or directly from Apple. Either way you'll need a voice and broadband account with AT&T Wireless in the United States, or with Rogers in Canada, the O2 network in Britain, T-Mobile in Germany, or Orange in France (or the service provider that supports the iPhone in your country when it becomes available).

Since the iPhone was introduced in 2007, several other manufacturers including Nokia, Hewlett-Packard, and HTC have also created phones that use similar touch screen controls, like the one shown in Figure 14-5. If you don't care about all the iPhone features (such as a music and video player), or if you want a different set of bundled programs, you might find a less costly alternative from another manufacturer. However, Apple has successfully marketed the iPhone as *the* high-status smartphone to own. Even if your Nokia or HP smartphone does everything you want it to do including cooking breakfast, it might not impress your friends like an iPhone will.

Symbian

Symbian is jointly owned by half a dozen major mobile telephone manufacturers, including Ericsson, Nokia, Panasonic, Samsung, Siemens, and Sony Ericsson. The majority of the world's smartphones use Symbian OS, but it's less common in North America than some other operating systems. Symbian OS version 9.5 (the current version in 2007) supports EDGE broadband connections. Figure 14-6 shows the screen from a smartphone that uses Symbian OS.

Linux

Motorola, NEC, and Samsung are among the long list of mobile phone makers who offer smartphones based on Linux in some parts of the world, but only a few of these devices have been approved for use in the United States. You can find a partial list of Linux smartphones at *http://www.linuxdevices.com/articles/AT9423084269.html*. Unlike the other smartphone operating systems that each has a single set of features and functions, there are several separate groups working with Linux. As a result, the screen layouts and command sets of Linux smartphones are not always consistent from one hardware manufacturer to another.

Another Linux-powered offering is the Internet Tablet series from Nokia. While they are not actually smartphones because they contain no cellular telephone hardware, the Nokia tablets have Wi-Fi and Bluetooth support and can use both hot spots or a tethered phone for Internet access.

Figure 14-7 shows a smartphone that uses Qtopia, a version of Linux developed by Trolltech. This particular phone was made by Wistron, a Taiwanese original design manufacturer (ODM) whose products are rebranded by many other companies.

Photo courtesy of Nokia

Figure 14-5: Nokia's N95 smartphone offers many similar features, but it's not an iPhone.

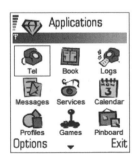

Photo © 2006 Symbian Software Ltd. or its Licensors

Figure 14-6: Symbian provides software for smartphones made by many hardware manufacturers.

Photo courtesy of Trolltech

Figure 14-7: Qtopia is one of several Linux smartphone developers. This Qtopia phone was made by Wistron.

Which Is Best?

Choosing the right smartphone for your needs can be confusing because each hardware manufacturer and each operating system offers a different combination of features in a slightly different package. If access to the Internet is an important reason to have a smartphone, you can apply the same criteria that apply to adapters for laptops and other portable computers: Look for a service provider whose coverage footprint includes all the places you're likely to use the device, and look for the fastest possible data transfer speed.

A smartphone is often a compromise between the convenience of a single device that works as a telephone and an Internet access device and performs several other functions, with the small size and simplicity of a single-purpose mobile telephone or PDA. The phone's software reflects this compromise.

Remember that a broadband wireless network doesn't care what kind of data is moving through it or what kind of client device is sending and receiving it. As long as the frames and packets and the radio modulation methods meet the Wi-Fi specifications or they're compatible with the EDGE or EV-DO standards, the network will pass it along. So the same technology that connects your laptop computer to the Internet today will appear tomorrow in embedded modules that perform completely new services. For example, home appliances, office machines, and cars will transmit diagnostic information to central monitoring centers that will identify problems and dispatch a repair technician before the problems become visible to the people using those machines. Pollable water and electric meters will allow a public utility's remote data collector to gather billing information without the need to send a human meter reader to every account location.

People seem to view smartphones in one of two very different ways: either they cannot imagine the need for such a thing, or they embrace them as a vital part of their daily lives. Many people who use smartphones say that they would never want to give them up. A single pocket-size device that can perform all those functions is enough to spoil them for life—or at least until the next generation of electronic assistants with even more features comes along.

On the other hand, as Freud might have said, sometimes a phone is just a phone. If telephone calls and maybe the occasional text message are all you need, you don't need the expense and complications of a smartphone.

15

VIRTUAL PRIVATE NETWORKS

The security tools in the Wi-Fi specification are not good enough to protect data transmitted through a wireless network. What's the fix? A virtual private network (VPN) can add another effective form of security to data that moves from a wireless network client to a host that can be located anywhere with a network connection.

A VPN uses a *data tunnel* to connect two points on a network through an encrypted channel. The end points can be a single network client and a network server, a pair of client computers or other devices, or the gateways to a pair of LANs. Data that passes through a public network such as the Internet is completely isolated from other network traffic. It uses login and password authentication to restrict access to authorized users; it encrypts the data to make it unintelligible to intruders who intercept it; and it uses data authentication to maintain the integrity of each data packet and to assure that all data originates with legitimate network clients.

VPN functions occur at the IP or network layer of the ISO model. Therefore, they can operate on top of the Wi-Fi or other wireless protocols, which operate at the physical layer. VPNs can also pass data across a network connection that includes more than one physical medium (for example, a wireless link that passes data onward to a wired Ethernet network). In other words, a VPN is an end-to-end service; it doesn't matter whether data uses a wireless link, an Ethernet cable, an ordinary telephone line, or some combination of those and other transmission media. This adds another level of security to (or provides an alternative to) WEP or WPA encryption, which only applies to the wireless portion of the network.

In a traditional VPN, a remote user can log in to a distant LAN and obtain all the same network services that are available to local clients. VPNs are commonly used to extend corporate networks to branch offices and to connect users to the LAN from home or from off-site locations such as a client or customer's office.

A connection through a VPN server presents the same appearance to the rest of the network as a client device connected directly to the LAN. The only difference is that the data from the VPN passes through a VPN driver and a public network instead of moving directly from the network adapter to the LAN. Figure 15-1 shows a typical VPN connection to a remote network.

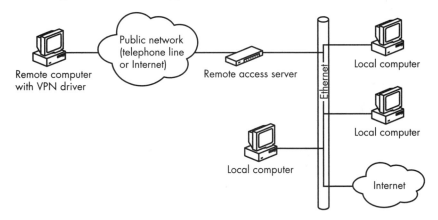

Figure 15-1: A remote network can connect to a LAN through a VPN.

All of the same security benefits also apply to a short-range VPN that tunnels through a wireless link and a longer-range VPN that starts on a wireless network and relays the data to a remote server. These are two different uses for a VPN: a *local* VPN that only extends across the wireless portion of a network between the client devices and the access point and an *extended network* that carries VPN-encoded data beyond the access points to a VPN server through a public network, such as the Internet or a dial-up telephone connection.

An extended network is a traditional VPN that happens to originate from a wireless network client. The same VPN can also support connections that don't include a wireless segment and logins from public wireless services, such as the ones at airports or coffee shops. This is the conventional way to use a VPN.

Local, short-range VPNs are interesting to people who operate wireless networks because they add another layer of security to wireless links. Because the data moving between wireless clients and the network access point is encrypted (using an algorithm that is more secure than WPA encryption), it is unintelligible to any third party who might be monitoring the radio signal; because the VPN server at the access point won't accept data links from wireless clients that are not using the correct VPN drivers and passwords, an intruder can't break into the network by associating a rogue client with the access point.

The goal of a wireless VPN is to protect the wireless link between the clients and the access point and to lock out unauthorized users. Therefore, the isolated and encrypted data can only move across a single room rather than hundreds or thousands of miles. Of course, the access point might also relay VPN-encoded data onward through the Internet to a network host in another location.

Figure 15-2 shows a wireless connection to a VPN. The VPN server is located between the wireless access point and the host LAN, so all of the packets that move through the wireless portion of the network are encoded. For clarity, the diagram shows the VPN server as a separate component, but the most practical way to add VPN security to a wireless LAN is to use a router or gateway that incorporates VPN support. VPN-enabled routers are available from several vendors, including Cisco, NETGEAR, and TRENDnet.

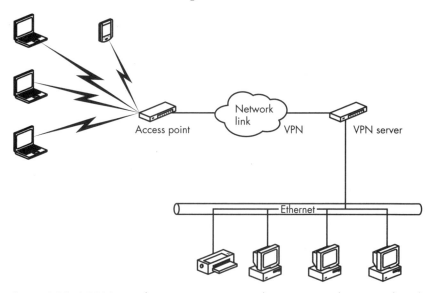

Figure 15-2: A VPN provides a secure connection between a wireless network and an Internet gateway or a local LAN.

VPN Methods

A VPN moves data through one or more intermediate networks to a destination on another network. The VPN's tunneling client encapsulates the existing data packets or frames by adding a new header with the routing information that instructs them how to reach the end point of the VPN. The transmission path through the intermediate networks is called a tunnel. At the other end of the tunnel, the VPN server removes the tunneling header and forwards the data to the destination specified by the next layer of headers. The exact form of the tunnel doesn't make any difference to the data because the data treats the tunnel as a point-to-point connection.

The tunneling headers can take several forms. The methods used most widely in VPNs are Point-to-Point Tunneling Protocol (PPTP), Layer Two Tunneling Protocol (L2TP), and IP Security (IPsec) mode. PPTP and L2TP can move data through IP, IPX, and NetBEUI networks; IPsec is limited to IP networks. Both the client and the server must use the same protocol.

In PPTP and L2TP, the client and server must configure the tunnel for each transmission before they begin to exchange data. The configuration parameters include the route through the intermediate network and the encryption and compression specifications. When the transmission is complete, the client and server terminate the connection and close the tunnel. Unfortunately, several data security analysts have identified significant flaws in PPTP that can allow intruders to break into a VPN based on PPTP and sniff passwords, decode encryption, read data, or inflict damage to a network server. Therefore, PPTP headers are not secure and should not be used.

In an IPsec network link, the client and server must establish the tunnel through the intermediate networks in a separate transaction before they begin to exchange data.

Both L2TP and IPsec offer specific advantages and disadvantages, but they're both good enough to create a secure link between a wireless network client and an access point. The differences among the three are technical rather than practical. You can find an excellent explanation of the internal operation of all three protocols in Microsoft's white paper entitled *Virtual Private Networking in Windows 2000: An Overview*, which is available online at *http://www.microsoft.com/windows2000/docs/VPNoverview.doc* (but remember that the flaws in PPTP networks were identified after that white paper was written).

VPN Servers

A VPN server (or host) can be part of a Unix or Windows server, or it can be built into a stand-alone network router or gateway. If your network already uses a separate computer as a dedicated server, you can use that computer as the VPN server. A separate piece of hardware might be a better choice if your network does not already have a full-blown network server.

Dozens of VPN equipment makers offer routers, gateways, and other products that support one or more of the VPN protocols. Each of these products has a different feature set, so it's essential to test the specific combination of client and server that you intend to use on your own network before you commit to them. The Virtual Private Network Consortium (VPNC) is moving toward a set of interoperability tests and certification standards (much like the Wi-Fi standards for wireless Ethernet equipment). The VPNC website, *http://www.vpnc.org*, lists the products that have passed the interoperability tests, and it also provides links to sources of information about a long list of VPN products.

Configuring a Windows Server for a Wireless VPN

If you're committed to using a Windows server, you can use either L2TP or IPsec with Windows Server 2003 or Windows Server 2008; if your server runs the older Windows NT Server 4.0 or Windows 2000 Server software, you're limited to L2TP (or the seriously flawed PPTP). The server also requires two network interface cards: one connected to the wired LAN or the Internet gateway and the other connected to the wireless network. The interface card that is connected to the wireless port normally connects directly to the wireless access point's Ethernet port. The exact process of installing an L2TP host on a Windows server is slightly different in each version of Windows, but the general steps are the same. For specific information about configuring a particular operating system, consult the online Help screens and Microsoft's Resource Kit and other online documentation for your server's operating system. The following sections describe the configuration steps in general terms.

NOTE   *For more information about deploying and using VPNs with Microsoft servers, see the Microsoft TechNet articles linked from* http://technet.microsoft.com/en-us/network/bb545442.aspx.

Configure the Connection to the Wired Network

The link to the LAN or other network is a dedicated connection through a network adapter. The network connection profile for this connection must include the IP address and subnet mask assigned to this connection and the default gateway address assigned to the network gateway.

Configure the VPN Connection

The VPN connection is usually an Ethernet link to one or more access points. The connection profile on the server for the VPN connection must include the IP address and subnet mask assigned to this port and the addresses of the DNS and WINS name servers used by this network.

Configure the Remote Access Server as a Router

The server must use either static routes or routing protocols that make each wireless client reachable from the wired network.

Enable and Configure the Server for L2TP Clients

Windows uses Remote Access Service (RAS) and Point-to-Point Protocol (PPP) to establish VPN connections. The Routing and Remote Access service enables RAS. A VPN connection requires these RAS configuration options:

Authentication Method   Encrypted PPTP connections use the MS-CHAP or EAP-TLS authentication methods.

Authentication Provider   Either Windows 2000 security or an external RADIUS server can verify network clients.

IP Routing   IP Routing and IP-based remote access must be active. If the wired network acts as a DHCP server for the wireless clients, DHCP must be active.

Configure L2TP Ports

Set each L2TP port to accept remote access.

Configure Network Filters

Input and output filters keep the remote access server from sending and receiving data that does not originate at a VPN client. These filters will reject data to or from unauthorized users, so those intruders will not be able to obtain an Internet connection (or a connection to the wired LAN) through the wireless network.

Configure Remote Access Policies

The remote access permission for each wireless client must be set to allow access to the RAS server. The port type must be set to the correct VPN protocol (e.g., PPTP or L2TP), and the profile for each connection must include the type of encryption in use. In Windows, the three encryption strength options are:

Basic   Uses a 40-bit encryption key

Strong   Uses a 56-bit encryption key

Strongest   Uses a 128-bit encryption key

VPN Servers for Unix

All of the BSD variations (including FreeBSD, NetBSD, OpenBSD, and Mac OS X) include an IPsec VPN client and server as part of the release package.

Linux FreeS/WAN is the most popular implementation of IPsec for Linux. Go to *http://www.freeswan.org* for downloads, documentation, and access to the community of FreeS/WAN users.

OpenVPN is an SSL-based VPN solution for Linux, BSD, OS X, and Windows. It is easy to configure and offers both routed VPN (traffic to specific destinations is sent through the VPN) and tunneled virtual interfaces (emulating a physical layer Ethernet device, which can pass non-IP traffic through the VPN). OpenVPN can be found at *http://openvpn.net.*

If you are using a Linux firewall, you might want to consider VPN Masquerade. Linux uses the IP Masquerade function in the Linux kernel to share a single connection to the Internet among multiple clients. VPN Masquerade is the section of IP Masquerade that supports IPsec clients. The HOWTO for Linux VPN Masquerade is at *http://tldp.org/HOWTO/VPN-Masquerade-HOWTO.html.*

Network Hardware with Built-in VPN Support

A dedicated computer running Linux or one of the BSD versions of Unix can be an inexpensive VPN server; if you're using a Windows server for other purposes, it can also provide VPN support at little or no additional cost. But a full-size network server is often a bigger and more complicated solution to a relatively simple problem. They're not always the best choice. Many switches, routers, gateways, and firewall devices also include VPN support. Cisco, 3COM, Intel, and many other manufacturers make VPN products that are often easier to install and maintain than a separate computer.

In a wireless network, the VPN server does not need all the same bells and whistles as a server in a larger corporate network. As Figure 15-3 shows, a router located between the wireless access point and the wired portion of an enterprise network can easily double as a VPN server. In a home network, the VPN server can operate between the access point and a DSL or cable modem.

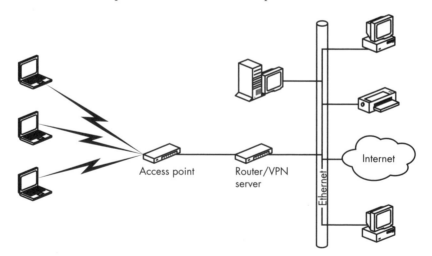

Figure 15-3: A network router can also act as a VPN server for a wireless network.

Stand-alone VPN client hardware that sits between the computer and the network is also available, but it's not as practical in a wireless network because the wireless network adapter is almost always plugged directly into the computer itself.

VPN Client Software

A wireless client connects to a VPN server through its wireless Ethernet link to the network access point, which the operating system sees as a LAN connection. To set up a VPN tunnel through that connection, you must install the tunneling protocol as a network service.

Configuring Windows for VPN

Windows XP and Vista include support for VPNs, but it's not part of the default installation, so the first step in setting up a VPN client is to install the protocol.

In Windows XP and Windows Vista, a wizard makes the whole process easy. In XP, follow these steps to set up a VPN connection:

1. From the Control Panel, open **Network Connections**.
2. Double-click the **New Connection Wizard** icon.
3. When the Network Connection Type window shown in Figure 15-4 appears, choose the **Connect to the network at my workplace** option.

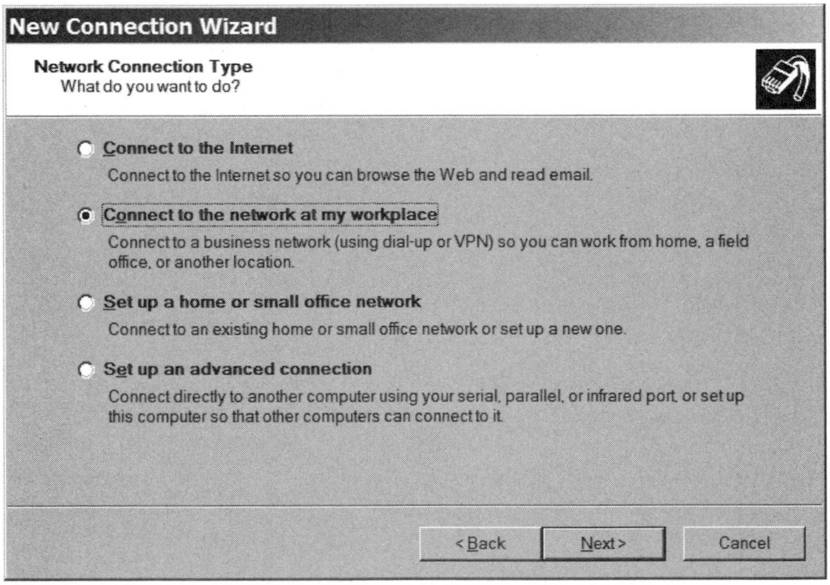

New Connection Wizard

Network Connection Type
What do you want to do?

○ **Connect to the Internet**
Connect to the Internet so you can browse the Web and read email.

◉ **Connect to the network at my workplace**
Connect to a business network (using dial-up or VPN) so you can work from home, a field office, or another location.

○ **Set up a home or small office network**
Connect to an existing home or small office network or set up a new one.

○ **Set up an advanced connection**
Connect directly to another computer using your serial, parallel, or infrared port, or set up this computer so that other computers can connect to it.

< Back   Next >   Cancel

Figure 15-4: The option for creating a VPN link specifies connecting to a workplace network, but it also applies to a wireless VPN.

4. In the Network Connection window (shown in Figure 15-5), choose the **Virtual private network connection** option and click the **Next** button.
5. In the Connection Name window, type a name for the Wireless VPN connection. This name will appear on desktop shortcuts to this connection. Click the **Next** button.

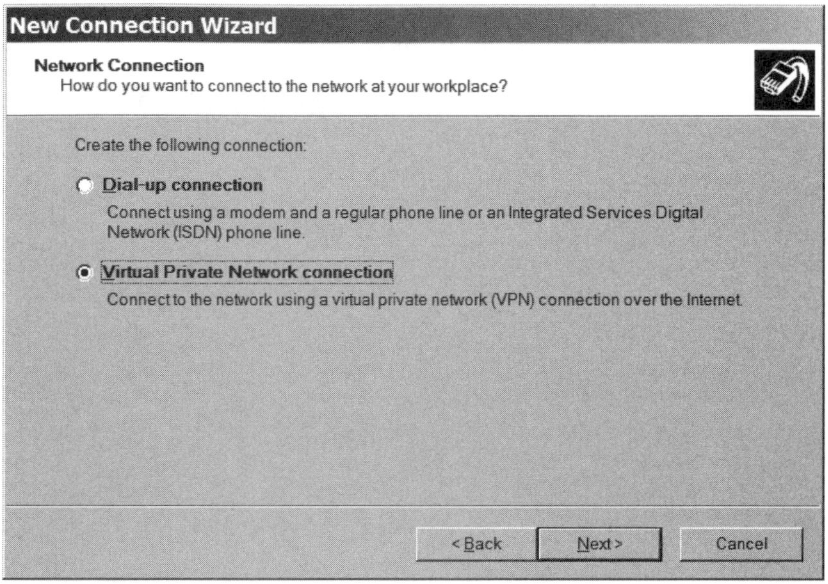

Figure 15-5: Select the Virtual private network connection option to create a VPN connection.

6. In the Public Network window (shown in Figure 15-6), choose the **Do not dial the initial connection** option because you don't need to connect through a telephone line. Click the **Next** button.

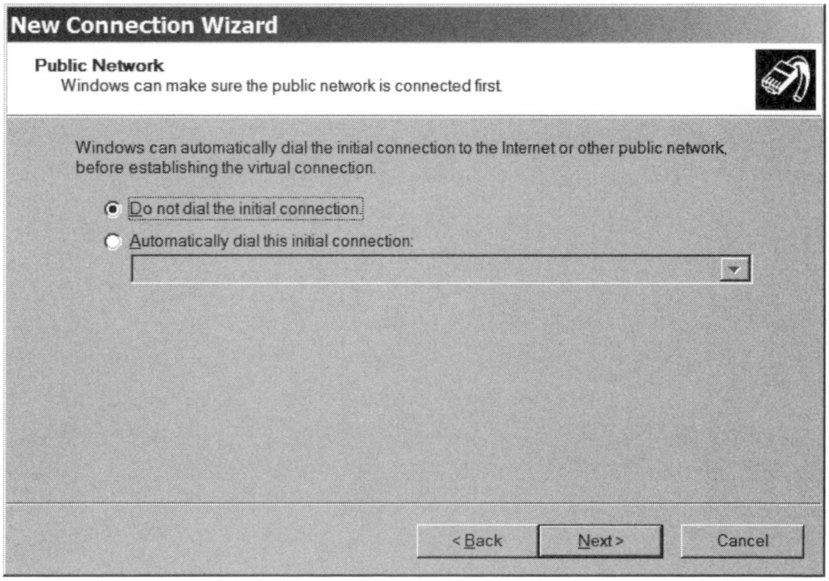

Figure 15-6: In a wireless network, the VPN does not require a dial-up connection.

7. In the VPN Server Selection window shown in Figure 15-7, type the IP address of the VPN server.

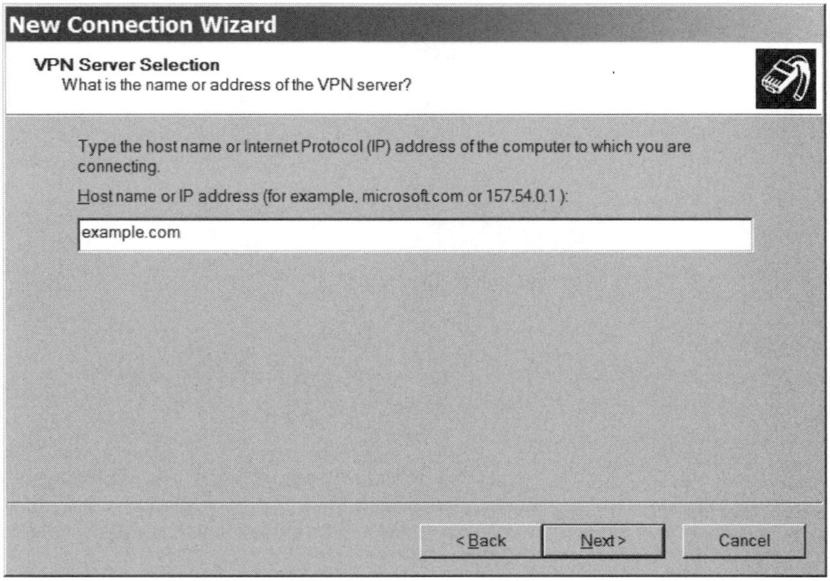

Figure 15-7: The Host Name or IP Address identifies the VPN server at the other end of the wireless link.

8. Click the **Next** button and then the **Finish** button to complete the wizard.

In Vista, follow these steps:

1. Open the **Control Panel**.
2. Open the **Network and Sharing Center**.
3. In the list of Tasks on the left side of the Network and Sharing Center shown in Figure 15-8, choose the **Set up a connection or network** option. A Choose a Connection Option window will open.
4. Choose the **Connect to a workplace** option and click the **Next** button. The wizard will ask if you want to use an existing connection.
5. Choose the **No, create a new connection** option. The wizard will ask if you want to use a VPN or a dial-up connection.

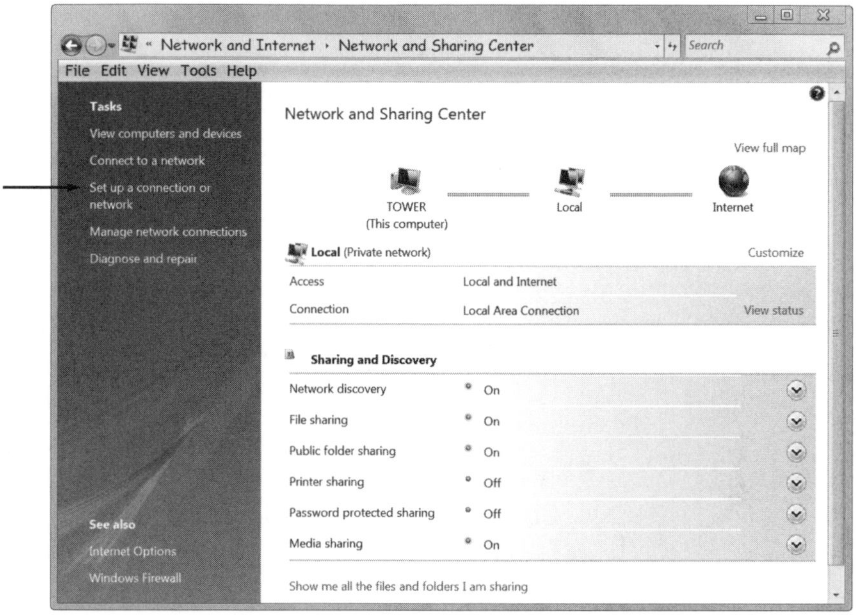

Figure 15-8: Use the Set up a connection or network option to create a VPN link.

6. Choose the **Internet connection (VPN)** option. The wizard will ask for details in the screen shown in Figure 15-9.

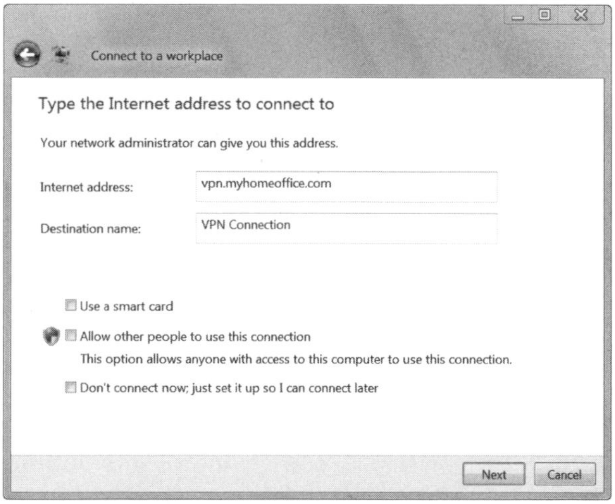

Figure 15-9: Use this screen to configure your VPN.

7. Type the VPN server's address provided by the network manager in the Internet Address field. This can be either a numeric address or a name.

8. Type the name you want to use on your own computer for this VPN connection in the Destination Name field.

9. If you want to test the connection, click the Next button. If you don't want to connect, select the Don't connect now option and click Next. The wizard will ask for your name and password.

10. Type the name and password you use for this VPN account. If you want your computer to automatically send your password, turn on the **Remember this password** option. Click the **Create** button to establish the VPN connection and close the wizard.

To create a shortcut to a VPN on your desktop in Windows, follow these steps:

1. In XP, open the Control Panel and choose **Network Connections**. In Vista, open the Control Panel, choose the **Network and Sharing Center**, and select **Manage Network Connections** from the list of Tasks.

2. From the Network Connections window, right-click the icon or listing for the VPN and choose **Create Shortcut** from the pop-up menu.

3. A pop-up window will ask if you want to place the shortcut on the desktop. Click the **Yes** button. A shortcut will appear on the desktop.

The Microsoft L2TP/IPsec VPN Client

Microsoft includes a client for Layer Two Tunneling Protocol (L2TP) connections with Internet Protocol security (IPsec) in Windows 2000, Windows XP, and Windows Vista. A similar client program for Windows 98, Windows Me, and Windows NT Workstation 4.0 is available for free download from *http:// download.microsoft.com/download/win98/Install/1.0/W9XNT4Me/EN-US/ msl2tp.exe*.

Making the Connection in Windows

When the VPN connection profile is in place, it's easy to connect a Windows client to the host LAN or the Internet through the wireless VPN link: Just double-click the icon for the connection profile. Windows will ask for a login and password and then make the connection.

If your wireless connection is the method you use most often to connect to the Internet, you can make it the default connection, which will open whenever you run a network application such as a web browser or email client program. To make the VPN profile the default, follow these steps:

1. Open the **Internet Properties** window from the Control Panel.

2. Select the **Connections** tab.

3. In the Dial-Up Settings section, select the VPN connection profile from the list and click the **Set Default** button.

4. Click the **Settings** button. In the Dial-Up Settings section, type your login and password on the VPN server.

5. Choose the **Dial whenever a network connection is not present** option.

Windows XP Options

Windows XP and Windows Vista offer many VPN options that were not available in earlier versions of Windows. To set these options, follow these steps:

1. Open the **Network Connections** window from the Control Panel. If you have a shortcut to your VPN connection on the desktop, you can skip this step.

2. Double-click the VPN icon. A Connect VPN to Internet window like the one in Figure 15-10 will appear.

Figure 15-10: Use the Connect VPN to Internet window to configure a VPN in Windows XP.

3. Click the **Properties** button. The Properties window for your VPN client will appear. Figure 15-11 shows the General tab of the VPN to Internet Properties window.

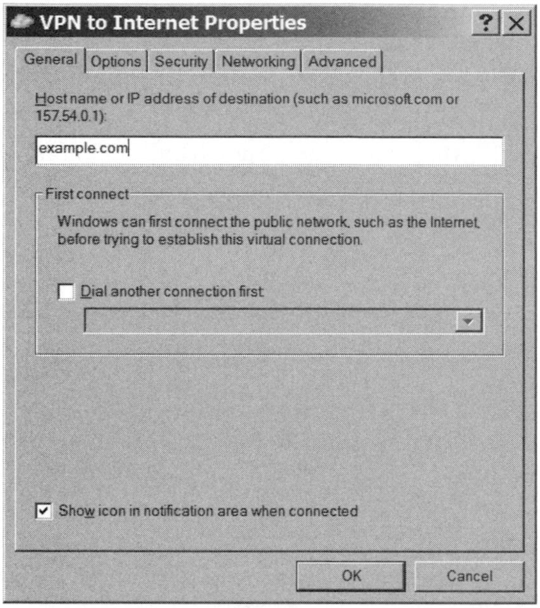

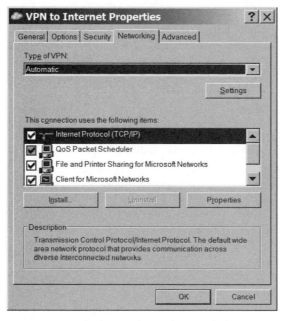

Figure 15-11: The General tab controls the destination
of a VPN connection.

4. The IP address of the VPN server should already be visible in the Host
    Name or IP Address of Destination field. The **Dial another connection
    first** option should be disabled. Click the **Networking** tab to view the dia-
    log box shown in Figure 15-12.

Figure 15-12: The Networking tab controls the VPN's
network configuration options.

5. Choose the type of VPN server your network will use from the Type of VPN menu. If you don't know the VPN type, choose the Automatic option.

6. Select Internet Protocol (TCP/IP) or Internet Protocol Version 4 from the list of connection items, and click the **Properties** button to change the network settings, including the use of a DHCP server or manual settings for IP address and DNS.

7. Click the **Advanced** tab to open the dialog box shown in Figure 15-13. If your network is not already protected by a firewall, select the Internet connection firewall option. This will protect the wireless client from attacks coming through the Internet.

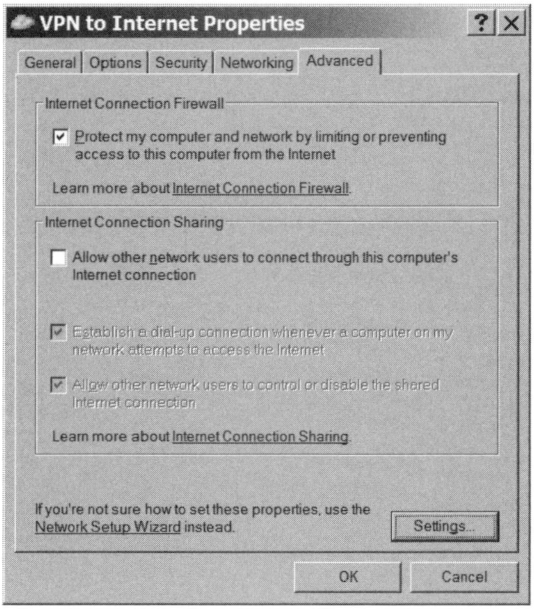

Figure 15-13: The Advanced tab controls the use of a firewall on the VPN.

The Options and Security tabs in the VPN to Internet Properties window control connection options that normally don't change from the default settings. Network managers who want to change the security settings should instruct their users how to configure these options to comply with the network's specific requirements.

VPN Clients for Unix

Using a VPN client on a computer running Unix is more complicated than running a VPN from a Windows machine because the client is not integrated into the kernel. Therefore, you must find a client program that works with the version of Unix *and* the VPN protocol you are trying to use. No single program offers a universal VPN client, and some combinations, such as PPTP on BSD Unix versions, don't seem to exist at all.

IPsec Clients

Linux users can choose from several IPsec implementations:

FreeS/WAN *http://www.freeswan.org*

pipsec *http://perso.enst.fr/~beyssac/pipsec*

NIST Cerberus *http://w3.antd.nist.gov/tools/cerberus*

IPsec is included in the OpenBSD distribution. You can find a tutorial that explains how to use it at *http://www2.papamike.ca:8082/tutorials/pub/obsd_ipsec.html*.

The IPsec implementation for FreeBSD is at *http://www.r4k.net/ipsec*.

For information about NetBSD IPsec, take a look at *http://www.netbsd.org/Documentation/network/ipsec*.

Using a Wireless VPN

When you design a VPN to protect the data on your network as it passes through the wireless link, it's important to understand exactly where the end points of the VPN tunnel are located. If the VPN only tunnels through the wireless link, as shown in Figure 15-14, the network will look exactly the same as it does without a VPN.

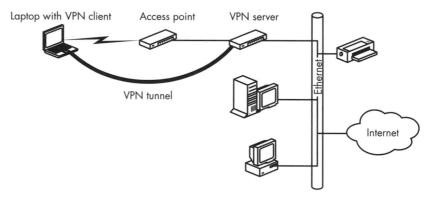

Figure 15-14: A wireless VPN with the server at the access point protects data through the wireless link, but it does not extend the network.

If the VPN extends beyond the wireless access points to pass through a wide area network (such as the Internet), like the one in Figure 15-15, the wireless network client can appear to be part of a LAN in another building or halfway across the continent.

So how far should your wireless VPN extend? It depends on what you want the network to accomplish. If your wireless network is in place to support laptop and other portable computers at your office, factory, or campus, it makes sense to place the server between the network of access points and the connection to your corporate LAN. This will protect your wireless users' data and keep unauthorized users off the network, but it won't affect the other users whose computers connect to the LAN through cables.

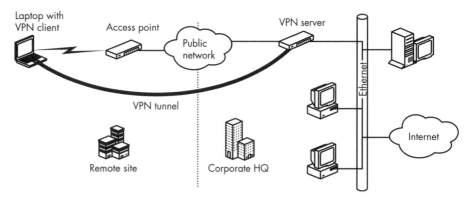

Figure 15-15: A VPN can include both the wireless link and an intercity connection through the Internet to a corporate network.

At home or in a small business network, the access points probably connect to an Internet gateway router that provides Internet access to all the computers in the office or the house. If the access point and the gateway are separate devices, you can place the VPN server between the two. If the access point and gateway are combined in the same box, you'll either have to use VPN clients on all your computers, including the desktop machines that are hardwired to the gateway, and place the client between the gateway and the Internet modem like the network in Figure 15-16, or you'll have to ignore the wired Ethernet ports on the gateway and add a new hub or switch between the VPN server and the Internet modem, as shown in Figure 15-17.

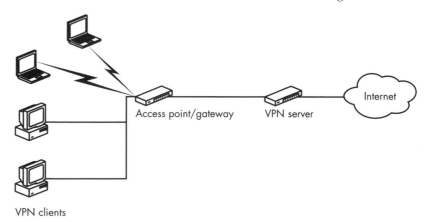

Figure 15-16: In a small LAN, you can use VPN clients on every computer.

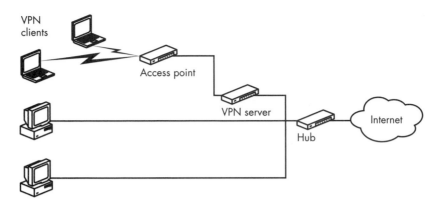

Figure 15-17: In this network, the VPN only protects the wireless links.

Making the Connection

If you use the wireless LAN with VPN protection most of the time, you should make the VPN profile your default connection. Whenever you run a network application, the computer will try to connect through the VPN unless you open a different connection (such as a dial-up telephone line) first.

To set a connection profile as the default in Windows, open the **Network Connections** window. Right-click the icon for the profile you want to choose, and select the **Set as default** option from the menu.

To connect to a VPN that isn't your default, double-click the icon for the VPN's connection profile. You will see a login window like the one in Figure 15-18. Type your name and password, and click the **Connect** button. If the VPN server recognizes your account, it will set up the connection.

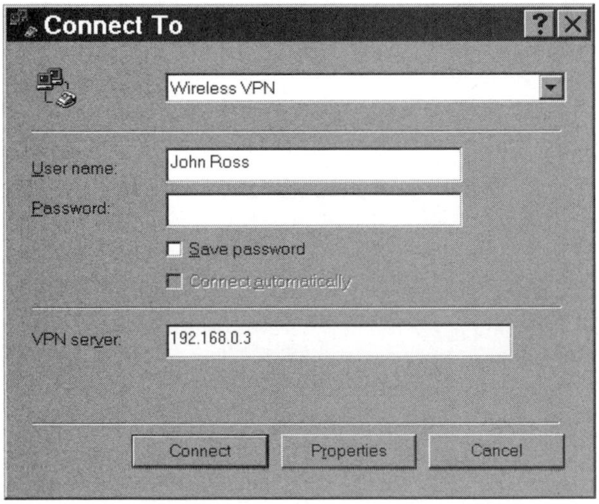

Figure 15-18: A VPN connection normally requires a login name and password.

Bypassing the VPN

Even though you normally use a VPN to protect your wireless data, you might sometimes want to send data in the clear without using the VPN. For example, you might use a local VPN at your own office or at home between your computer and your Internet gateway router, but when you use the same computer at an airport or a coffee shop, or some other location that isn't protected by a VPN, you can use the same computer and network adapter to connect directly to the Internet.

If you're a network manager, you might occasionally have to change your Wi-Fi network's internal settings. The configuration programs that control the Wi-Fi network's operating channel, SSID, and other options are web-based utilities that originate on the access point. Because the access point is inside the VPN tunnel, it is not possible to send commands to the access point through the VPN. It's important to remember that you can use a VPN when you need it and bypass it when you want to make a direct connection.

Using a VPN Through a Public Network

When you connect your laptop to your corporate LAN through a public network at an airport or in a conference center, or if you're using a broadband wireless service, you can connect through their network to the Internet and onward to your corporate VPN server. Because you will have to log in to the public network before you initiate the VPN connection, you should create a separate *VPN via Public Network* connection profile in addition to the one you use from your own office. The profile should point to your corporate VPN server, but it should not be your default connection.

To connect through a public network on a computer running Windows, follow these steps:

1. Turn on the computer with the wireless network adapter in place.

2. Use your wireless configuration utility to select the public network you want to use.

3. Start Internet Explorer, Netscape Navigator, or some other web browser. You will see the public network's login screen.

4. If the computer doesn't do it automatically, enter your account name and password. The public network will acknowledge your login.

5. Minimize the browser window and open the **Network Connections** window or find the VPN shortcut on your desktop.

6. Double-click the icon for your VPN via Public Network profile. The computer will connect through the Internet to your corporate LAN.

7. Enter the login and password for your corporate network.

If this procedure doesn't work for your VPN, ask your network manager for help.

VPNs are an important part of many networks' security plans for off-site users. When a VPN is up and running, it's also an extremely convenient way to connect to your LAN. With just a few keystrokes or mouse clicks, you can establish the same access to your network resources from anywhere with Internet access that you can get from your own office. If any Internet technique can eliminate the apparent distance between you and your LAN, your office, and your colleagues, a VPN is that technique.

16

USING BROADBAND FOR TELEPHONE CALLS

 For more than a century, a dedicated collection of cables, switches, and radio links known as the *public switched telephone network (PSTN)* has connected the world's telephones. When you place a telephone call, the PSTN creates a direct link between your phone and the phone assigned to the unique telephone number you requested. The telephone industry calls this kind of basic connection POTS (plain old telephone service, pronounced like *pots* and pans). The Internet is a separate system that uses a different set of rules and methods to connect computers to one another. Computer data (including digital audio) does not require a continuous connection, so Internet connections can use packet switching (as described in Chapter 1) to move data more quickly and more efficiently than the older PSTN.

When you connect a telephone or a microphone to a computer and convert the sound of your voice to a sequence of digital packets, you can send those packets through the Internet to a specific destination, where the recipient's computer converts the packets back into an analog audio stream and plays the audio through a speaker or a telephone handset. The technology that moves voice communication through the Internet is known as *VoIP (Voice over Internet Protocol)*.

If the recipient of your call has a computer connected to the Internet, you can completely bypass the PSTN and route the call through the Internet, using the recipient's Internet address to identify the call's destination. But it's also possible to transfer a call between the Internet and the PSTN in either direction. You can originate a call on the Internet and direct it to the PSTN, or you can use your POTS line to call a phone attached to a computer.

There are several possible ways to use VoIP:

- Place a computer-to-computer call entirely through the Internet.

- Originate a call on a computer connected to the Internet and transfer it to the PSTN as close to the destination as possible, then complete the call to the recipient's telephone line.

- Originate a call on a telephone line and call a local VoIP service provider, then connect through the Internet to the recipient's computer.

- Originate a call on a telephone line, connect to a local VoIP provider, then connect the call through the Internet to a distant VoIP center, where it transfers back to the PSTN and on to the recipient's telephone line.

VoIP offers several possible advantages over calling through the traditional telephone system. First, it's often significantly cheaper because there are no toll charges for long distance calls. Second, in places where telephone service is not reliable, the Internet's error-correcting packet data switching can sometimes provide connections with better sound and fewer dropped calls than a bad telephone line (but the emphasis is on *sometimes*—just as often, a POTS call will be clearer than VoIP). And third, it's possible to use VoIP through a Wi-Fi or broadband wireless link in places where a conventional telephone line or mobile telephone signal might not be available.

On the other hand, VoIP is often less reliable and less consistent than the PSTN because VoIP packets (and other live audio or video streams) can be interrupted or delayed by all the sources of interference and noise that other data ignores. It makes no difference if your email message takes several minutes to arrive, but you expect a phone call to reach its recipient *right now*. And the sound quality of VoIP calls can sometimes be noticeably worse than a call through the PSTN. In practice, the reduced cost of long distance calls is generally the most compelling reason to use VoIP.

Dozens of service providers offer local or long distance telephone services that use VoIP instead of the old PSTN. Some are marketed as alternatives to the local dial tone company, others are low-cost worldwide long distance services, and still others offer a local telephone number in one or more distant locations, so people who call you don't have to pay long distance charges. You can find directories and user reviews of VoIP services at several websites, including *http://www.voipreview.org*, *http://www.voip-info.org*, and *http://www.voipmonitor.net/VoIP+Providers.aspx*.

NOTE *There are two important safety issues related to VoIP telephone calls. Even if your VoIP phone or portable computer runs on batteries, the access point and the Internet gateway almost certainly use domestic AC power; if your electricity fails, you won't be able to use your VoIP telephone, but a conventional telephone will probably continue to work. And VoIP networks create special challenges when you call 911 (or the comparable telephone number in your country) in an emergency because a VoIP call to 911 might not connect you to the nearest Public Safety Answering Point (PSAP), or if it does, it might not accurately transmit your telephone number and address to the PSAP operator.*

There are many ways to use VoIP, but this is a book about broadband wireless, so we'll limit this discussion to VoIP services that use Wi-Fi or broadband data services to connect to the Internet. These services fall into two categories: software and services that allow a user to originate telephone calls from a portable computer or PDA using Wi-Fi or broadband wireless data networks, and wireless voice over Wi-Fi telephones that use Wi-Fi links to send and receive VoIP calls through the Internet. You don't need Wi-Fi or broadband wireless to use VoIP, but if wireless is part of your arsenal of Internet connection tools, you should know that VoIP is available and that the two technologies can work together.

VoIP over Broadband Wireless and WiMAX

Any VoIP service that can place telephone calls through the Internet can use a portable computer with a broadband wireless connection to originate those calls.

In general, the process goes something like this:

1. Attach a microphone and a speaker or earpiece to the computer (or use the computer's internal microphone and speakers).
2. Open up a wireless connection to the Internet.
3. Use a web browser or the wireless service provider's control program to log in.
4. Use the VoIP service provider's software to place a telephone call.

After the computer has established its connection to the Internet, the VoIP software treats the connection just like any other Internet link. For example, Figure 16-1 shows the Skype calling screens for Windows, Macintosh, and Linux. To place a call to a telephone number, choose the **Call Phones** or **Dial** tab, click the green telephone button to connect to Skype, and either type a telephone number or use your mouse to enter the number on the onscreen keypad. You can sign up for a Skype account and download the software at *http://www.skype.com*.

Skype's software also includes a personal telephone directory, so you can use the program's Contacts list to place a call without reentering the telephone number.

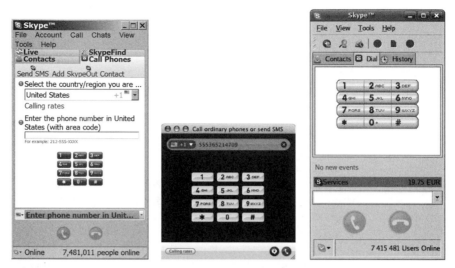

Figure 16-1: Skype offers calling software for Windows, Mac OS X, and Linux.

Vonage (*http://www.vonage.com*) offers a similar service, but it uses a special USB flash drive (shown in Figure 16-2) preloaded with its calling software, along with a socket for a microphone and stereo earpiece. To place a call, insert the flash drive into a USB socket, put the earbuds into your ears, and wait for the Vonage Talk software to start.

Figure 16-2: Vonage's USB flash drive includes calling software and an earpiece microphone cable.

Many other VoIP service providers offer similar services. Each of them has organized its call origination software differently and each has a different pricing plan, so you might want to compare several before you commit to a long-term subscription. The reviews at *http://www.voipreview.org* can tell you about other users' experiences with many providers.

To receive calls through your VoIP account, you must choose an area code and telephone number from your VoIP service provider's website and follow their instructions for setting up an inbound account. A VoIP telephone number is just like any other phone number, so anybody with a telephone can use that number to call you. Most service providers either charge a flat rate for unlimited inbound calls, or they charge a few pennies per minute or per call.

You don't have to choose a telephone number based in your local area code or even in your own country. If you have customers or friends (or both) in a distant location, you can choose one or more numbers that allow them to reach you with a local call. For example, if you live in California, and you have family in Hong Kong, England, and Canada, you could choose local telephone numbers for your VoIP account based in Hong Kong, London, and Vancouver and allow your relatives to reach you without the need to place expensive international long distance calls.

Remember that you can only receive incoming calls through a wireless link when the link is active. Unlike a wired DSL or cable modem connection, your Wi-Fi or broadband data connection is only alive when the wireless control program is running. Therefore, if you expect to receive calls to your VoIP number, you will probably want to subscribe to your service provider's voicemail service.

NOTE   *Be sure to compare the real cost of VoIP service to your existing cell phone charges. If you already have both a mobile telephone and a broadband data account from the same service provider, there might not be any real advantage to using VoIP instead of your mobile phone. The mobile service provider uses the same base stations for both services, so you probably won't find wireless data coverage in places where your phone doesn't work. And if your mobile telephone billing plan includes long distance calls at no extra cost, VoIP might not offer any real savings.*

Voice over Wi-Fi

Wi-Fi phones are cordless telephones that communicate with Wi-Fi access points or hot spots and VoIP to send and receive calls through the Internet. When you combine a VoIP telephone instrument and a VoIP account with a Wi-Fi network, you can create a telephone connection that does not require a dedicated telephone line or cellular telephone account. You also get a truly ugly abbreviation: either VoWiFi or wVoIP, depending on where you look.

Most VoIP services use the Session Initiation Protocol (SIP) specification to control Internet telephone calls and other multimedia services. SIP is comparable to the Hypertext Transfer Protocol (HTTP) that controls the World Wide Web. A VoWiFi telephone must either support SIP or connect to a computer or router that supports SIP. A VoWiFi telephone call uses SIP to control a wireless telephone that sends and receives calls through a Wi-Fi base station that is connected to the Internet. Among other things, the SIP configuration settings specify the IP address of your VoIP service provider and the telephone number assigned to your VoIP account.

Figure 16-3 shows typical VoWiFi connections using a D-Link VoIP phone. The wireless telephone uses a Wi-Fi link at home or on the road to connect to a VoIP service provider through the Internet, and the service provider relays the call to a VoIP subscriber or a PSTN telephone number.

Skype is among the first VoIP providers to offer VoWiFi telephones. The NETGEAR SPH101 Wi-Fi Phone (shown in Figure 16-4) and similar phones made by SMC, Belkin, Linksys, and Panasonic connect to the Internet through a Wi-Fi access point, and they use Skype's VoIP network to send and receive telephone calls.

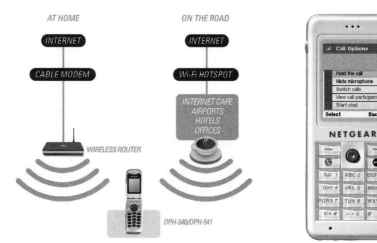

Diagram courtesy of D-Link

Figure 16-3: A VoIP over Wi-Fi phone can connect to the Internet through a home network or a Wi-Fi hot spot.

Photo courtesy of NETGEAR

Figure 16-4: NETGEAR's SPH101 Skype Wi-Fi Phone handles telephone calls through the Internet.

The Nokia N800 Internet Tablet (shown in Figure 16-5) combines a VoWiFi telephone with a web browser, media player, and a client for email and instant messaging. The Skype subscription associated with the Wi-Fi Phone includes free calls to other Skype users and very low cost calls to conventional telephones.

Other VoIP networks, including BroadVoice (*http://www.broadvoice.com*), also offer preconfigured VoWiFi phones. Other phones are not limited to a single VoIP service. These phones have SIP configuration screens that allow a user to specify the VoIP service provider, account information, and other settings, either through the phone's keypad or from a computer connected to the phone through a USB port.

NOKIA
N800
Contacts
Joe Smith
€0.09
Paul Eastwood
bob.palmer1 Holiday = Me h...
Dawn November
Graham Bell
Harry White My daughter"s b...
John Black
Laura Hilton
mike.king7
Peter Towns Hi, I"m in Frisco ...
Rob Hope
Sam Bullman Jihaa, leaving t...
echo123
Eddie House
Paul Eastwood
I'm on business trip in London at the moment
Call
Chat
NOKIA

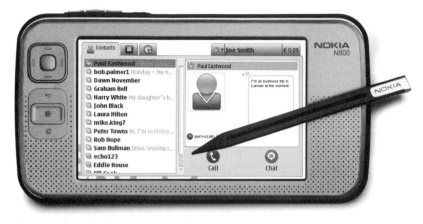

Photo courtesy of Nokia

Figure 16-5: The Nokia N800 Internet Tablet includes Skype telephone service along with other Internet functions.

For example, Figure 16-6 shows the SIP Settings web screen for the D-Link DPH-540S VoIP Phone. Every make and model of VoIP phone seems to organize the configuration screens differently, so you'll have to consult the user's manual for specific instructions that apply to your phone. Your VoIP service provider will supply the specific information needed in each configuration field.

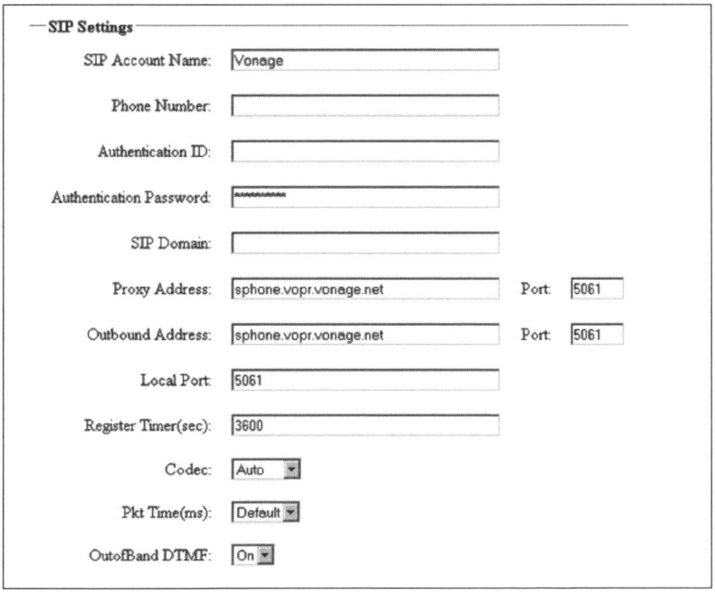

SIP Settings
SIP Account Name: Vonage
Phone Number:
Authentication ID:
Authentication Password: **********
SIP Domain:
Proxy Address: sphone.vopr.vonage.net
Port: 5061
Outbound Address: sphone.vopr.vonage.net
Port: 5061
Local Port: 5061
Register Timer(sec): 3600
Codec: Auto
Pkt Time(ms): Default
OutofBand DTMF: On

Figure 16-6: The SIP Settings screen contains the information your VoIP phone needs to connect to a specific service provider.

NOTE *When you're evaluating VoIP service providers for use with a VoWiFi phone, be sure that the service provider does not require a web-based login because you won't be able to log in to the service using your phone. Another downside to VoWiFi phones is that you will be unable to use Wi-Fi networks that require a web-based login, including many hot spots in airports and hotels.*

In most cases, placing VoIP telephone calls through your computer or a VoWiFi phone is not a good enough reason to set up a new Wi-Fi access point or a broadband wireless data account, but if you already have some kind of wireless connection, VoIP might be a handy supplement to email, instant messaging, and other Internet communications channels. If you don't carry a conventional mobile phone along with your laptop computer or PDA, VoIP can provide a convenient and inexpensive way to send and receive telephone calls when you're within range of a Wi-Fi signal.

17

TIPS AND
TROUBLESHOOTING

 When everything in your wireless network connection is working properly, you won't even know it's there—just fire up the wireless network adapter and go online. Plug and play, right? Don't hold your breath.

Like everything else related to computers, wireless networking works just fine when everything is set up correctly. But that essential setting is often hidden under three layers of windows, screens, and dialog boxes. If some obscure configuration option is wrong, the network connection won't work properly, if at all. This chapter contains descriptions of common problems and advice for solving them.

My computer doesn't detect my network adapter.

Windows should automatically detect a PCMCIA or USB adapter when you connect the adapter to the computer or when you turn on the computer with the adapter already connected. If you're using a PC Card, you should hear a *boo-deep* sound when the PCMCIA controller detects it, and the system tray (next to the clock) should show a PC Card icon like the one in Figure 17-1.

2:36 PM

Figure 17-1: The PC Card icon appears when a device in the computer's PCMCIA slot is active.

If Windows doesn't detect a PC Card or USB device, try removing and replacing the card or unplugging and reconnecting the USB connector. If it's a PC Card, make sure the card is firmly seated in its socket. If it's a USB adapter, disconnect any other USB devices that are connected to the same computer and try connecting the wireless adapter again. If the adapter works, connect the other USB devices one at a time; if connecting another USB device kills the wireless adapter, the two devices are competing with each other for the same resources.

Try connecting a USB adapter to a different USB connector. The problem might be a bad internal connection to the first USB socket.

If Windows does not automatically recognize your network adapter, it probably can't find the right driver, either for your PCMCIA socket or for the adapter itself. The Device Manager (as shown in Figure 17-2) will display an icon with a yellow exclamation point or a red *X* for any device that is currently not working properly. Right-click the listing with the exclamation point or *X*, and choose **Properties** from the menu to restore the device or reinstall the driver.

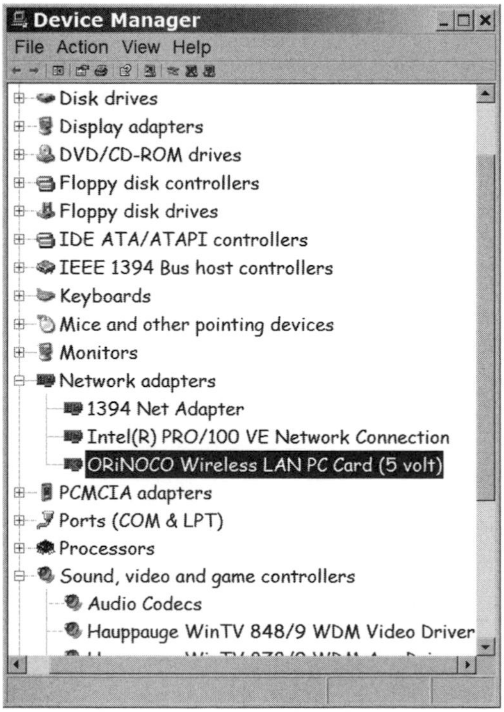

Device Manager

File   Action   View   Help

- ⊞ ⟶ Disk drives
- ⊞ ⟶ Display adapters
- ⊞ ⟶ DVD/CD-ROM drives
- ⊞ ⟶ Floppy disk controllers
- ⊞ ⟶ Floppy disk drives
- ⊞ ⟶ IDE ATA/ATAPI controllers
- ⊞ ⟶ IEEE 1394 Bus host controllers
- ⊞ ⟶ Keyboards
- ⊞ ⟶ Mice and other pointing devices
- ⊞ ⟶ Monitors
- ⊟ ⟶ Network adapters
  - ⟶ 1394 Net Adapter
  - ⟶ Intel(R) PRO/100 VE Network Connection
  - ⟶ ORiNOCO Wireless LAN PC Card (5 volt)
- ⊞ ⟶ PCMCIA adapters
- ⊞ ⟶ Ports (COM & LPT)
- ⊞ ⟶ Processors
- ⊟ ⟶ Sound, video and game controllers
  - ⟶ Audio Codecs
  - ⟶ Hauppauge WinTV 848/9 WDM Video Driver

Figure 17-2: The Device Manager identifies devices that are not working properly. There's a red X over the icon next to the listing for the ORiNOCO Wireless LAN card.

If there is no listing for the PCMCIA socket or the network adapter, install a driver from the disk that was supplied with the adapter, or download a new driver from the manufacturer's website.

In Linux, the PC Card requires PCMCIA services and Wireless Extensions. In Unix, you must install the specific driver for your network adapter. After connecting your device, use `dmesg` to view the kernel logs, which will indicate whether or not the device was properly detected. For CardBus cards (but not PCMCIA cards), `lspci` should show the device and information about the type of drivers it needs. For USB cards, `lsusb` will display all detected USB devices and provide information about them.

If you're using a laptop computer, confirm that wireless operation is turned on. Check both the hardware switch and the software controls in your wireless configuration and control program.

The wireless control program tries to run, even if I'm not using my adapter.

Some wireless configuration and control programs automatically try to load every time you start your computer. Running the wireless programs at startup is fine for a desktop computer that uses them to connect to a LAN all the time, but it makes less sense on a laptop computer that often operates without a wireless network connection.

To remove the autostart function, follow these steps:

1. From the Start menu in Windows, choose **Run**.

2. Type `msconfig` in the Open field and click the **OK** button.

3. Select the **Startup** tab to display a list of programs that automatically run every time you start Windows.

4. Find the entry in the list for the wireless configuration program, and remove the checkmark from the box on the same line.

5. Most Windows systems have several other unnecessary programs that start automatically. While you have the program open, look for other programs that you don't need to open at startup and disable them.

6. Click the **OK** button and restart your computer when Windows asks you to do so.

If you have removed several programs from the Startup list, you will probably notice that Windows starts a lot faster than it did before.

Even though the configuration program no longer runs every time you run Windows, you can start the program when you need it. You will probably see a shortcut to one or more wireless programs on your desktop or in the Program menu.

My computer won't associate with the local network.

If you can't find the network, check these items:

- Confirm that the wireless network adapter PC Card is firmly inserted into the PCMCIA socket.

- Confirm that the cable between the USB adapter and the computer is plugged in at both ends.

- If you are using an access point, confirm that your network adapter is configured as an infrastructure network; if you are trying to link directly to another wireless adapter, confirm that both systems are configured for an ad hoc network.

- Confirm that you are using the correct encryption key.

- Confirm that the IP address setting is correct. If the access point or some other DHCP server automatically assigns IP addresses, confirm that the computer's TCP/IP settings are set to obtain an address automatically.

- Test with encryption and authentication turned off, then *be sure to enable them again when you are finished.*

My computer connects to the wrong network.

In an environment where signals from more than one wireless network are within range of the radio in a network adapter, the adapter will detect all of them. If the SSID option is set to join *ANY* network, the client will automatically associate with the strongest local signal; if the configuration program includes a list of two or more SSIDs, it will search for SSIDs in the order specified by the list.

To configure your computer to join a specific network, change the list of preferred networks in the wireless configuration program, and change the name of the workgroup. Both the SSID and the workgroup should match the SSID of the access point you want to use.

If another network in the area uses the same SSID as yours, the wireless control software will assume it's part of your network. Change your SSID to something unique.

To change the workgroup name in Windows XP, follow these steps:

1. Open the **System** window from the Control Panel.
2. Choose the **Computer Name** tab.
3. Click the **Change** button.

I can see the local network, but I can't connect to the Internet.

Most LANs use a gateway server to convert the internal IP addresses that are used within the LAN to a separate IP address that identifies this network to the Internet. To establish an Internet connection, your computer's TCP/IP network configuration settings must specify the addresses of the gateway and one or more DNS servers.

Check that your computer has received an address by following these steps:

1. Open a command prompt (run `cmd`).
2. Look at the network configuration with `ipconfig /all`.
3. Reinitialize DHCP (request a new address) with `ipconfig /release` and `ipconfig /renew`.

I can see the Internet, but I can't see other computers on my LAN.

Some firewall programs normally block inbound attempts to view files and directories. This prevents unauthorized access to your computer, but it also blocks other computers on the LAN unless you specifically allow access from those computers (using their IP addresses). The firewall controls should include a function where you can identify trusted computers or allow local access (it's different for each firewall program); consult the firewall program's documentation for specific instructions.

If the firewall isn't blocking access, it's possible that the computer you're trying to reach is not configured properly, the access point doesn't recognize that computer's MAC address, or the other computer has filesharing turned off.

The signal strength is weak or signal quality is low.

Assuming there's an access point close to your computer, a weak signal is probably caused by some kind of obstruction between your network adapter and the access point. To improve the signal quality and signal strength, try moving the adapter (and the computer if the adapter is on a PC Card) to a different location. The wavelength of radio signals at 2.4 GHz is extremely short (they're called *microwaves* for a reason!), so moving the adapter even a short distance can be enough to make a noticeable difference.

If you're using a USB adapter, you can be more flexible about its location. Try placing the adapter on top of a bookcase or in some other location with a clean shot to the access point. And try turning the adapter (or the external antenna) sideways so it's on its side rather than upright; this might bring the polarity of the adapter's antenna closer to the polarity of the antenna in the access point.

I can't find a public network.

Before your computer can connect to a public wireless network, your network adapter must associate itself with that network's access point. If the adapter doesn't automatically join the network, check these configuration settings:

- Confirm that the TCP/IP settings are configured to accept an IP address from a DHCP server.

- Run your web browser before you try to use some other Internet client program, such as a mail reader. Most commercial public networks display a login screen through the browser, and they won't make any other connection until you identify yourself to them (and start their billing clock). If your default home page is a blank screen, choose a website from your Favorites or Bookmarks list, or type a URL in the address field. The local login screen will appear before the computer connects you to the site you requested.

I don't know if I'm within range of a network.

Some wireless utilities detect and display the SSIDs of all nearby network signals, so you can often check for a signal by simply plugging in an adapter and running the status program.

For more detailed information about nearby networks, including their SSIDs, try using NetStumbler (available at *http://www.netstumbler.com*) to identify all the signals that your network adapter can find.

The network is slow.

Any time a single network segment slows down, the overall performance of the network will suffer. A slow file transfer or download could be caused by an overloaded server or too many people trying to use the network at the same time. Within the wireless segment of the network, slow performance could be caused by high demand for access to the network or interference from other wireless networks and other radio services operating on the same frequency. Signal fading and multipath interference can also cause the wireless network data speed to drop.

To reduce interference, try to shift the access point to a different channel at least five steps away from the original channel. For example, if you're currently using channel 2, try shifting the access point to channel 7. This requires access to the access point's configuration software, so it's normally something that only a network administrator can do.

If you're the manager of a Wi-Fi network that's overloaded because too many users are online at the same time, add more access points that use different channels.

My computer drops its connection.

It doesn't happen often, but a wireless network connection can occasionally disappear for no obvious reason. This disappearance could be caused by a very brief burst of radio interference, an intermittent failure at the base station, or some other short-lived problem. There is always a reason, but it's often easier to simply restore the link than to spend hours searching for the cause.

Windows offers a quick fix for this kind of problem. To restore a dropped connection, try this method first:

1. From the Control Panel, open **Network Connections**.
2. Right-click the icon or listing for the connection profile that failed. For a Wi-Fi connection, the name is probably *Wireless Network Connection*.
3. Click **Repair** from the pop-up menu. Windows will clear anything that remains from the failed connection, turn off the wireless adapter, and try to establish a new connection.
4. Try connecting to a website or some other Internet destination.

If the Repair command solves your problem, you can go back to what you were doing before you lost the connection. If you still can't connect to a nearby Wi-Fi hot spot or to your broadband data network, there might be some residual junk programs running on your computer that interfere with the wireless connection. To clean out the junk, try rebooting the computer: Shut down Windows (or any other operating system), turn off the computer, wait 10 seconds, and then turn it back on again.

IF ALL ELSE FAILS, REBOOT

Restarting the computer is often the only thing necessary to clear a problem. When you turn the computer off and then back on again, you will get rid of the shards and fragments of old programs that are taking up space—but not doing anything useful—in your computer's memory. A *cold reboot*, in which you turn the computer off (rather than a *warm reboot*, in which you use the Restart command), can solve a multitude of apparent problems.

My Wi-Fi network has crashed.

If you're a network manager and several of your users tell you that they can't connect to your Wi-Fi network, it's possible that the access point has temporarily flaked out (that's the technical term) or your wired connection to the Internet has dropped out. Take a look at the lights on the access point and the Internet gateway router to confirm that the Power and WAN indicators are on. If you can't find an obvious problem, try restarting the access point by unplugging and reconnecting the power plug.

Can I improve performance with an external antenna?

As a rule of thumb, an external antenna will improve the signal strength of a wireless network signal by at least 15 percent because it can be placed in a position free of obstructions to the signal path. The external antenna can be attached to either the access point (in which case it will increase signal strength to every network client) or to a wireless network adapter. If you can place external antennas on both ends of the link, the total improvement will be about 32.5 percent.

This assumes that the captive antenna and the external antenna have exactly the same characteristics. If the external antenna is directional, or if it has more gain than the captive antenna, the performance improvement could be even greater. On the other hand, many network adapters and access points use two captive antennas in a *diversity* system that constantly compares the signals from each antenna and selects the stronger one. In a noisy environment, a diversity antenna system might be more effective than a single antenna.

What else can I do to improve performance?

Energy radiated from a transmitting antenna is often polarized in either the horizontal or the vertical plane, so a receiving antenna will detect a stronger signal from an antenna with the same polarity. In other words, if the transmitter uses a vertical antenna, the receiving antenna will detect a stronger signal if it is also vertical. If the transmitting antenna is horizontal, a horizontal receiving antenna will perform best.

At short range, polarity won't make a significant difference to the performance of a Wi-Fi link. Even if the two antennas have different polarity, they will still exchange signals that are strong enough to keep the data moving at full speed. But when you are trying to squeeze every possible data bit out of a weak or noisy signal, you might see some improvement when both antennas are polarized the same way.

The captive antennas built into most PC Card adapters are difficult or impossible to move without turning the whole computer on its side, but many access points have antennas mounted on swivels, so it's easy to move them from a vertical to a horizontal position.

If you are using a laptop computer with an internal network adapter, the antenna is probably built into the upper half of the "clamshell" alongside the screen. You can sometimes improve wireless performance by changing the angle of the screen or by rotating the entire computer on its base. You don't have to make a huge adjustment to the screen angle; a slight change can make the difference between a poor signal and one you can use.

When I move to a different access point, the adapter loses the connection.

In a Wi-Fi network with more than one base station, wireless adapters are supposed to detect all nearby access points and automatically shift their association to an access point with a clean, strong signal when you move from one place to another. However, the transfers don't always work properly. Sometimes an adapter will just drop the network connection when the signal from the nearest access point fades out. If that happens, try connecting again. If that doesn't work, try rebooting your computer.

Where can I find a copy of the Wi-Fi standards?

IEEE standards are written by engineers for other engineers, so they don't make particularly exciting reading. However, they are the defining documents for wireless Ethernet networks, so you might want to take a look at them. They're available online at *http://standards.ieee.org/reading/ieee/std/lanman.*

How can I find out who made my network adapter?

In spite of the labels on the packages, many wireless network adapters and access points are private label versions of some other company's products. It's often much easier for a company to add wireless products to their catalogs by buying them from somebody else rather than creating and building their own designs.

Some companies that sell private label versions of adapters and access points might tell you who made them, but many salespeople will insist that they make everything themselves, and even if they don't, they stand by the warranty, so why should you care?

As a user or network manager, the name of the original equipment manufacturer (OEM) should not make any difference to you, as long as the device carries Wi-Fi certification. If it has passed the Wi-Fi tests, you can assume that it will work reasonably well with the other equipment in your network, but sometimes it helps to know what's inside that sealed PC Card package. If you're using the adapter with a computer running Unix or Linux, the manufacturer's tech support people might not know where to find the right drivers and configuration tools for their devices, but when you know whose components are inside, you can find the drivers on your own. As a network manager, it can be useful to know which adapters are identical to the ones you're already using so you can keep a few spares on hand that will work with the existing drivers in your users' computers.

How do you find the name of the original manufacturer? You'll have to do your own detective work. Every piece of electronic equipment sold in the United States that can emit radio energy must carry a registration number issued by the Federal Communications Commission (FCC). This applies to radio transmitters such as wireless network devices, and also to most other computer components, because they emit radio energy as a side effect to whatever function they're supposed to perform.

There's an FCC ID number on just about every wireless network device. For example, Figure 17-3 shows the label on a Xircom PC Card adapter. The FCC ID number is LDK102038.

Figure 17-3: Every wireless adapter has a unique FCC ID number.

The FCC maintains a searchable database at *https://gullfoss2.fcc.gov/oetcf/eas/reports/ GenericSearch.cfm* that lists every ID number, with links to copies of all the technical exhibits that the manufacturer supplied with their application for registration. (If you get a security warning when you try to connect to this site, don't worry about it. Just click OK to continue to this website.) Most of this information is boring technical stuff, but if you look around the exhibits, you can often find something that identifies the original manufacturer or the maker of an adapter's internal chip set.

The FCC database is also a great tool for people like me who have a junk box full of old computer circuit cards that seemed important enough to save but don't have labels that explain what they were good for. The database maps each card to a listing with a description of the card and maybe even a copy of the user's manual. With a make and model number, it's usually possible to find a manufacturer's website that provides even more details.

If you already have the device, often the easiest way to find out what it is, especially in an operating system like Linux or BSD, is to plug it in and see what happens. Typically, dmesg, lspci, or lsusb will give you enough information about the device specifics to plug into a search engine and find the original manufacturer and which drivers to use.

Is the software that came with my network adapter or access point up to date?

The software supplied with wireless network adapters exists in two forms: programs that run on the computer connected to the adapter and internal firmware that controls the adapter itself. All the software that runs on an access point is internal firmware.

The manufacturers of wireless networking hardware (and most other computer-related products) often issue new versions of the software that supports their products. Updated software might include fixes for bugs that were discovered after the product shipped, support for new operating systems, and additional features and functions such as improved encryption.

Therefore, it's always useful to check the manufacturer's website to see what might be available. For updates to wireless broadband data adapters, look in the technical support section of your service provider's website.

Installing new configuration and status programs is easy; just load the new software over the older version. In most cases, the manufacturer supplies the software in an executable file that automatically deletes earlier versions and runs a complete installation routine. It's always a good idea to read the README file or other instructions that were provided as part of the download package.

Updating firmware is more complicated. The manufacturer or service provider always includes detailed instructions, which you should follow as closely as possible. Before you update the firmware in an access point, remember to warn all your users that the network will be offline for maintenance.

I'm having trouble connecting to a broadband network.

If you're trying to connect for the first time, make sure your new account has been activated. Telephone your service provider's support center to check.

If your broadband connection stops working after you have been using it for a few weeks or more, check with your service provider to confirm that your account is still active. If you're at the end of a free trial period, make sure the service provider hasn't cancelled your account.

Most broadband networks use DHCP to automatically assign an IP address and DNS address. Make sure the broadband network profile has DHCP enabled.

If your broadband connection still doesn't work, try removing and reinstalling the service provider's connection manager software from the original CD or from a copy on your hard drive. Most service providers have copies of the latest software available for download from their websites (you'll need either a Wi-Fi or wired Ethernet connection to reach the Internet when your broadband service isn't working).

If you are using a non-Windows operating system, such as OS X, Linux, or BSD, many broadband vendors require the first connection to be made using their Windows proprietary software. After the first connection is made, the device will usually work on other operating systems. Ask your vendor's support center for help with alternative operating systems.

I'm having trouble connecting to my VPN.

If you can't connect to your LAN through a VPN, the problem could be either in the VPN settings on your computer or at the VPN host. Either way, your best bet is to telephone or email the network manager or help desk staff who are responsible for the network. They'll have the exact codes and settings necessary to make your connection work properly.

How can I extend the life of my computer's battery?

A radio transmitter consumes electric power as it sends and receives radio signals, so the battery in a portable computer with a wireless adapter will run down much faster than the same computer without the adapter. Fortunately, there are a few things you can do to keep the power drain down to an absolute minimum.

First, turn off or disconnect the adapter when you're not using it. If you're on an airplane or a train, or anywhere else where you're outside the range of a wireless signal, or if you're using the computer for some purpose that doesn't require network access, remove the PC Card adapter from its socket or unplug the USB cable. If your computer has an internal wireless adapter, turn it off.

This is good advice for any plug-in device on a PC Card. If you're not using it, remove it. Modems, Ethernet adapters, and storage cards all consume power any time they're plugged into the computer, so your battery will keep going longer if the socket is empty.

When you use your wireless network adapter, you can reduce power consumption by using the Power Saving Protocol that's part of the 802.11 specification. Someplace in the adapter's configuration utility, there's a set of power management options that can instruct the adapter to enter a power saving mode:

- Constantly Awake Mode (CAM) consumes the most power and provides the fastest response. In CAM mode, the adapter is on all the time. It receives all incoming messages as soon as the access point gets them.

- Power Saving Protocol (PSP) mode consumes less power, but it also provides slower response. In PSP mode, the adapter instructs the access point to hold messages for this network node in a buffer, and it enters a low-power sleep mode. At regular time intervals (several times each minute), the adapter wakes up and polls the access point for messages. Because there's a delay between the time the access point receives each message and the time it sends the message on to the sleeping adapter, data and messages will take longer to move through the network.

Can I use my access point as a network bridge?

An access point is a bridge between a wireless network and a wired LAN. If a single access point is not adequate to reach the entire area to be served by the wireless network, connecting additional access points to the wired LAN can extend the coverage area. But a *wireless bridge*, in which the wireless link connects two LANs together, is a more specialized device. Many access points offer wireless bridging as an option, but not as part of the basic feature set. If you plan to use an access point as a bridge between networks, check the specifications before you buy it. Your best bet is to buy a separate wireless bridge rather than trying to jury-rig a generic wireless adapter.

I've heard that radio signals from cellular phones might be dangerous. What about Wi-Fi?

Some people believe the jury is still out on the safety of cellular telephones. Others are convinced that they're a serious health threat. Scientists and engineers have performed studies and published papers that claim to prove that extended use of a cell phone can—or can't possibly—cause cancer, make milk go sour, or have some other terrible effect. Human exposure to electromagnetic fields at the frequencies used by cell phones and wireless network adapters is within the levels that most organizations and regulatory agencies that have studied the matter consider safe. The dissenters believe that those levels are too high.

Even if you think cell phones are potentially dangerous, it's likely that the radios in wireless adapters are safer, for several reasons. First, when a cellular telephone is transmitting, it's usually just an inch or two from the user's brain, but a wireless adapter is probably a foot or more away (even though they're called *laptops*, most people use them on a table rather than on their laps). The effect of nonionizing radiation (a fancy name for radio waves) decreases at a rate equal to the square of the distance, so a transmitter located two inches from your head will have about 36 times more effect on your body than a radio located a foot away, assuming that both radio signals are equally strong at the antenna.

Second, the radio in a cell phone is 20 times more powerful than a radio in a wireless adapter (0.60 watts versus 0.03 watts), so the intensity of the signal is more than 700 times stronger.

Finally, the effect of radio frequency radiation on organic matter is cumulative—the longer the body is exposed to radiation, the greater the effect. Most cell phones transmit a continuous stream of packets as long as the phone conversation is going on, but wireless LANs are bursty services that are only active when they are actually transmitting data. The total amount of transmission time for a wireless adapter is just a fraction of the time that a cell phone is active.

Therefore, the total amount of radiation your body receives from a wireless network adapter is just a tiny fraction of the amount you receive from a cell phone. There are plenty of other, more serious, threats to your health and safety.

INDEX

pre-WiMAX services, 250–251
Pringles potato chips canister, antenna
    made from, 69, 192
print sharing, in Windows, 102
PRISM chip sets, drivers for, 139
privacy filter, 200
private access points, unprotected,
    208–209
private IP addresses, 99
private networks, 40
private-label adapters, 118, 301
/proc/net/wireless, 126
    graphic display of information from,
    127–128
Properties window
    of wireless adapter, 102
        Advanced tab, *103*
ProSet/Wireless program (Intel),
    86–88, *87*, *88*, *91*
    excluding bogus ad hoc network, *207*
Proxim, 118
    Harmony AP Controller, 225
    Outdoor Router, 189
PSK (Pre-Shared Key), 151
    passphrases, 223
PSP (Power Saving Protocol), 304
PSTN (public switched telephone
    network), 285–286
public access, to wireless network,
    235–236
public DNS servers, 102
public name servers, 148
public networks, 40
    finding, troubleshooting, 298
    protecting files while logged into, 216
    VPN through, 283–284
public switched telephone network
    (PSTN), 285–286
public Wi-Fi hot spots, 202–203
    finding, 197–199
    firewall when using, 199–200
    "Free Public WiFi," 205–207, *206*
    municipal Wi-Fi networks, 204–205
    security issues, 196–197

Q

Qtopia, *262*
Qualcomm, 243
Qwest, 212
    Wireless, 245

R

radio frequency (RF), 33–36
    for wireless, 15
radio line of sight, 173
radio signals, 13–14
    improving quality, 65
radio spectrum, 13
RADIUS (Remote Authentication Dial-
    In User Service), 151–152, 223
railroads
    broadband wireless from, 251–254
    hot spots on, 203
Ralink chip sets, drivers for, 139
range expander, 153
RAS (Remote Access Service), 270
RC4 algorithm, 214
rebooting, troubleshooting by, 299
receiver, for radio waves, 13
reflectors, 191
registration number, of electronic
    equipment, 302
Rehm, Greg, 193
relays, in point-to-point wireless link,
    189–190
Remote Access Service (RAS), 270
Remote Authentication Dial-In
    User Service (RADIUS),
    151–152, 223
remote monitoring, 128
remote network, VPN for connection
    to LAN, *266*
repeaters, 189
    in point-to-point link, 184
reputation, 57–58
residential gateways, 59
Rev. A signals, 243
Revision B chip sets, 243
RF (radio frequency), 33–36
RF amplifier, 169, 172
Rice University, 222
roaming, 40
    international broadband data ser-
    vices and, 248
    Wi-Fi specification on, 64, 65
Robust Security Network, 225
routers
    access point as, and gateway
    addresses, 101
    broadband, network connections, 62
    VPN-enabled, 267
    as VPN server, *271*
Routing Address, in AirPort, 140
RTS/CTS threshold, in Unix, 131

S

Electronic Frontier Foundation
Defending Freedom in the Digital World

Free Speech. Privacy. Innovation. Fair Use. Reverse Engineering. If you care about these rights in the digital world, then you should join the Electronic Frontier Foundation (EFF). EFF was founded in 1990 to protect the rights of users and developers of technology. EFF is the first to identify threats to basic rights online and to advocate on behalf of free expression in the digital age.

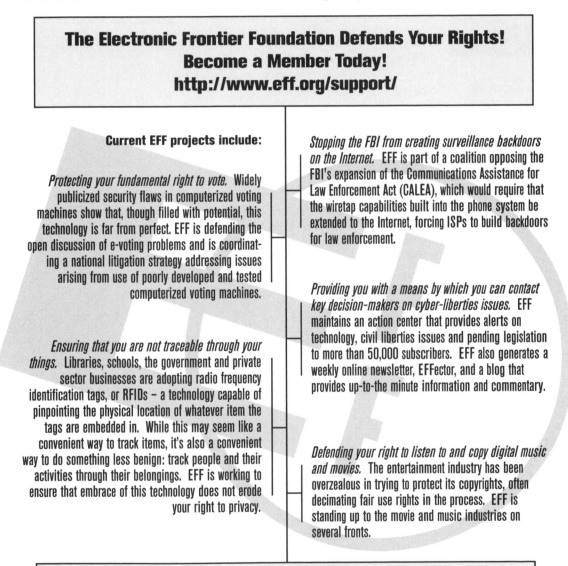

The Electronic Frontier Foundation Defends Your Rights!
Become a Member Today!
http://www.eff.org/support/

Current EFF projects include:

Protecting your fundamental right to vote. Widely publicized security flaws in computerized voting machines show that, though filled with potential, this technology is far from perfect. EFF is defending the open discussion of e-voting problems and is coordinating a national litigation strategy addressing issues arising from use of poorly developed and tested computerized voting machines.

Ensuring that you are not traceable through your things. Libraries, schools, the government and private sector businesses are adopting radio frequency identification tags, or RFIDs – a technology capable of pinpointing the physical location of whatever item the tags are embedded in. While this may seem like a convenient way to track items, it's also a convenient way to do something less benign: track people and their activities through their belongings. EFF is working to ensure that embrace of this technology does not erode your right to privacy.

Stopping the FBI from creating surveillance backdoors on the Internet. EFF is part of a coalition opposing the FBI's expansion of the Communications Assistance for Law Enforcement Act (CALEA), which would require that the wiretap capabilities built into the phone system be extended to the Internet, forcing ISPs to build backdoors for law enforcement.

Providing you with a means by which you can contact key decision-makers on cyber-liberties issues. EFF maintains an action center that provides alerts on technology, civil liberties issues and pending legislation to more than 50,000 subscribers. EFF also generates a weekly online newsletter, EFFector, and a blog that provides up-to-the minute information and commentary.

Defending your right to listen to and copy digital music and movies. The entertainment industry has been overzealous in trying to protect its copyrights, often decimating fair use rights in the process. EFF is standing up to the movie and music industries on several fronts.

Check out all of the things we're working on at http://www.eff.org and join today or make a donation to support the fight to defend freedom online.

ELECTRONIC FRONTIER FOUNDATION · 454 SHOTWELL STREET · SAN FRANCISCO, CA 94110 · 415.436.9333

STEAL THIS COMPUTER BOOK 4.0
What They Won't Tell You About the Internet

by WALLACE WANG

This offbeat, non-technical book examines what hackers do, how they do it, and how readers can protect themselves. Informative, irreverent, and entertaining, the completely revised fourth edition of *Steal This Computer Book* contains new chapters that discuss the hacker mentality, lock picking, exploiting P2P file-sharing networks, and how people manipulate search engines and pop-up ads. Includes a CD with hundreds of megabytes of hacking and security-related programs that tie in to each chapter of the book.

MAY 2006, 384 PP. W/CD, $29.95 ($38.95 CDN)
ISBN 978-1-59327-105-3

STEAL THIS FILE SHARING BOOK
What They Won't Tell You About File Sharing

by WALLACE WANG

Steal This File Sharing Book peels back the mystery surrounding file-sharing networks such as Kazaa, Morpheus, and Usenet, showing how they work and how to use them wisely, and revealing potential dangers, including viruses, spyware, and lawsuits, and how to avoid them.

NOVEMBER 2004, 296 PP., $19.95 ($27.95 CDN)
ISBN 978-1-59327-050-6

UBUNTU FOR NON-GEEKS, 2ND EDITION
A Pain-Free, Project-Based, Get-Things-Done Guidebook

by RICKFORD GRANT

This newbie's guide to Ubuntu lets readers learn by doing. Using immersion-learning techniques favored by language courses, step-by-step projects build upon earlier tutorial concepts, stimulating the brain and increasing the reader's understanding. This book covers all the topics likely to be of interest to an average desktop user, such as installing new software via Synaptic; Internet connectivity; working with removable storage devices, printers, and scanners; and handling DVDs, audio files, and even iPods. It also eases readers into the world of commands, thus allowing them to work with Java, Python, or other script-based applications; convert RPMs to DEB files; and compile software from source.

JUNE 2007, 352 PP. W/CD, $34.95 ($43.95 CDN)
ISBN 978-1-59327-152-7